Fast, Fun & Fabulous Quilts

30 **Terrific Projects from the Country's** Most Creative Designers

Edited by Suzanne Nelson

Rodale Press, Inc.
Emmaus, Pennsylvania

The designers and editors who compiled this book have tried to make all of the contents as accurate and as correct as possible. Plans, illustrations, photographs, and text have all been carefully checked and cross-checked. However, due to the variability of local conditions, construction materials, personal skill, and so on, neither the author nor Rodale Press, Inc., assumes any responsibility for any injuries suffered or for damages or other losses incurred that result from the material presented herein. All instructions and plans should be carefully studied and clearly understood before beginning construction.

Printed in the United States of America on acid-free ∞, recycled ♻ paper

Technical Editor: *Sharon Rose*
Editor: *Suzanne Nelson*
Cover and Interior Designer: *Lisa Palmer*
Book Layout: *Lisa Palmer and Robin Hepler*
Technical Artists: *Tanya L. Lipinski and Nancy J. Smola*
Interior Illustrators: *Jack Crane, Sandy Freeman, Sue Gettlin, and Martin Lemelman*
Cover and Interior Photographer: *Mitch Mandel*
Interior Photo Stylist: *Marianne Grape Laubach*
Cover Quiltmaker: *Suzanne Nelson*
Studio Manager: *Leslie Keefe*
Copy Editor: *Sarah Dunn*
Manufacturing Coordinator: *Jodi Schaffer*
Editorial Assistance: *Stephanie Wenner*

Rodale Home and Garden Books
Editorial Director: *Margaret J. Lydic*
Managing Editor, Quilt Books: *Suzanne Nelson*
Art Director: *Michael Mandarano*
Associate Art Director: *Mary Ellen Fanelli*
Copy Director: *Dolores Plikaitis*
Office Manager: *Karen Earl-Braymer*

We're happy to hear from you.

For questions or comments concerning the editorial content of this book, please write to:
 Rodale Press, Inc.
 Book Readers' Service
 33 East Minor Street
 Emmaus, PA 18098

For more information about Rodale Press and the books and magazines we publish, visit our World Wide Web site at **http://www.rodalepress.com**

Library of Congress Cataloging-in-Publication Data

Fast, fun and fabulous quilts : 30 terrific projects from the country's most creative designers / edited by Suzanne Nelson.
  p. cm.
ISBN 0–87596–709–4 (hardcover : alk. paper)
1. Quilting—Patterns. 2. Patchwork—Patterns. I. Nelson, Suzanne.
TT835.F37 1996
746.46—dc20
                                         95–38002

Distributed in the book trade by St. Martin's Press

4 6 8 10 9 7 5   hardcover

*T*hank you to all the very talented designers who so enthusiastically jumped on board this project and were so conscientious about getting things in on time. It was a true pleasure to work with all of you.

The photographs throughout the book were taken at the following locations. A special note of gratitude to all the owners for welcoming the photography crew into their homes.

> *Harmony Barn Antiques*
> Karen and Ted Johns
> 2481 Belvidere Road
> Phillipsburg, NJ 08865
> (908) 859-6159

> *The Bucksville House*
> Barbara and Joe Szollosi
> 4501 Durham Road, Route 412
> Kintnersville, PA 18930
> (610) 847-8948

> *The Simon Butler House*
> 116 East Butler Avenue
> Chalfont, PA 18914
> (215) 822-3582

Thank you to Debbie Heeps of Allentown, Pennsylvania, for so graciously offering the use of her collection of antique sewing chickens, seen in the photo on page 10. Also thanks to Julie Powell of Vintage Textiles and Tools for the use of the wonderful political memorabilia in the photograph on page 28.

A giant note of gratitude to Sarah Dunn and Lisa Palmer for always being there to pick up the loose ends.

And last, a thank you to Emmy and Liana for taking it easy on their dad on the nights when I had to work late to finish this book.

Contents

RODALE PRESS MEMO

To:

From: Date:

Subject:

Back row, left to right: Sandy Gervais, Marilyn Reardon, Mary Ellen Von Holt, Jill Kemp, Juanita Simonich, Gerry Kimmel, Paula Kemperman, Connie Tesene, Debbie Mumm, Lynette Jensen, Johanna Wilson.

Front row, left to right: Kathy Boudreau, Sylvia Johnson, Toni Phillips, Judith Hughes Marte, Mary Tendall, Susan Rand.

Not pictured: Glenda Carr, Alice Berg, Virginia Robertson, Retta Warehime.

Photograph taken at the International Quilt Market in Houston, Texas by Sam Pierson. Quilts in the background are, from left to right, Starshine by Sally Saulmon; The Odense Album by Elly Sienkiewicz; and Journey through Time by Suzanne Marshall.

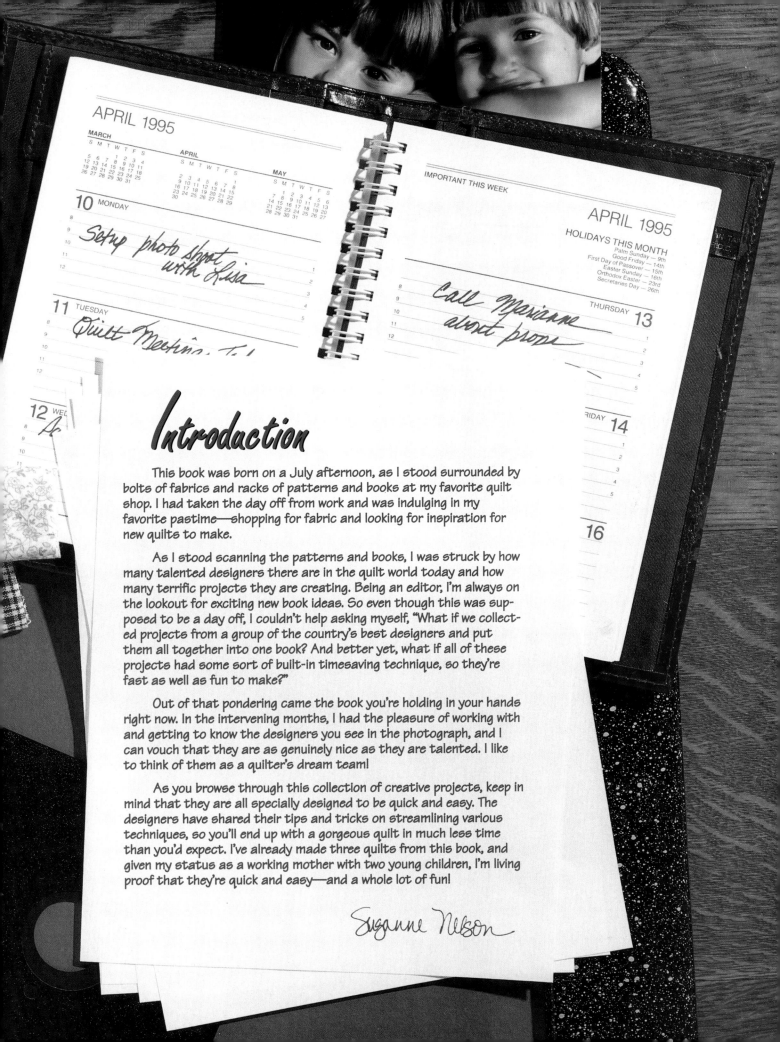

APRIL 1995

MARCH
S M T W T F S

APRIL
S M T W T F S

MAY
S M T W T F S

10 MONDAY

Setup photo shoot
with Lisa

11 TUESDAY

Quilt Meeting, T...

12 WED

IMPORTANT THIS WEEK

APRIL 1995

HOLIDAYS THIS MONTH
Palm Sunday — 9th
Good Friday — 14th
First Day of Passover — 15th
Easter Sunday — 16th
Orthodox Easter — 23rd
Secretaries Day — 26th

Call Marianne
about prose

THURSDAY **13**

FRIDAY **14**

16

Introduction

This book was born on a July afternoon, as I stood surrounded by bolts of fabrics and racks of patterns and books at my favorite quilt shop. I had taken the day off from work and was indulging in my favorite pastime—shopping for fabric and looking for inspiration for new quilts to make.

As I stood scanning the patterns and books, I was struck by how many talented designers there are in the quilt world today and how many terrific projects they are creating. Being an editor, I'm always on the lookout for exciting new book ideas. So even though this was supposed to be a day off, I couldn't help asking myself, "What if we collected projects from a group of the country's best designers and put them all together into one book? And better yet, what if all of these projects had some sort of built-in timesaving technique, so they're fast as well as fun to make?"

Out of that pondering came the book you're holding in your hands right now. In the intervening months, I had the pleasure of working with and getting to know the designers you see in the photograph, and I can vouch that they are as genuinely nice as they are talented. I like to think of them as a quilter's dream team!

As you browse through this collection of creative projects, keep in mind that they are all specially designed to be quick and easy. The designers have shared their tips and tricks on streamlining various techniques, so you'll end up with a gorgeous quilt in much less time than you'd expect. I've already made three quilts from this book, and given my status as a working mother with two young children, I'm living proof that they're quick and easy—and a whole lot of fun!

Suzanne Nelson

Americana Quilts

Bird Parade

✪

Friendship Plaids

✪

Plaid Patches

✪

Sew So Easy

✪

Flying Flags

Bird Parade

Gerry Kimmel, *Red Wagon*

*W*ho could resist this parade of endearing, folk-art inspired birds? (Especially when there's one feathered individualist marching to the beat of his own drum!) Homespun plaids and a rustic color scheme enhance the look of this appealing wall quilt—the perfect complement to a country decor.

SIZE

Finished quilt is 39 × 45 inches
Finished block is 15 × 11 inches

FABRICS and SUPPLIES

Yardage based on 44-inch-wide fabric

- ½ yard (or one fat quarter) *each* of 6 different background fabrics
- ½ yard black solid for feet and binding
- ¼ yard *each* of 11 different fabrics for borders, bodies, wings, and neck bands
- Scraps of 6 different fabrics for heads
- Scraps of gold for eyes and beaks
- 1⅜ yards for backing
- Batting, larger than 39 × 45 inches
- Template plastic or fusible web, depending on appliqué technique
- Rotary cutter, ruler, and mat

GETTING READY

COLOR and FABRIC TIPS:

Since each bird is made up of four different fabrics (head, neck band, body, and wing), have fun playing with different combinations. Don't be afraid to mix polka dots with plaids, or stripes with checks. The more daring the fabric combinations, the more outstanding your birds will be. Use contrasting scale fabrics. Put a busy plaid on top of a calm and repetitive print. Cut the plaids and stripes for the heads and bodies off-grain so the lines in the fabric are slightly off kilter.

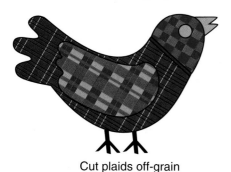

Cut plaids off-grain

- Wash, damp dry, and press all fabrics before using.
- All seam allowances are ¼ inch and should be pressed to one side.
- See "Appliqué Basics" on page 238 and choose a method. Trace pattern pieces for the bird (**Body, Wing, Neck Band, Head, Eye, Beak, Leg,** and **Feet**) on pages 7–9 onto template plastic or fusible web. (Trace the two parts of the Wing/Body pattern and join them together to make a master pattern before tracing.) When using fusible web, *reverse* the patterns first before tracing onto the web.
- Save time by rotary cutting the block backgrounds, sashing strips, borders, and binding. First trim the selvages off these fabrics and square off one crosswise edge of each fabric, as described on page 236.
- Cutting directions for each part of the quilt are provided in the sections indicated by the yellow rotary cutters. This format allows you to cut what you need as you get ready to assemble each part of the quilt. If you prefer to cut all the pieces at once, skip ahead, looking for the yellow rotary cutters, and cut all the pieces before starting to sew.

ASSEMBLING the BLOCKS

Cutting for Blocks (make 6)

From each of the six background fabrics, cut:

◆ One 15½ × 11½-inch piece

From the remaining fabrics:

◆ Cut out the pieces for the birds, following the directions for the appliqué method you have chosen. (For fusible web, cut pattern pieces *without* seam allowances.)

NOTE: For the one bird marching in the opposite direction, cut one complete set of pattern pieces *reversing* the templates.

Assembling the Bird

STEP 1. Sew the neck band to the head. Sew this unit to the body, as shown in **Diagram 1**.

STEP 2. Appliqué or fuse the wing to the body. Trim out the fabric from behind the wing (for traditional appliqué).

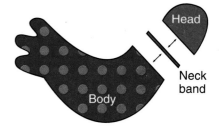

Diagram 1

STEP 3. Appliqué or fuse the eye to the head.

STEP 4. Repeat to make five more birds. (Remember that one will be facing the opposite direction from the other five.)

Make It EASY

Here's a trick to try for preparing the birds' eyes for appliqué. Use the Eye pattern to make a circle out of lightweight cardboard. Cut the fabric circles a scant ¼ inch larger than this cardboard circle. Baste along the outside edge of each fabric circle, then place the cardboard circle inside and gently pull up the thread. Keeping the fabric drawn up around the cardboard, press. When you remove the cardboard and basting, you're left with a perfect circle with seam allowances already turned under, ready to appliqué. ■

Appliquéing the Bird

STEP 1. Referring to the photograph on page 2 for placement, pin the body onto the background block. Make sure the bird doesn't extend into the ¼-inch seam allowance on all sides of the background.

STEP 2. If you are using hand or machine appliqué, pin the beak, legs, and feet in position, making sure the edges that meet the bird will be covered when it is appliquéd in place. Appliqué the feet first, then add the legs on top. Appliqué the beak. Then stitch the body to

the background, being sure to completely cover the raw edges of the legs and beak with the turned-under seam allowance of the body. Repeat five times, reversing one bird so it faces in the opposite direction.

If you are using fusible web, place all the bird pieces on the background block without pinning. Make sure the edges of the beak and legs will be covered by the body. First fuse the feet, then add the legs. Next fuse the beak, then add the body. Repeat five times, reversing one bird.

ASSEMBLING the CENTER

Cutting for Setting Pieces

From the remaining bird fabrics, cut a total of:

◆ Four 3½ × 15½-inch strips (Horizontal Sashing Strips)
◆ One 3½ × 39½-inch strip (Vertical Sashing Strip; may be pieced as in the photograph on page 2)

Piecing the Center

STEP 1. Sew horizontal sashing strips to the bottom of four of the bird blocks. Join two of these units, adding a bird block at the bottom. Repeat to make two vertical rows of three birds each, as shown in **Diagram 2**. Press the seam allowances toward the sashing strips.

Diagram 2

Make It FUN

Borrow a common feature from antique quilts to enhance the gentle, time-honored look of your quilt by patching together different fabrics for one of the background blocks. Look at the center right background block on the quilt in the photograph on page 2. A couple of light-colored patches were added, purposely re-creating the random look of a quilt that had to be pieced together from leftovers in the scrap bag. ■

STEP 2. Sew a row to each long side of the vertical sashing strip to complete the center, as shown in **Diagram 3**. Press toward the sashing strip.

Diagram 3

BORDERS

Cutting for Borders

From the remaining bird/border fabrics, cut a total of:

◆ Two 3½-inch crosswise strips (Top and Bottom Borders; Bottom Border is pieced in the photograph)

◆ Two 3½ × 47½-inch strips (Side Borders; will need to be pieced as in the photograph)

Attaching the Borders

STEP 1. Measure through the center of your quilt horizontally. Cut the top and bottom border strips to this exact measurement.

STEP 2. Attach these strips to the quilt top, as shown in the **Quilt Diagram**. Press toward the border.

STEP 3. Measure across the center of the quilt vertically. Include the top and bottom borders in your measurement. Cut the remaining two border strips to this exact measurement.

STEP 4. Attach these strips to the sides of your quilt top. Press the seam allowances toward the border.

Make It FUN

To add a charming scrappy look to the quilt, you can piece together two fabrics for the central sashing strip, and even do the same for one or two of the borders. ■

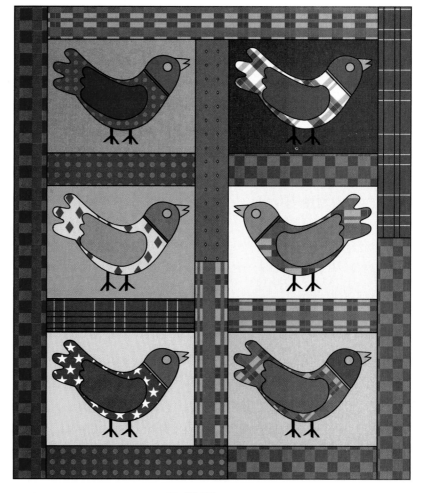

Quilt Diagram

QUILTING

STEP 1. Press the finished quilt top. Mark the quilting design, using one of your own or following these suggestions.

■ Outline quilt the bodies and wings.

■ Stitch a stylized feather pattern inside the wings.

■ Quilt diagonal lines 1½ inches apart in the bird backgrounds. (Note in the photograph on page 2 that the direction of the lines alternates from block to block.)

■ Quilt lines 1½ inches apart across the sashing strips and borders.

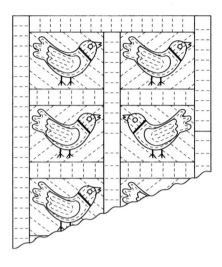

STEP 2. Layer the quilt top, batting, and backing. Baste the layers together.

STEP 3. Quilt by hand or machine.

STEP 4. Trim the batting and backing even with the quilt top. Remove the basting.

BINDING

STEP 1. Cut four 2-inch crosswise strips to prepare 180 total inches of double-fold straight-grain binding. (You may need a bit more fabric—cut another short strip and attach it, if necessary.)

STEP 2. Join the strips end to end with diagonal seams. Fold in half lengthwise with wrong sides together and press. Attach the binding to the quilt, following the instructions on page 242.

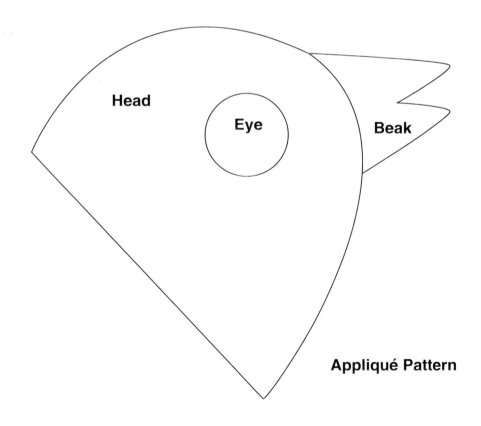

Head

Eye

Beak

Appliqué Pattern

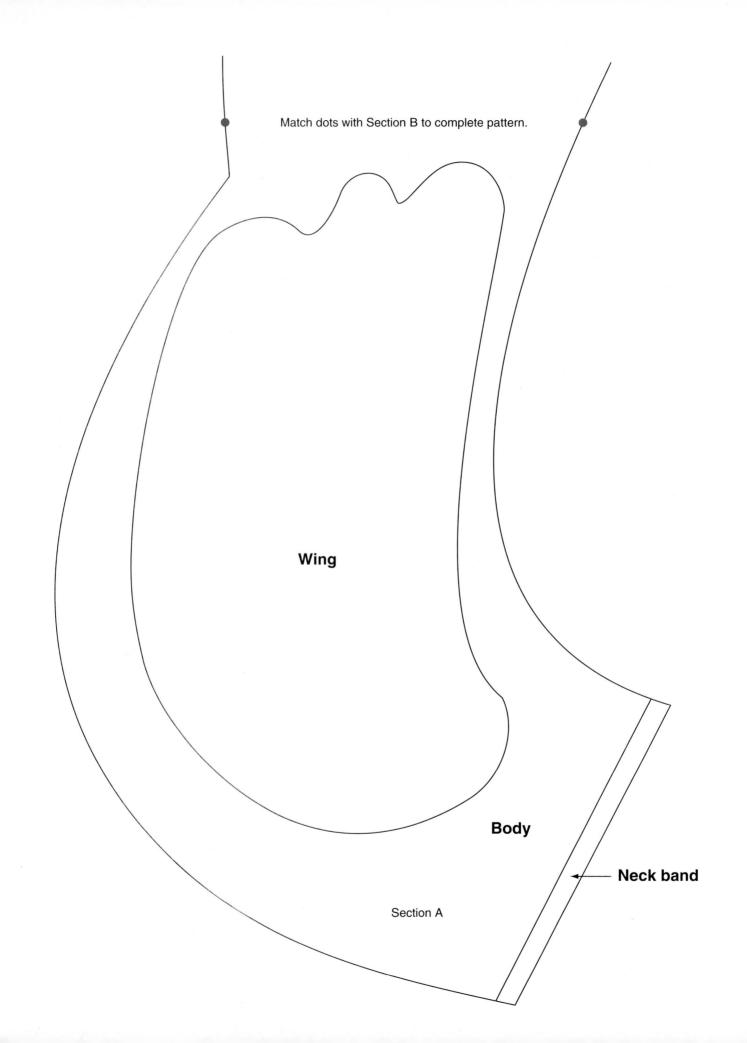

Match dots with Section B to complete pattern.

Wing

Body

Neck band

Section A

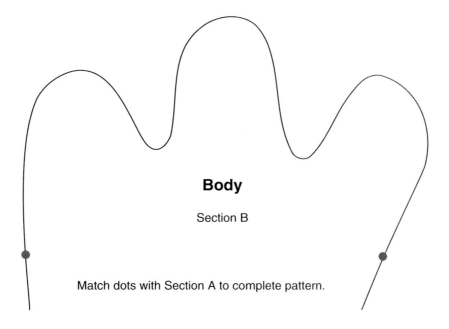

Body

Section B

Match dots with Section A to complete pattern.

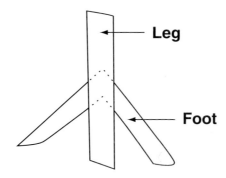

Leg

Foot

Appliqué Patterns

CHURN DASH DESIGNS

Friendship Plaids

Marilyn Reardon, *Churn Dash Designs*

*T*his large wall quilt would be an excellent showcase for your collection of treasured "old-time" fabrics. If you love a truly scrappy look, why not exchange fabric squares with your quilting friends until you have collected enough to make this quilt?

SIZE

Finished quilt is 50 × 60 inches
Finished block is 6 inches square

FABRICS and SUPPLIES

Yardage based on 44-inch-wide fabric
- 1⅝ yards navy solid for outer border (1 yard for pieced border)
- 1½ yards gold solid for inner border (⅜ yard for a pieced border)

If purchasing block fabrics (these amounts assume you will use all of the 25 different fabrics; if you don't mind leftovers, go ahead and buy more than the 25 listed here for more variety):
- ¼ yard *each* of 10 different darks
- ⅛ yard *each* of 15 different lights. (If the fabric store won't make ⅛-yard cuts, think about going in on ¼-yard cuts with a quilting friend and then splitting the pieces.)

If exchanging block fabrics:
- Scraps of *at most* 30 darks (each at least 12 inches square)
- Scraps of *at most* 60 lights (each at least 7 inches square)
- ½ yard for binding
- 3¼ yards for backing
- Batting, larger than 50 × 60 inches
- Rotary cutter, ruler, and mat

GETTING READY

COLOR and FABRIC TIPS:

Using plaids and stripes in your quilt gives you lots of opportunities to play with colors and visual textures. Combining these fabrics with other prints can achieve the look of antique quilts, which often mixed many plaids and stripes.

Plaid and striped fabrics can be used two ways. *On-grain* (where the lines of the fabric run parallel with or perpendicular to the sides of the pattern piece) creates a "calm" or "quiet" spot. *Off-grain* (where the lines run at random angles to the sides of the pattern pieces) creates movement or excitement. You can range from slightly off-grain to very off-grain for different results. To experiment with your directional plaids and stripes, try cutting the pattern piece shapes you'll be using out of paper to leave a window. Lay the window over your fabric and move it around to see where you would like to cut out your pattern pieces to achieve the desired results.

■ Wash, damp dry, and press all fabrics before using.

■ All seam allowances are ¼ inch and should be pressed to one side, unless otherwise indicated. Press seam allowances toward the darker fabric.

■ In preparation for rotary cutting, trim the selvages off the dark and light block fabrics, the border fabric, and the binding fabric, and square off one crosswise edge of each fabric, as described on page 236.

■ Cutting directions for each part of the quilt are provided in the sections indicated by the yellow rotary cutters. This format allows you to cut what you need as you get ready to assemble each part of the quilt. If you prefer to cut all the pieces at once, skip ahead, looking for the yellow rotary cutters, and cut all the pieces before starting to sew.

Window for Viewing Plaids and Stripes

· ·

ASSEMBLING the BLOCKS

Whole blocks are used in the center of the quilt; partial blocks fill in along the sides and bottom of the quilt top. Dark fabric triangles fill in along the top.

Cutting
for Blocks (make 50 whole and 16 partial)

From the darks, cut:

◆ Twenty-seven 6⅞-inch squares; cut the squares in half diagonally to make 54 large triangles. Set 4

triangles aside for the setting triangles along the top of the quilt.

◆ Eighty-one 2⅞-inch squares; cut the squares in half diagonally to make 162 triangles. Cut 3 squares from each fabric so you will have enough triangles (6) for two blocks. Set 12 triangles (4 matching sets of 3 triangles each) aside for the partial blocks on the bottom row.

Select three darks. From these, cut and set the following aside for the partial blocks along the quilt sides:

◆ Six 2⅞-inch squares (cut *two* from each fabric). Cut the squares in half diagonally to make 12 triangles.

Make It FUN

Each 6-inch whole block is made of one large dark triangle, three small dark triangles, and six small light triangles. For variety, some blocks use one dark for the large triangle, another dark for the three small triangles, and a light fabric for the six small triangles. For a more uniform look, match the three dark triangles to the large one in every block. ■

◆ Three 3¼-inch squares (cut *one* square from each fabric). Cut the squares in half *twice* diagonally to make 12 triangles.

◆ Six 5⅜-inch squares (cut *one* square from each fabric). Cut the squares in half diagonally to make 12 triangles.

From the lights, cut:

◆ One hundred sixty-two 2⅞-inch squares. Cut 3 squares from each fabric so you will have enough matching triangles (6) for one block. Cut the squares in half diagonally to make 324 small triangles. Set 24 triangles (4 matching sets of 6 triangles each) aside for the partial blocks on the bottom row.

Select six lights. From these, cut and set the following aside for the partial blocks along the quilt sides:

◆ Twelve 2⅞-inch squares (cut *two* squares from each fabric). Cut the squares in half diagonally to make 24 triangles.

◆ Six 3¼-inch squares (cut *one* square from each fabric). Cut the squares in half *twice* diagonally to make 24 triangles.

Piecing the Blocks

Whole Blocks

STEP 1. Referring to the diagram of the **Whole Block**, lay out all the light and dark small triangles and the large dark triangle for your block. Following **Diagram 1**, join light and dark small triangles to form squares. Press the seams toward the darker fabric. Remember to use matching fabrics for all the dark and light triangles in each block.

Make 50

Whole Block

Diagram 1

STEP 2. Join squares 1/2 and 3/4. Press. Add triangle 5 to the right side of this unit, as shown in **Diagram 2**. Press. This completes Row 1.

Row 1

Diagram 2

STEP 3. Add triangle 8 to the right side of square 6/7, as shown in **Diagram 3**. Press. This completes Row 2.

Row 2

Diagram 3

STEP 4. Sew Row 2 to the bottom of Row 1, and add triangle 9 to the bottom of this unit to complete the large pieced triangle, as shown in **Diagram 4**. Press.

STEP 5. Sew this pieced triangle to a large dark triangle (10) to

complete the whole block, as shown in **Diagram 5**. Press. Repeat to make a total of 50 whole blocks.

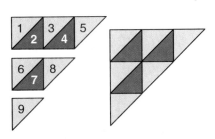

Diagram 4

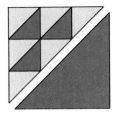

Diagram 5

Make It EASY

As you cut the triangles for the partial blocks, place them in labeled bags. Label one "Bottom Row" and put the light and dark triangles inside. Label another "2⅞-inch Squares/Sides" and put in the light and dark triangles cut from the 2⅞-inch squares. Label a third "3¼-inch Squares/Sides" and add the light and dark triangles cut from those squares. Organizing the pieces this way will make it quicker and easier to assemble the partial blocks later on. ■

Partial Blocks

STEP 1. For the four partial blocks needed for the bottom row, repeat Steps 1 through 5 above to make four large pieced triangles. Use the light and dark triangles cut from the 2⅞-inch squares.

Bottom Row (Make 4)

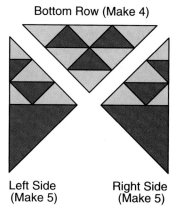

Left Side
(Make 5)
Right Side
(Make 5)
Partial Blocks

STEP 2. Partial blocks for the sides consist of a small pieced unit joined to a small triangle. Use the pieces cut and set aside earlier. Referring to **Diagram 6**, join triangles cut from 3¼-inch squares to make six each of the two mirror-image 1/2 units. Use triangles cut from 2⅞-inch squares to make twelve 3/4 units. Press.

Make 6   Make 6   Make 12

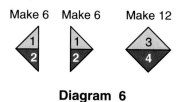

Diagram 6

STEP 3. Join units, sewing 1/2 units to the upper *left* corner of unit 3/4 for six of the blocks and to the upper *right* corner

for the other six, as shown in **Diagram 7**. Be sure to use the correct 1/2 units for each side, matching the positioning shown. Press. Add triangles 5 and 6, carefully noting their placement, as shown. Press.

Make 6   Make 6

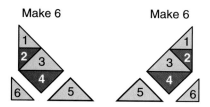

Diagram 7

STEP 4. Add a dark triangle (7) to the bottom of *ten* of the units (five left and five right) to complete the partial blocks for the sides, as shown in **Diagram 8**. Press. You should have two dark triangles and two small pieced triangles left over for the corners of the quilt.

Make 5   Make 5

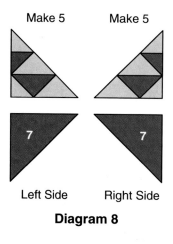

Left Side   Right Side
Diagram 8

ASSEMBLING the CENTER

STEP 1. Gather all the whole blocks, partial blocks, and setting triangles. Referring to the

Quilt Diagram, lay them out in diagonal rows and move them around until you are satisfied with the arrangement.

STEP 2. Join the blocks together in diagonal rows. Begin in the upper left corner, as shown in **Diagram 9**. Press, alternating the direction of the seam allowances from row to row. Join the rows. Press.

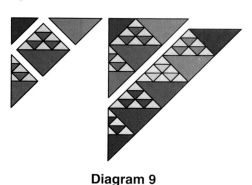

Diagram 9

BORDERS

Cutting for Borders

From the gold, cut:

♦ Four 1½-inch-wide lengthwise strips (Inner Borders). For a pieced border, cut five 1½-inch crosswise strips; cut one strip in half and sew half to each of two other strips. Press the seams open.

From the navy, cut:

♦ Four 4-inch-wide lengthwise strips (Outer Borders). For a pieced border, cut seven 4-inch crosswise strips. Join two strips together for each side border. Cut one strip in half and sew half to each of the two other strips for the top and bottom borders. Press the seams open.

Attaching the Borders

STEP 1. Measure through the center of your quilt vertically. Cut the two long pieced inner border strips to this exact measurement. Save the leftovers.

STEP 2. Attach these strips to the sides of your quilt top. Press the seam allowances toward the border.

STEP 3. Attach one of the leftover pieces you set aside to each of the remaining two inner border strips. Press the seams open.

STEP 4. Measure across the center of the quilt horizontally. Include the side borders in your measurement. Cut the remaining two inner border strips to this exact measurement. Attach to the top and bottom of your quilt top. Press the seam allowances toward the border.

STEP 5. Repeat Steps 1, 2, and 4 for the outer borders.

QUILTING

STEP 1. To prepare the backing, cut the fabric in half crosswise (from selvage to selvage). Remove the selvages and sew the halves together side by side to make a piece approximately 58 × 84 inches. Press the seam open.

STEP 2. Press the finished quilt top. Mark the quilting design, using one of your own or following these suggestions.

■ Quilt ¼ inch from the seams around the inside of all the small triangles.

■ Fill the large triangles with diamond cross-hatching.

■ Extend the lines from the pieced blocks into the borders with lines of quilting.

STEP 3. Layer the quilt top, batting, and backing. Baste the layers together.

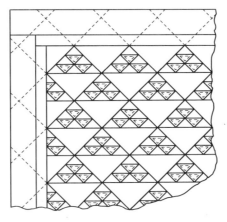

Quilting Diagram

STEP 4. Quilt by hand or machine.

STEP 5. Trim the batting and backing even with the quilt top. Remove the basting.

BINDING

STEP 1. Cut six 2-inch crosswise strips to prepare 240 total inches of double-fold straight-grain binding.

STEP 2. Join the strips end to end with diagonal seams. Fold in half lengthwise with wrong sides together and press. Attach the binding to the quilt, following the instructions on page 242.

Quilt Diagram

Plaid Patches

Connie Tesene and Mary Tendall, *Country Threads*

*T*his small wall quilt could easily be a satisfying weekend project. The nine-patch blocks go together in a snap with speedy cutting and piecing techniques. Once the top is together, finish it with machine quilting. The size of this quilt and the homespun look of the plaid nine-patch blocks make it perfect to use as a table topper on a country pine sideboard or draped over the side of a big, rustic harvest basket.

SIZE

Finished quilt is 27 inches square
Finished block is 3 inches square

FABRICS and SUPPLIES

Yardage based on 44-inch-wide fabric

- 1 yard light plaid for background
- ¼ yard plaid for binding
- Scraps of 9 different plaid fabrics, each at least 9½ inches square (or ⅛ yard each)
- 1 yard for backing
- Batting, larger than 27 inches square
- Rotary cutter, ruler, and mat

GETTING READY

COLOR and FABRIC TIPS:

For a softer, more antique look, choose a tan background fabric instead of unbleached muslin. Or, you might try dyeing the background fabric with a light tan Rit dye or with a Dylon cold-water dye kit (ask for both at your local quilt shop) to add a warm brown tone. Dipping the fabrics in solutions of coffee or tea is also a way to add the mellow tones of a gently aged quilt to your weekend masterpiece. See page 63 for instructions on tea dyeing.

- Wash, damp dry, and press all fabrics before using.
- All seam allowances are ¼ inch and should be pressed to one side, unless otherwise indicated. Press the seam allowances toward the darker fabric.
- In preparation for rotary cutting, trim the selvages off the muslin, the scraps, and the binding fabric and square off one crosswise edge of each fabric, as described on page 236.
- Cutting directions for each part of the quilt are provided in the sections indicated by the yellow rotary cutters. This format allows you to cut what you need as you get ready to assemble each part of the quilt. If you prefer to cut all the pieces at once, skip ahead, looking for the yellow rotary cutters, and cut all the pieces before starting to sew.

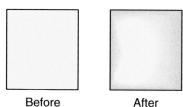

Before   After

Tea-dye for a mellow look

ASSEMBLING the BLOCKS

Cutting for Blocks

From the muslin, cut:

◆ Eight 1½-inch crosswise strips; cut two 9½-inch pieces from the end of one strip. Set this strip and the pieces aside.

From each of the plaids, cut:

◆ Five 1½ × 9½-inch strips

Piecing the Blocks

STEP 1. Join plaid strips end to end to form eight pieced units made up of five strips each. See **Diagram 1.** Press. (Hold on to the five extra plaid strips; they come up in Step 3.)

STEP 2. Referring to **Diagram 2,** join muslin strips and pieced

strips to make two A Units and three B Units. Don't worry if your muslin strips aren't quite long enough; you won't be using the full length of the units anyway. Press the seam allowances toward the plaids.

STEP 3. Using the two 9½-inch muslin pieces set aside earlier and one plaid strip, make one

Make 8

←—— 9" ——→

1½"

Diagram 1

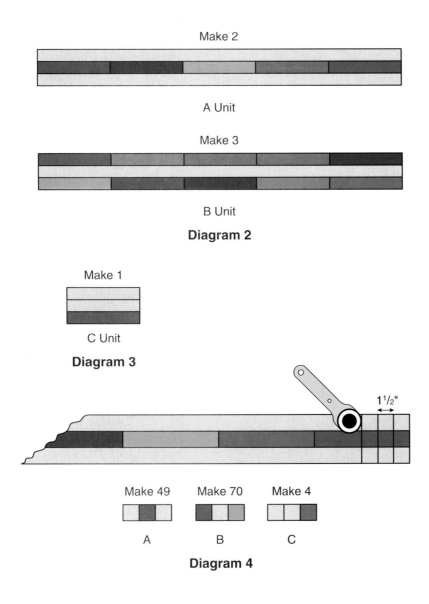

Make 2

A Unit

Make 3

B Unit

Diagram 2

Make 1

C Unit

Diagram 3

1½"

Make 49   Make 70   Make 4

A   B   C

Diagram 4

C Unit, as shown in **Diagram 3**. Press. (You should have four plaid strips left over—save them for another project or use them to create a scrappy binding as described in "Make It Fun" on page 21.)

STEP 4. Crosscut the A, B, and C Units into 1½-inch strips, as shown in **Diagram 4**. Avoid the seams between plaids, unless you don't mind some pieced squares. You need a total of 49 A strips, 70 B strips, and 4 C strips.

STEP 5. Referring to **Diagram 5**, join A, B, and C strips into blocks, taking care to match up seams. You need a total of 29 of Block 1, 8 of Block 2, and 4 of Block 3.

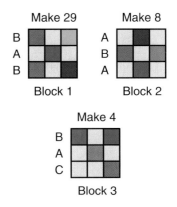

Make 29   Make 8

B   A
A   B
B   A

Block 1   Block 2

Make 4

B
A
C

Block 3

Diagram 5

Piecing the Center

STEP 1. To make the large center block, join one Block 1, four of Block 2, and four of Block 3 into horizontal rows, following the order in **Diagram 6** on page 20. (Block 1 is in the center.) Pay particular attention to the way Block 3 is placed in each corner. Press, alternating the direction of the seam allowances from row to row. Join the rows. Press.

Make It EASY

To keep long strip sets from sliding around on your ironing board, put a terry towel down. Strips set on the towel won't shimmy away from the iron, and you'll find that it's a lot easier to press the seams fully open and flat. ■

ASSEMBLING the CENTER

Cutting for Setting Pieces

From the muslin, cut:

◆ Four 3½-inch crosswise strips; from these strips, cut sixteen 3½-inch squares and eight 9½ × 3½-inch pieces

Make 1

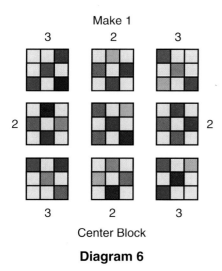

Center Block

Diagram 6

STEP 2. To make the large corner blocks, join five of Block 1 and four 3½-inch muslin squares into three horizontal rows of three blocks each, as shown in **Diagram 7**. Press, alternating the direction of the seam allowances from row to row. Join the rows. Press. Repeat to make a total of four corner blocks.

Make 4

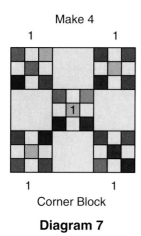

Corner Block

Diagram 7

STEP 3. To make the pieced side bars, sew a Block 1 to each side of a Block 2, as shown in **Diagram 8**. Press. Sew a muslin rectangle to each long edge to complete the block. Press seams

toward the muslin. Repeat to make a total of four side blocks.

Make 4

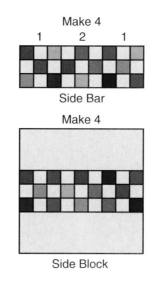

Side Bar

Make 4

Side Block

Diagram 8

STEP 4. Join the large sections into three rows of three sections each, as shown in **Diagram 9**. Press, alternating the direction of the seam

allowances from row to row. Join the rows to complete the quilt top, as shown in the **Quilt Diagram**. Press.

QUILTING

STEP 1. Press the finished quilt top. Mark the quilting design, using one of your own or following these suggestions.

■ The quilt in the photo was quilted in a simple all-over crosshatch design. The small size of this project would make it an easy one to quilt by machine. Use a walking foot or even-feed attachment on your sewing machine. Thread your machine with regular sewing thread in a light color in the top and the bobbin, then stitch along the cross-hatching lines.

Make 2

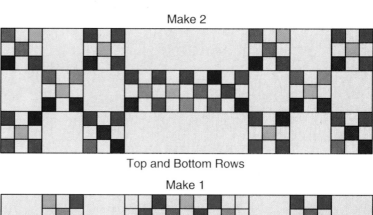

Top and Bottom Rows

Make 1

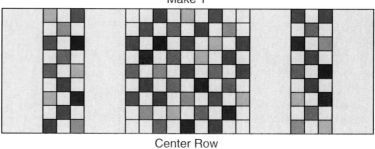

Center Row

Diagram 9

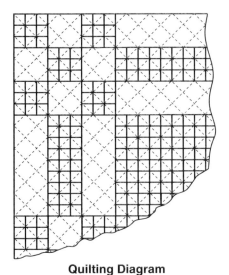

Quilting Diagram

■ If you have some experience machine quilting, it could be fun to do some free-motion meander quilting all over the surface of the quilt, or even fill the muslin areas with stipple quilting.

Make It FAST

Marking the crosshatch quilting design is quick work when you use a rotary ruler and mechanical pencil. Use a light touch with the pencil, and place a cutting mat underneath as you mark to provide a firm surface. ■

STEP 2. Layer the quilt top, batting, and backing. Baste the layers together.

STEP 3. Quilt by hand or machine.

STEP 4. Trim the batting and backing even with the quilt top. Remove the basting.

BINDING

STEP 1. Cut three 1½-inch crosswise strips to prepare 120 total inches of single-fold straight-grain binding.

STEP 2. Join the strips end to end with diagonal seams. Fold in half lengthwise with wrong sides together and press. Attach the binding to the quilt, following the instructions on page 242.

Make It FUN

Put those four 1½-inch plaid strips left over from the blocks to good use in the binding. Cut each of the plaid binding strips in half and intersperse the plaid leftovers with the plaid strips as you join them together to make the single length of binding. The random appearance of all the plaids in the binding will create a pleasingly scrappy look that complements the overall look of the quilt. (Plus, you can feel virtuous about using up leftover scraps!) ■

Quilt Diagram

Wild Goose Chase®

Sew So Easy

Paula Kemperman and Susan Rand, *Wild Goose Chase*

*T*his delightful miniature quilt is the perfect solution for itchy stitching fingers. Every quilter recognizes those moments when you want to play around with your stash of fabrics, yet not tackle something too big or time-consuming. Dig into your scrap bag, pick up your rotary cutter, and before you know it you'll have a sweet little quilt that you can tuck into a crock or basket for display, put under a wooden bowl of potpourri on the coffee table, or use as a backdrop for a collection of dolls or miniature chairs.

SIZE

Finished quilt is 9 × 10 inches
Finished block is 1½ × 2½ inches

FABRICS and SUPPLIES

Yardage based on 44-inch-wide fabric

- ⅛ yard dark fabric for binding*
- Scraps of light neutrals for block centers (you need 24, each at least 3 × 4 inches; ¼ yard total)
- Scraps of darker fabrics for block corners (you need 48, each at least 2 inches square; ⅛ yard total)

- Scraps of wool for appliqué (optional)
- Buttons (optional)
- Black perle cotton thread (optional)
- ⅜ yard (or one fat quarter) for backing
- Thin batting, larger than 9 × 10 inches (try Thermore, baby flannel, or Pellon fleece)
- Rotary cutter, ruler, and mat

*Some fabric shops will not cut ⅛-yard pieces. Purchase ¼ yard and save the extra for other projects, or check your scrap bag to see if you have any suitable leftovers on hand. Check the size of the scrap against the size of the pieces that need to be cut to confirm that you have enough fabric.

GETTING READY

COLOR and FABRIC TIPS:

This is a perfect pattern for all the new "made to look old" fabrics that we find in quilt shops today. It's also a great opportunity to use up those odd little bits in the scrap bag! As you can see from the quilt in the photograph on page 22, light background plaids and stripes can serve as "neutral" block centers, accentuated by the darker colors in the corners. When the fabric list calls for a neutral, you don't always have to play it safe with a solid or a plain, small-scale print. Use this little quilt as a chance to play around with some unexpected print combinations. You might be pleasantly surprised!

- Wash, damp dry, and press all fabrics before using.
- All seam allowances are ¼ inch and should be pressed to one side, unless otherwise indicated. Press seam allowances toward the darker fabric.
- One of the trio of quilts in the photo features a heart-and-hand appliqué. If you decide to include the appliqué, prepare templates using the **Appliqué Pattern** on page 27. Or, use the heart but trace the hand of your favorite small child to personalize this little quilt.
- Cutting directions for each part of the quilt are provided in the sections indicated by the yellow rotary cutters. This format allows you to cut what you need as you get ready to assemble each part of the quilt. If you prefer to cut all the pieces at once, skip ahead, looking for the yellow rotary cutters, and cut all the pieces before starting to sew.

Jewel Tones   Country Colors

■ ■

ASSEMBLING the BLOCKS

Cutting for Blocks (make 24)

From the light scraps, cut:

♦ Twenty-four 2 × 3-inch background rectangles

From the darker scraps, cut:

♦ Forty-eight 1¼-inch squares

NOTE: The designers used matching triangles on all the background rectangles. To duplicate this, you will need to cut two squares from each fabric.

Piecing the Blocks

STEP 1. Lay two matching corner squares right sides together on the upper left and lower right corners of a background rectangle, as shown in **Diagram 1.**

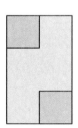

Diagram 1

STEP 2. Sew diagonally across the corner squares, as shown in **Diagram 2.**

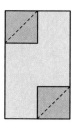

Diagram 2

STEP 3. Press half of each square toward the corner, as shown in **Diagram 3**.

Diagram 3

STEP 4. Cut off the excess fabric (background and square) that extends beyond the stitching line, leaving a ¼-inch seam, as shown in **Diagram 4**. Repeat to make a total of 24 blocks.

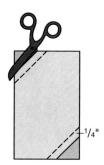

¼"

Diagram 4

ASSEMBLING the CENTER

STEP 1. Arrange the finished blocks in four rows of six, as shown in the **Quilt Diagram** on page 26.

STEP 2. Sew the blocks together into horizontal rows. Press, alternating the direction of the seam allowances from row to row. Join the rows. Press.

OPTIONAL APPLIQUÉ

STEP 1. Using black perle cotton and a whipstitch, appliqué the heart onto the hand.

STEP 2. Pin the hand onto the quilt top and whipstitch in place using the black perle cotton.

QUILTING

STEP 1. Press the finished quilt top. Quilt ⅛ inch from the seam line on the light background pieces (there's no need to mark this design). This quilt would be a snap to machine quilt; be sure to use an even-feed or walking foot attachment to keep the layers from shifting. If there's a budding quilter in your house, this small project might be a nice first try at hand quilting, in keeping with the tradition of mothers teaching daughters to quilt on small or doll-size quilts.

STEP 2. Layer the quilt top, batting, and backing. Baste the layers together.

STEP 3. Quilt by hand or machine.

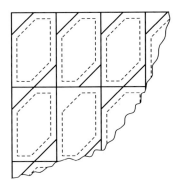

Quilting Diagram

STEP 4. Trim the batting and backing even with the quilt top. Remove the basting.

Make It FUN

If you've used lots of home-spun plaids and stripes in your quilt, you might want to add a few finishing touches that play up that folksy look. Instead of quilting, consider tying the quilt, using black or brown strands of yarn. Slide a button onto the strands and tie it to the quilt surface. Or, even if you quilt instead of tying, sew on a few buttons as embellishments. ■

Quilt Diagram

BINDING

STEP 1. Cut two 1¼-inch crosswise strips to prepare 50 total inches of single-fold straight-grain binding.

STEP 2. Join the strips end to end with diagonal seams. Fold in half lengthwise with wrong sides together and press. Attach the binding to the quilt, following the instructions on page 242.

Appliqué Pattern

Flying Flags

Retta Warehime, *Sew Cherished*

*S*how your patriotic pride with this snappy, up-to-date rendition of the flag, inspired by Betsy Ross's original but embellished with a quilter's touch. Ingeniously easy sewing and piecing techniques let you put together the blue "stars" and Flying Geese strips in a flash.

SIZE

Finished quilt is 37 × 38 inches

FABRICS and SUPPLIES

Yardage based on 44-inch-wide fabric
- ½ yard red print for border
- ⅜ yard gold print for accent strips
- ⅜ yard blue print for binding
- ⅜ yard red print for flag
- ⅜ yard white print for flag
- ⅛ yard *each* of five different tan prints for geese and stars

- ⅛ yard *each* of five additional reds for geese (or one 10-inch-square scrap of each)
- ⅛ yard dark blue for stars[*]
- ⅛ yard medium blue for stars[*]
- 1¼ yards for backing
- Batting, larger than 37 × 38 inches
- Twelve ½-inch buttons
- Fusible web
- Rotary cutter, ruler, and mat

[*] Some fabric shops will not cut ⅛-yard pieces. Purchase ¼ yard and save the extra for other projects, or check your scrap bag to see if you have any suitable leftovers on hand. Check the size of the scrap against the size of the pieces that need to be cut to confirm that you have enough fabric.

GETTING READY

COLOR and FABRIC TIPS:

This quilt is an exuberant display of reds, tans, and blues. For a less scrappy look, choose just one red, but vary the tans in the Flying Geese strips. Or, work with the same tan, but vary the reds. To create a more coordinated look, use just one red and one tan fabric in the Flying Geese strips.

Very scrappy Moderately scrappy Controlled color scheme

- Wash, damp dry, and press all fabrics before using.
- All seam allowances are ¼ inch and should be pressed to one side, unless otherwise indicated.
- In preparation for rotary cutting, trim the selvages off all but the backing fabric and square up one crosswise edge of each fabric, as described on page 236.
- Trace the **Star** pattern on page 35 onto fusible web, following the directions on page 238.
- Cutting directions for each part of the quilt are provided in the sections indicated by the yellow rotary cutters. This format allows you to cut what you need as you get ready to assemble each part of the quilt. If you prefer to cut all the pieces at once, skip ahead, looking for the yellow rotary cutters, and cut all the pieces before starting to sew.

ASSEMBLING the BLOCKS

Cutting for Flag Blocks (make 4)

From one of the tans, cut:

◆ One 3¾-inch crosswise strip; from this strip, cut four 3¾-inch squares and eight 3-inch squares

From the dark blue, cut:

◆ One 3¾-inch crosswise strip; from this strip, cut four squares

From the medium blue, cut:

◆ One 3-inch crosswise strip; from this strip, cut eight squares

From the red, cut:

◆ Seven 1½-inch crosswise strips

From the white, cut:

◆ Six 1½-inch crosswise strips

Piecing the Flag Blocks

STEP 1. With right sides together, lay a 3¾-inch tan square on a 3¾-inch dark blue square.

STEP 2. Draw an X from corner to corner on the tan square.

STEP 3. Using your presser foot as a guide, sew ¼ inch from the drawn lines, as shown in **Diagram 1**. If the edge of your presser foot is not exactly ¼ inch from the needle, try moving the needle position until it gives you the ¼ inch measurement. If your machine can't make this sort of adjustment, draw the sewing lines ¼ inch from the X. Another trick is to put a piece of ¼-inch masking tape along each line and use the edge of the tape as your sewing guide.

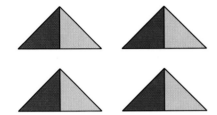

Diagram 1

Make It EASY

Before stitching, take a moment to press the squares together. This simple trick helps hold them in place while you're sewing, so there's no need to pin! ■

STEP 4. With a rotary cutter, cut apart on the drawn lines. Open, press, and set aside. Repeat with the remaining 3¾-inch tan and dark blue squares for a total of 16 pieced triangles.

STEP 5. Repeat Steps 1 through 4 with 3-inch tan and medium blue squares. Make a total of 32 pieced triangles.

STEP 6. Join two tan/medium blue units from Step 5, as shown in **Diagram 2**. Press. Repeat to make a total of 16 pieced squares. Each square will measure 2¼ inches.

Make 16

Diagram 2

STEP 7. Sew four pieced squares together to make a large square, as shown in **Diagram 3**. Be sure to note the fabric placement. Press. Repeat to make a total of four large squares. Each large square will measure 4 inches.

Make 4

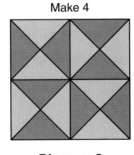

Diagram 3

STEP 8. Join one of the dark blue/tan units from Step 4 to each side of a large square from Step 7 to complete the star, as shown in **Diagram 4**. Attach triangles to the top and bottom first, then to the sides. If necessary, re-press the center seams in the triangles so that the seam allowances lie in the opposite direction from those in the large square. Repeat with the remaining pieced triangles and large squares to make a total of four stars. Each star will measure 5½ inches square.

Make 4

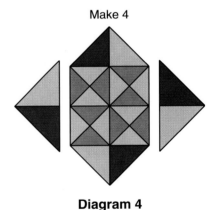

Diagram 4

STEP 9. Join three red strips and two white strips along the long edges, as shown in **Diagram 5**. Press. Crosscut this strip set into four 7½-inch units.

Make 1

7½"   7½"   7½"

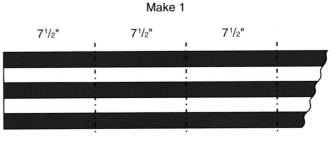

Diagram 5

STEP 10. Join the remaining red and white strips along the long edges to make *two* additional strip sets, as shown in **Diagram 6.** Press. Crosscut these sets to make a total of four 12½-inch units.

Make 2

12½"   12½"

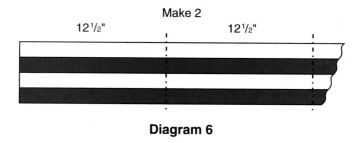

Diagram 6

Make It FUN

Save the leftover red-and-white strip sets to use in a pieced backing for the quilt. ■

STEP 11. Join a star unit to one end of a 7½-inch red-and-white striped unit. Then add a 12½-inch red-and-white striped unit to the bottom to complete the flag, as shown in **Diagram 7.** Repeat to make a total of four flags. Each flag will measure 9½ × 12½ inches.

Make 4

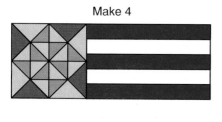

Diagram 7

Cutting for Flying Geese
(make 36)

From the various tans, cut a total of:
◆ Seventy-two 2-inch squares

From the various reds, cut a total of:
◆ Thirty-six 3½ × 2-inch rectangles

Piecing the Flying Geese

STEP 1. Draw a diagonal line from corner to corner on the wrong side of each 2-inch tan square, as shown in **Diagram 8.**

Diagram 8

STEP 2. With right sides together, lay a tan square on one end of a 3½ × 2-inch red rectangle, as shown in **Diagram 9.** Note the placement of the diagonal line. Sew along the line.

Diagram 9

STEP 3. Trim the outside corner of the tan square to ¼ inch from

the seam, as shown in **Diagram 10.** Do *not* cut the red. Open out and press the seam allowance toward the square. (Leaving the red rectangle intact prevents distortion.)

Trim ¼"

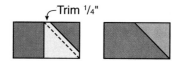

Diagram 10

STEP 4. Repeat Steps 2 and 3 with a second square on the other end of the rectangle, as shown in **Diagram 11.** Note the placement of the diagonal sewing line. Repeat to make a total of 36 flying geese units.

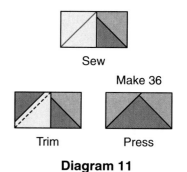

Sew

Make 36

Trim   Press

Diagram 11

STEP 5. Assemble the completed geese into two rows of 8 geese and one row of 20 geese, as shown in **Diagram 12.** Press all seam allowances in the direction indicated.

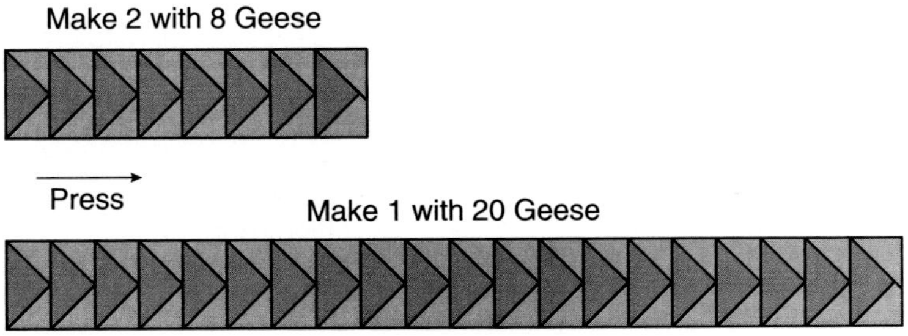

Make 2 with 8 Geese

→ Press

Make 1 with 20 Geese

Diagram 12

ASSEMBLING the CENTER

Cutting for the Center

From the remaining tans, cut:

♦ Four 12½ × 3-inch pieces (Star Background)

From the gold, cut:

♦ Eight 1½-inch crosswise strips; from these strips, cut the following:

  ♦ Twelve 12½-inch pieces (Horizontal Sashing)

  ♦ Two 3½-inch pieces (Horizontal Sashing)

  ♦ Four 32½-inch pieces (Vertical Sashing)

Using the pattern pieces traced onto fusible web and the dark blue fabric scraps, prepare the following (directions for fusible appliqué are on page 238).

♦ Twelve Stars from the dark blue

Piecing and Appliquéing the Center

STEP 1. Join flags, 8-geese units, star backgrounds, and 12½-inch sashing strips into two vertical rows, as shown in **Diagram 13**. Press.

STEP 2. Sew a 3½-inch sashing strip to each end of the 20-geese unit. Press.

Make It FAST

This speedy method for the Flying Geese moves along even more quickly when you do the same step for all 36 geese at the same time. Mark all the squares at once; sew, trim, and press the first seam on all the geese at the same time; then finish up with the second seam, and you'll have a finished flock of three dozen geese before you know it. ∎

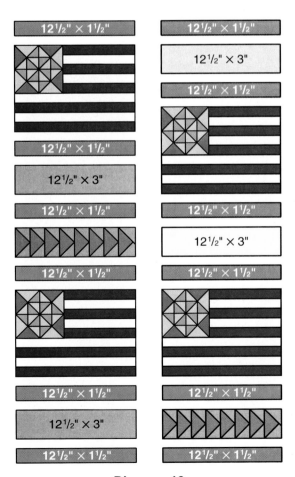

Diagram 13

STEP 3. Join vertical rows, the 20-geese unit, and the 32½-inch vertical sashing strips, as shown in **Diagram 14**. Press.

STEP 4. Referring to the **Quilt Diagram** and the photograph on page 28 for placement, fuse three dark blue stars to each tan background piece. Sew a button in the center of each star.

BORDERS

Cutting for Borders

From the red, cut:

◆ Four 3½-inch crosswise strips

Attaching the Borders

STEP 1. Measure across the center of the quilt horizontally. Cut two border strips to this exact measurement.

STEP 2. Attach these strips to the top and bottom of the quilt top. Press toward the border.

STEP 3. Measure through the center of the quilt vertically. Include the top and bottom borders in your measurement. Cut the remaining two border strips to this exact measurement.

STEP 4. Attach these strips to the sides of the quilt top. Press toward the border.

Diagram 14

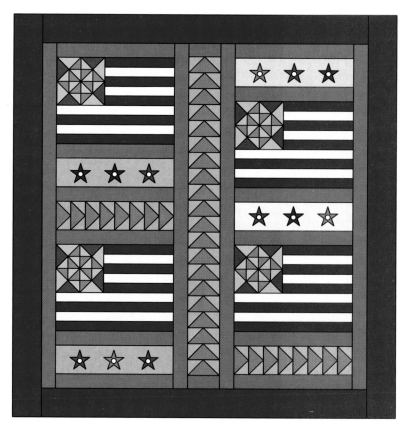

Quilt Diagram

QUILTING

STEP 1. Press the finished quilt top. Mark a quilting design, using one of your own ideas or following these suggestions.

■ Quilt in the ditch between all sections of the quilt, including the stripes in the flags.

■ Stitch along all seams in the star sections.

■ Quilt along the edge of the geese and ¼ inch inside.

■ Randomly scatter five-pointed stars throughout the outer border, having some of the star points extend into the gold sashing.

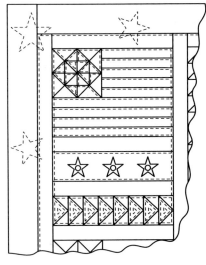

Quilting Diagram

STEP 2. Layer the quilt top, batting, and backing. Baste the layers together.

STEP 3. Quilt by hand or machine.

STEP 4. Trim the batting and backing even with the quilt top. Remove the basting.

BINDING

STEP 1. Cut four 2½-inch crosswise strips to prepare 165 total inches of double-fold straight-grain binding.

STEP 2. Join the strips end to end with diagonal seams. Fold in half lengthwise with wrong sides together and press. Attach the binding to the quilt following the directions on page 242.

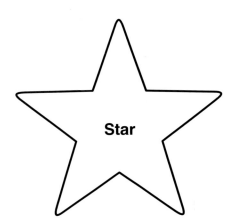

Star

Stars

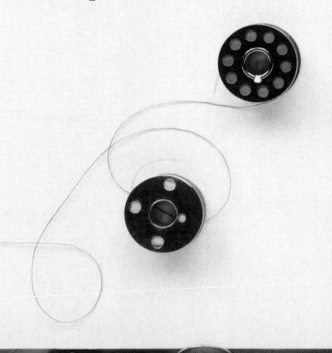

1776

Gerry Kimmel, *Red Wagon*

A charming wall quilt with the look of a homemade eighteenth-century flag, 1776 goes together almost as fast as you can say "Betsy Ross." This patriotic project, with its slightly askew scattering of stars and chunky, wide strips, fits in nicely with today's popular homespun, folk-art style of decorating.

SIZE

Finished quilt is 39 × 47 inches
Finished block is 4¼ inches
    square

FABRICS
and SUPPLIES

Yardage based on 44-inch-wide fabric
- ⅔ yard red print for border
- ¾ yard dark blue print for star backgrounds
- ⅔ yard white-and-blue plaid for sashing strips
- ⅜ yard blue solid for binding
- ⅓ yard gold solid for stars
- 1½ yards for backing
- Batting, larger than 39 × 47 inches
- Template plastic
- Rotary cutter, ruler, and mat

GETTING READY

COLOR and FABRIC TIPS:

Although red, white, and blue are an obvious choice for a quilt with this patriotic motif, other color schemes would work equally well. Just be sure to provide enough contrast between the star fabrics and their backgrounds or you risk losing the stars. Another place to think about contrast is between the plain vertical strips and the star-studded strips. The quilt shown has high contrast between these strips; for a more subtle effect with less contrast, you might consider using dark- and medium-value fabrics in these areas.

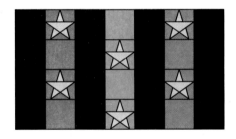

Amish Color Scheme

- Wash, damp dry, and press all fabrics before using.
- All seam allowances are ¼ inch and should be pressed to one side, unless otherwise indicated.
- Trace the pattern pieces on page 43 onto template plastic and cut them out.
- This quilt includes some templates that must be used both right side up and reversed. This is always specified in the instructions, and is denoted on the pattern pieces with (r) following the pattern letter name.
- In preparation for rotary cutting, trim the selvages off the plaid, red print, and dark blue print fabrics and square off one crosswise edge of each fabric, as described on page 236.
- Cutting directions for each part of the quilt are provided in the sections indicated by the yellow rotary cutters. This format allows you to cut what you need as you get ready to assemble each part of the quilt. If you prefer to cut all the pieces at once, skip ahead, looking for the yellow rotary cutters, and cut all the pieces before starting to sew.

ASSEMBLING the BLOCKS

Cutting for Blocks (make 14)

From the blue print, cut:

- Two 4¾-inch crosswise strips; from these strips cut a total of thirteen 4¾-inch squares (Alternate Blocks)
- 14 each of D, D Reverse, E, E Reverse, and F

From the gold, cut:

- 14 A
- 14 B
- 28 C

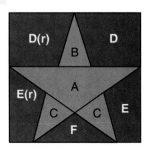

Block Diagram

Rotary Cutting with Templates

Trace around the plastic templates onto the right sides of the blue and gold fabrics, using pattern pieces **A, B, C, D, D Reverse, E, E Reverse,** and **F.** Align the edge of a rotary ruler exactly along the lines you've drawn and cut with the rotary cutter. For more accurate pieces, use the thin lead of a mechanical pencil to draw the cutting lines.

Make It FAST

Save time by not making separate patterns for reverse pieces. Instead, just trace the plastic templates for pieces D and E onto the fabric with wrong sides folded together. For each D and E you trace and cut from the top layer of the fabric, you will automatically create a reverse piece from the bottom fabric layer. ∎

Piecing the Blocks

STEP 1. Referring to **Diagram 1**, sew D and D Reverse to B to make Section 1.

STEP 2. Sew C to E Reverse. Sew this unit to A to make Section 2.

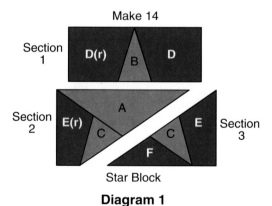

Make 14

Section 1 D(r) B D

Section 2 E(r) A C E Section 3

F

Star Block

Diagram 1

STEP 3. Sew E and F to the remaining C to make Section 3.

STEP 4. Sew Section 3 to Section 2. Sew Sections 2 and 3 to Section 1 to complete the block. Repeat to make a total of 14 blocks.

ASSEMBLING the CENTER

Cutting for Setting Pieces

From the plaid, cut:

◆ Four 4¾ × 38¾-inch strips

Piecing the Center

STEP 1. To make the two outer pieced rows, join five Star Blocks and four dark blue Alternate Blocks, beginning and ending with stars, as shown in **Diagram 2**. Press.

Make 2

Outer Pieced Row

Diagram 2

STEP 2. To make the inner pieced row, join four Star Blocks and five dark blue Alternate Blocks, beginning and ending with Alternate Blocks, as shown in **Diagram 3**. Press.

STEP 3. Referring to the **Quilt Diagram** on page 42, sew plaid sashing strips to the pieced strips, beginning and ending with plaid strips. Press.

Make 1

Inner Pieced Row

Diagram 3

Make It FUN

Depending on how you orient the star blocks, you can make the stars look perfectly balanced or tilted slightly to the left or slightly to the right. As you join the star blocks into the vertical rows, play around with their placement. In the quilt in the photograph on page 38, you'll notice there's a playful randomness to the way the stars are tilted. ∎

BORDERS

Cutting for Borders

From the red, cut:

◆ Four 4¾ × 44-inch strips

Attaching the Borders

STEP 1. Measure through the center of your quilt vertically. Cut two border strips to this exact measurement.

STEP 2. Attach these strips to the sides of your quilt top. Press the seam allowances toward the border.

STEP 3. Measure across the center of the quilt horizontally. Include the side borders in your measurement. Cut the remaining two border strips to this exact measurement. Attach to the top and bottom of your quilt top. Press toward the border.

QUILTING

STEP 1. Press the finished quilt top. Mark the quilting design, using one of your own or following these suggestions.

- Quilt diagonal lines 1 inch apart in the blue backgrounds.

- Channel quilt in the red borders 1 inch apart.

- Stitch a smaller star shape inside each of the gold stars.

- Quilt seven lines of parallel stitching, about ¾ inch apart, in the blue plaid areas.

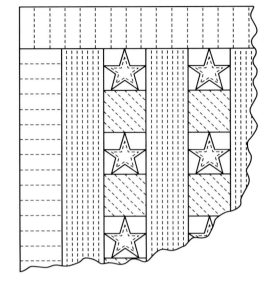

Quilting Diagram

- Quilt small stars randomly across the surface of the quilt.

STEP 2. Layer the quilt top, batting, and backing. Baste all the layers together.

STEP 3. Quilt by hand or machine.

STEP 4. Trim the batting and backing even with the quilt top. Remove the basting.

BINDING

STEP 1. From the binding fabric, cut five 2-inch crosswise strips to prepare 190 total inches of double-fold straight-grain binding.

STEP 2. Join the strips end to end with diagonal seams. Fold in half lengthwise with wrong sides together and press. Attach the binding to the quilt, following the instructions on page 242.

Quilt Diagram

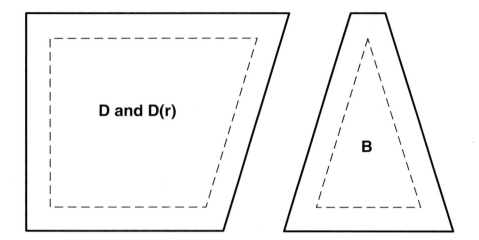

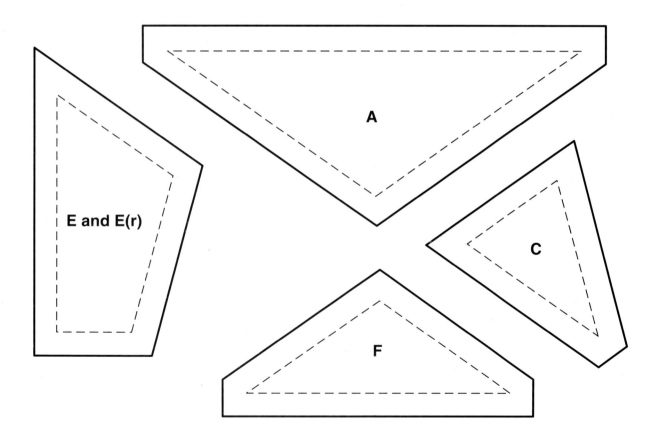

Starry Night

Glenda Carr, *Blue Whale Designs*

*L*ike a magician pulling a rabbit out of a hat, reach into your stash of fabrics and pull out a happy mix of celestial prints to make this star-studded quilt. Two easy variations on a traditional pieced star block, plus two simple appliqué star clusters, create a small quilt with a lot of interesting variety. Mix and match fabrics to your heart's content to work your own quiltmaking magic.

SIZE

Finished quilt is 25 × 32 inches
Finished block is 6 inches square

FABRICS and SUPPLIES

Yardage based on 44-inch-wide fabric
- ⅝ yard navy star print for sashing and binding
- ⅝ yard navy solid for background
- ½ yard white print for blocks
- ⅜ yard *each* of three different lavender prints

NOTE: Use one lavender print for the narrow outer border. You will need a little more than ⅜ yard of this print, and also of any fabric you think you will use more than another.

- ⅜ yard lavender solid for blocks
- ⅞ yard for backing
- Batting, larger than 25 × 32 inches
- Template plastic or fusible web, depending on appliqué method
- Rotary cutter, ruler, and mat

GETTING READY

COLOR and FABRIC TIPS:
For a totally different look from the quilt shown, use bright or richly colored fabrics with stars, moons, and other celestial motifs. Many of these have gold highlights, which will create a more elegant feeling. Keep a good level of contrast between the background and the fabrics you choose for the stars.

Warm colors like red can alter the mood of the quilt

■ Wash, damp dry, and press all fabrics before using. To create a warm, country look, some of the fabrics in this quilt were tea-dyed before they were cut and sewn together into the blocks. (A recipe for tea dyeing appears on page 63.) Tan fabric dye also works; follow the manufacturer's instructions.

■ All seam allowances are ¼ inch and should be pressed to one side, unless otherwise indicated.

■ In preparation for rotary cutting, trim the selvages off all fabrics and square up one crosswise edge of each fabric, as described on page 236.

■ See "Appliqué Basics" on page 238 and choose a method. Then, trace the patterns for the **Large Star** and **Small Star** on page 51 onto template plastic or fusible web, depending on the method you've chosen.

■ Cutting directions for each part of the quilt are provided in the sections indicated by the yellow rotary cutters. This format allows you to cut what you need as you get ready to assemble each part of the quilt. If you prefer to cut all the pieces at once, skip ahead, looking for the yellow rotary cutters, and cut all the pieces before starting to sew.

ASSEMBLING the BLOCKS

The pieced star blocks (Blocks 1 and 2) are two variations of the Ohio Star. Different fabric combinations give each block a different look, even though the pattern is the same.

The cutting directions that follow are for one version each of Blocks 1 and 2, using three different lavenders (Fabrics #1, #2, and #3) and the navy background. For the rest of the blocks, vary the position of the different lavender prints, or try a block with two lavender fabrics plus the background. Use the white and solid lavender accent fabrics sparingly and vary their placement from block to block.

Cutting  for Block 1 (make 5)

From the navy solid, cut pieces for all five blocks at once. Cut:

◆ Two 2½-inch crosswise strips; from these strips, cut 20 squares (A)

◆ One 17 × 3¼-inch piece; from this piece, cut 5 squares. Cut each square in half *twice* diagonally to make 20 triangles (B).

For each of the five blocks, cut the following:

From Fabric #1:

◆ Two 3¼-inch squares; cut each square in half *twice* diagonally to make 8 triangles (B)

From Fabric #2:

◆ One 3¼-inch square; cut the square in half *twice* diagonally to make 4 triangles (B)

From Fabric #3:

◆ One 2½-inch square (A)

Make It FUN

The center squares in Blocks 1 and 2 give you a perfect place to feature a special motif from a favorite fabric. Make a handy viewing guide by cutting a square equal to the size of the finished square in the block (cut size minus ½ inch) from a piece of lightweight cardboard. Discard the square you've cut out and use the opening in the cardboard as your guide. Move it around the fabric until you've isolated the motif you want to use. You can lightly run a pencil around the edges of the square to mark the positioning on the fabric. Be sure to add ¼-inch seam allowances on all sides before cutting. ■

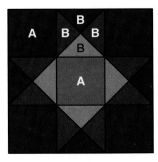

Block 1

Piecing for Block 1

STEP 1. Sew a navy B to a Fabric #1 B, as shown on the left in **Diagram 1**. Press. Sew a Fabric #1 B to a Fabric #2 B, as shown on the right. Press.

Diagram 1

STEP 2. Sew the two units from Step 1 together, as shown in **Diagram 2**. Press. Repeat to make a total of four pieced squares.

Make 4

Diagram 2

STEP 3. To make the top row, sew a navy A to each side of one pieced square, following the fabric placement in **Diagram 3**. Press toward A. Repeat to make the bottom row.

Make 2

Diagram 3

STEP 4. Sew a pieced square from Step 2 to each side of a Fabric #3 A, following the fabric placement in **Diagram 4**. Press toward A.

Make 1

Diagram 4

STEP 5. Referring to the diagram of **Block 1**, sew the three rows together, matching seams. By always pressing toward the A pieces, seams automatically face in opposite directions, making matching easy. The navy triangles should be on the outside edges of the block. Press.

STEP 6. Repeat to make a total of five blocks, changing fabrics for each block.

Make It FAST

To speed the assembly of these star blocks, join the "chain gang." Chain piecing, where you feed many similar units through the sewing machine without stopping in between, is a very efficient way to sew. Make sure you have all the pieces for the units ready next to your sewing machine, with right sides together and the edge to be sewn on the right. As you come to the end of the first unit, butt the second unit up against it and keep sewing. Repeat until all the units are sewn. You'll end up with a "chain" of pieces that's easy to pick up and carry to the ironing board. Some quilters find it handy to press the joined units first, then clip the threads to separate them. ■

Cutting for Block 2 (make 5)

From the navy solid, cut pieces for all five blocks at once. Cut:

♦ One 2-inch crosswise strip; from this strip, cut 20 squares (C)

♦ One 22 × 4¼-inch piece; from this piece, cut 5 squares. Cut each square in half *twice* diagonally to make 20 triangles (E).

For each of the five blocks, cut the following:

From Fabric #1:

♦ Four 2⅜-inch squares; cut each square in half *once* diagonally to make 8 triangles (D)

From Fabric #2:

♦ Two 2⅜-inch squares; cut each square in half *once* diagonally to make 4 triangles (D)

From Fabric #3:

♦ One 2⅝-inch square (F)

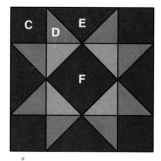

Block 2

Piecing for Block 2

STEP 1. Sew the long edge of a Fabric #1 D to each short side of a navy E, as shown in

Diagram 5. Press. Repeat to make a total of four units.

Make 4

Diagram 5

STEP 2. Sew the long edge of a Fabric #2 D to each edge of a Fabric #3 F, as shown in Diagram 6. Press.

Make 1

Diagram 6

STEP 3. To make the top row, sew a navy C to each end of one of the Step 1 units, as shown in Diagram 7. Press the seams toward the center. Repeat to make the bottom row.

Make 2

Diagram 7

STEP 4. To make the middle row, sew one of the units from Step 1 to each side of the square from Step 2, following the fabric placement in **Diagram 8**. Press toward the sides.

STEP 5. Referring to the diagram of **Block 2**, sew the three rows together, matching seams and points. Press.

Make 1

Diagram 8

STEP 6. Repeat to make a total of five blocks, changing fabrics for each block.

Cutting for Block 3 (make 1)

From the navy solid, cut:

♦ One 6½-inch square

From the white, cut:

♦ 4 Large Stars, following the directions for your appliqué method

From one of the lavender prints, cut:

♦ 1 Large Star, following the directions for your appliqué method

Block 3

Appliquéing Block 3

STEP 1. Referring to the diagram of **Block 3**, position the four white large stars in the corners of the 6½-inch navy square with the points touching. Be careful to stay within the ¼-inch seam allowances. Lay the lavender large star in the center.

STEP 2. Fuse or appliqué, following the directions for the method you have chosen.

Cutting  for Block 4 (make 1)

From the navy solid, cut:

◆ One 6½-inch square

From the white, cut:

◆ 7 Small Stars, following the directions for your appliqué method

Block 4

Appliquéing Block 4

STEP 1. Referring to the diagram of **Block 4**, position the seven white small stars on the navy square in a circle. Some of the points will overlap. Be careful to stay within the ¼-inch seam allowances.

STEP 2. Fuse or appliqué, following the directions for the method you have chosen.

ASSEMBLING the CENTER

Cutting for the Center

From the navy print, cut:

◆ Three 2-inch crosswise strips; from these strips, cut eight 6½-inch pieces (Vertical Sashing) and three 21½-inch pieces (Horizontal Sashing)

Piecing the Center

STEP 1. Refer to the **Quilt Diagram** as you follow these directions. Lay your finished blocks and the 6½-inch vertical sashing strips out in four horizontal rows. Move them around until you are satisfied with the arrangement. Balance placement of white and solid lavender accent fabrics, as well as placement of Blocks 3 and 4. Sew the blocks and strips into rows. Press toward the sashing.

Quilt Diagram

STEP 2. Join the four rows with the three 21½-inch sashing strips to complete the center. Press toward the sashing.

BORDERS

Cutting for Borders

From the navy print for the inner border, cut:

◆ Four 2-inch crosswise strips

From one of the lavender prints for the outer border, cut:

◆ Four 1-inch crosswise strips

Attaching the Borders

STEP 1. Refer to the **Quilt Diagram** as you follow these directions. Measure across the center of your quilt horizontally. Cut two 2-inch navy strips to this exact measurement.

STEP 2. Attach these strips to the top and bottom of the quilt top. Press toward the border.

STEP 3. Measure through the center of the quilt vertically. Include the top and bottom borders in your measurement. Cut the remaining two navy strips to this exact measurement.

STEP 4. Attach these strips to the sides of the quilt top. Press toward the border.

STEP 5. Repeat Steps 1 through 4 with 1-inch lavender outer border strips.

QUILTING

STEP 1. Press the finished quilt top. Mark the quilting design, using one of your own or following these suggestions.

- Using dark navy quilting thread, follow the shapes of the stars in Blocks 1 and 2, quilting ¼ inch inside and outside the seam lines.

- In Blocks 3 and 4, start in the center of each star and quilt in a straight line out to each point.

- In Blocks 3 and 4, working ¼ inch away from the edge of the stars, stitch in one continuous line around the entire star cluster.

- In Block 4, do the same on the inside of the star cluster.

- Quilt ¼ inch from both sides of the inner border.

STEP 2. Layer the quilt top, batting, and backing. Baste the layers together.

STEP 3. Quilt by hand or machine.

STEP 4. Trim the batting and backing even with the quilt top. Remove the basting.

BINDING

STEP 1. From the navy star print fabric, cut three 2-inch crosswise strips to prepare 125 total inches of double-fold straight-grain binding.

STEP 2. Join the strips end to end with diagonal seams. Fold in half lengthwise with wrong sides together and press. Attach the binding to the quilt, following the directions on page 242.

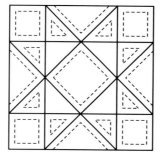
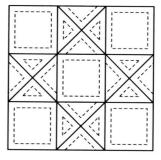
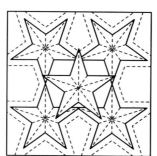

Quilting Diagram

Make It EASY

Thin batting gives your quilt an authentic look, with the added bonus of being extra-easy to hand quilt. Look for low-loft battings like Thermore or Quilt Light (both polyester). ■

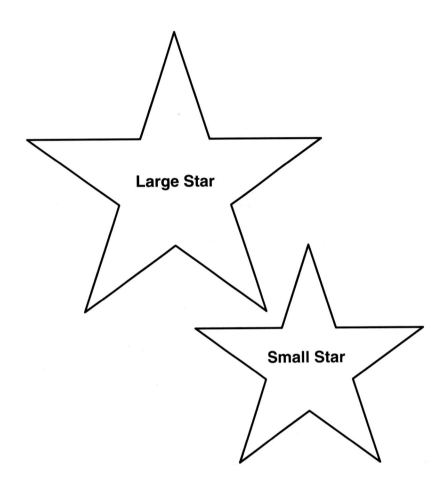

Large Star

Small Star

CHURN DASH DESIGNS

Stars & Stripes

Marilyn Reardon, *Churn Dash Designs*

*Y*ou might be tempted to hum "Yankee Doodle" as you work on this patriotic quilt that sizzles with bold contrast between the red, white, and blue fabrics. This snappy wall quilt combines All-American blocks like the eight-pointed star and diamond-in-a-square. These blocks are simple to rotary cut and piece, but no one else needs to know that!

SIZE

Finished quilt is 36 inches square
Finished block is 6 inches square

FABRICS and SUPPLIES

Yardage based on 44-inch-wide fabric

- ⅞ yard navy solid for outer border and binding
- ½ yard muslin for star backgrounds
- ¼ yard red solid for inner border
- Scraps of nine different navy prints (each at least 10 × 14 inches)
- Scraps of nine different red prints (each at least 2½ × 10 inches)
- 1¼ yards for backing
- Batting, larger than 36 inches square
- Rotary cutter, ruler, and mat

GETTING READY

COLOR and FABRIC TIPS:
Instead of a scrappy version, you could make this quilt using a single navy blue fabric and a single red fabric. This would require ¾ yard of the navy and ⅓ yard of the red *in addition to* the amounts required for the borders.

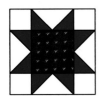

Repeating the same fabrics can have a soothing effect

- Wash, damp dry, and press all fabrics before using.

- All seam allowances are ¼ inch and should be pressed to one side, unless otherwise indicated. Press the seams toward the darker fabric.

- In preparation for rotary cutting, trim the selvages (if any) off the scraps and border fabrics and square off one crosswise edge of each fabric, as described on page 236.

- Cutting directions for each part of the quilt are provided in the sections indicated by the yellow rotary cutters. This format allows you to cut what you need as you get ready to assemble each part of the quilt. If you prefer to cut all the pieces at once, skip ahead, looking for the yellow rotary cutters, and cut all the pieces before starting to sew.

ASSEMBLING the BLOCKS

Cutting for Star Blocks (make 9)

From the muslin, cut:

- Two 2-inch crosswise strips; from these strips, cut 36 2-inch squares (B)

- Two 3-inch crosswise strips; from these strips, cut 18 squares. Cut the squares in half diagonally to make 36 triangles (D).

From each of the nine navy scraps, cut:

- One 3½-inch square (A)

From each of the nine red scraps, cut:

- One 2½ × 10-inch strip; cut each strip into 4 squares. Cut each square in half diagonally to make a total of 72 triangles (C).

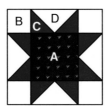

Star Block

Piecing the Star Blocks

STEP 1. Sew a C to each side of a D, as shown in **Diagram 1.**

Press. Repeat to make a total of four units.

Make 4

Diagram 1

STEP 2. Sew two Step 1 units to opposite sides of A, as shown in **Diagram 2.** Press the seams toward A.

Make 1

Diagram 2

STEP 3. Sew a B square to each end of the remaining two Step 1 units. See **Diagram 3**. Press the seams toward B.

Make 2

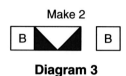

Diagram 3

STEP 4. Referring to the **Star Block** diagram, sew these sections together to complete the Star Block. Press. Repeat to make a total of nine Star Blocks.

Cutting
for Diamond Blocks
(make 4)

From the muslin, cut:

◆ One 4¾ × 19-inch strip; from this strip, cut 4 squares (E)

From each of four of the navy scraps, cut:

◆ One 5½-inch square; cut each square in half *twice* diagonally to make 16 triangles (F)

Diamond Block

Piecing
the Diamond Blocks

STEP 1. Sew an F to each side of E, as shown in **Diagram 4**. Press.

Diagram 4

STEP 2. Sew two F triangles to the remaining sides of E, as shown in **Diagram 5**. Press. Repeat to make a total of four Diamond Blocks.

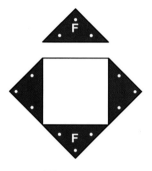

Diagram 5

ASSEMBLING
the CENTER

Cutting
for Setting Pieces

From the navy scraps, cut:

◆ Two 9¾-inch squares; cut each square in half *twice* diagonally for a total of 8 side setting triangles

◆ Two 5⅛-inch squares; cut each square in half *once* diagonally for a total of 4 corner setting triangles

Piecing the Center

STEP 1. Following the **Assembly Diagram**, lay out the Star Blocks, Diamond Blocks, and setting pieces. Play with the blocks until you are happy with the arrangement of the different reds and blues.

Side setting triangle

Corner setting triangle

Assembly Diagram

Make It EASY

Make sure the blocks are all a standard size before you assemble the quilt top. This ensures that the quilt will go together easily and be nice and flat. No matter how careful you are, there's bound to be some variance in size among the blocks. Measure and see which ones deviate the most from the group. Those are the blocks you should attend to. If they are within ⅛ inch of the average measurement, you can "fudge" as you sew the blocks together. But if they deviate more than that, you should be ready to resew. ■

STEP 2. Sew the blocks together in diagonal rows. Add the corner setting triangles last. Press, alternating the direction of the seams from row to row.

STEP 3. Join the rows. Press.

BORDERS

Cutting for Borders

From the red solid for the inner border, cut:

♦ Four 1½-inch crosswise strips

From the navy solid for the outer border, cut:

♦ Four 4½-inch crosswise strips

Attaching the Borders

STEP 1. Measure through the center of your quilt vertically. Cut two inner border strips to this exact measurement. Attach these strips to the sides of your quilt top. Press the seam allowances toward the border.

STEP 2. Measure across the center of the quilt horizontally, including the side borders. Cut the remaining two inner border strips to this exact measurement. Attach them to the top and bottom of the quilt top. Press the seam allowances toward the border.

STEP 3. Repeat Steps 1 and 2 for the outer border.

QUILTING

STEP 1. Press the finished quilt top. Mark the quilting design, using one of your own or following these suggestions.

■ Create an interesting effect by using triple rows of quilting, spaced ½ inch apart. These rows form an X through the Diamond Blocks, but appear only in the muslin background of the Star Blocks. To get your bearings as you mark these lines, have the center line of each trio run exactly through the V formed by the star points.

■ Quilt ¼ inch inside each center square in the Star Blocks.

■ Stitch in the ditch between the center of the quilt and the inner border, and again between the inner and outer border.

■ Fill the outer border with diagonal lines spaced 1 inch apart.

STEP 2. Layer the quilt top, batting, and backing. Baste the layers together.

STEP 3. Quilt by hand or machine.

STEP 4. Trim the batting and backing even with the quilt top. Remove the basting.

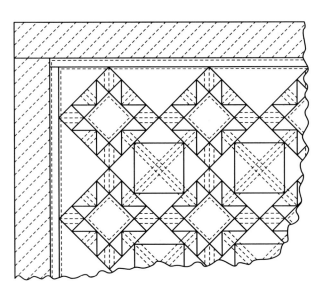

Quilting Diagram

BINDING

STEP 1. Cut four 1¼-inch crosswise strips to prepare 160 total inches of single-fold straight-grain binding.

STEP 2. Join the strips end to end with diagonal seams. Fold in half lengthwise with wrong sides together and press. Attach the binding to the quilt, following the instructions on page 242.

Quilt Diagram

Make It FUN

If your family has a reunion planned, turn this into a commemorative signature quilt. Bring either the individual blocks or the completed (but not yet layered or quilted) top to the gathering, along with some extra-fine point, permanent felt-tip pens. Set up a table for the signing area, and make sure people stop by to add their names to the muslin areas around the stars and in the diamond blocks. To make it easier to write on the fabric, press freezer paper onto the back of all the muslin pieces. When the quilt is all done, be sure to add a label giving the date, event, and location. If your family gets together every year, make this quilt signing a regular feature and hold a drawing to see who gets to go home with the family quilt. ■

Little Quilts.

Star & Nine Patch Quilt

Alice Berg, Mary Ellen Von Holt,
and Sylvia Johnson, *Little Quilts*

*T*his "little" (not miniature) quilt was designed
as a scrap quilt to resemble those of days gone
by. Doll quilts were often a little girl's first attempt
at quilting, using scraps from Mother's sewing basket. Have fun using your own scraps—or anyone
else's you can get your hands on!

SIZE

Finished quilt is 23 inches square
Finished block is 3 inches square

FABRICS and SUPPLIES

Yardage based on 44-inch-wide
fabric
- ¼ yard blue print for outer border
- ¼ yard black for binding
- ⅛ yard black print for star backgrounds*
- ⅛ yard dark plaid for setting triangles*
- ⅛ yard gold print for inner border*

- Scraps of a variety of prints for Nine Patch Blocks (at least 1½ inches wide and 12 inches long; need a total of 18)
- Scraps of gold-and-tan prints for stars
- ¾ yard for backing
- Thin batting, larger than 23 inches square
- Black embroidery floss (optional)
- Template plastic or fusible web, depending on appliqué method
- Rotary cutter, ruler, and mat
*Some fabric shops will not cut ⅛-yard pieces. Purchase ¼ yard and save the extra for other projects, or check your scrap bag to see if you have any suitable leftovers on hand. Check the size of the scrap against the size of the pieces that need to be cut to confirm that you have enough fabric.

GETTING READY

COLOR and FABRIC TIPS:

The more different fabrics you use, the better. Choose a variety of tiny, 100 percent cotton prints in reds, blues, greens, tans, golds, and pinks. Don't forget plaids and stripes! In the quilt in the photograph on page 58, only the setting triangles and star background blocks are cut from the same fabrics. Repeating the same fabrics in this way can help keep a scrappy quilt from becoming too busy.

Color variety makes the quilt!

- Wash, damp dry, and press all fabrics before using.

- All seam allowances are ¼ inch and should be pressed to one side, unless otherwise indicated. Accuracy in piecing is more important than ever when the pieces are so small.

- See "Appliqué Basics" on page 238 and choose a method. Then, trace the **Star** on page 63 onto template plastic or fusible web, depending on the method you've chosen.

- Cutting directions for each part of the quilt are provided in the sections indicated by the yellow rotary cutters. This format allows you to cut what you need as you get ready to assemble each part of the quilt. If you prefer to cut all the pieces at once, skip ahead, looking for the yellow rotary cutters, and cut all the pieces before starting to sew.

ASSEMBLING the BLOCKS

Cutting for Blocks

Nine Patch Blocks (make 16)

From the print scraps, cut:

◆ Eighteen 1½ × 12-inch strips

Star Blocks (make 9)

From the black, cut:

◆ Nine 3½-inch squares

From the gold-and-tan scraps, cut:

◆ 9 Stars, following the directions for the appliqué method you have chosen

Star Block

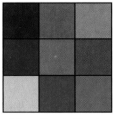

Nine-Patch Block

Block Diagrams

Make It FAST

The fastest and easiest way to collect a variety of different fabric strips for the Nine Patch Blocks is to plan ahead. Whenever you cut fabric for a project, cut several 1½-inch-wide strips to set aside in a basket to use for this or any other future project. You'll have a delightfully assorted selection of strips ready and waiting for you to piece together into nifty 3-inch Nine Patches. ■

Piecing the Nine Patch Blocks

STEP 1. Sew three strips together to form a strip set, as shown in **Diagram 1**. Be sure to use an accurate ¼-inch seam. Press all seams to one side. Repeat to make a total of six strip sets. Note that in this quilt, the placement of dark and light strips is random.

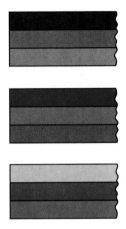

Diagram 1

STEP 2. Crosscut the strips into 1½-inch slices, as shown in **Diagram 2**. Sew three pieces together to make a Nine Patch Block, making sure to match seams between blocks. Ignore the seam direction if necessary, instead of trying to always alternate seam allowances. Press. As you combine slices from the various strip sets, don't worry about matching fabrics—be spontaneous!

STEP 3. Measure the first block. It should be 3½ inches square. Adjust your seam allowance if necessary. Repeat Steps 1 and 2 to make a total of 16 Nine Patch Blocks.

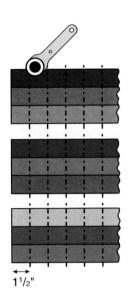

1½"

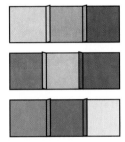

Alternate seam allowances when possible

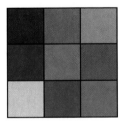

Diagram 2

Preparing the Star Blocks

Appliqué a gold-and-tan star to the center of each of nine black squares, using your favorite technique. If you chose fusible web, embroider around each star with a buttonhole stitch, following the **Buttonhole Stitch Diagram.**

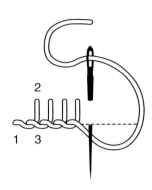

Buttonhole Stitch Diagram

Make It EASY

A design wall is invaluable in laying out your quilt. It allows you to stand back and position blocks so that the finished piece is well balanced. Take a 1½-yard piece of fleece or flannel and tack or tape it to a wall in your sewing room. Place the parts of your quilt on the fleece and stand back to "audition" the layout. Make changes as necessary, moving the pieces around before sewing. ■

ASSEMBLING the CENTER

Cutting for Setting Pieces

From the plaid, cut:

◆ Three 5½-inch squares; cut each square in half twice diagonally to make 12 triangles (Side Setting Triangles)

◆ Two 3-inch squares; cut the squares in half diagonally to make 4 triangles (Corner Setting Triangles)

Piecing the Center

STEP 1. Following the **Quilt Diagram**, lay out the Nine Patch Blocks, Star Blocks, and setting triangles.

STEP 2. Beginning at the top left corner, sew blocks together in diagonal rows, referring to **Diagram 3**, adding side and corner triangles as needed. Press, alternating the direction of the seam allowances from row to row.

Diagram 3

STEP 3. Join the rows. Press.

BORDERS

Cutting
for Borders

From the gold, cut:

◆ Two 1½-inch crosswise strips; cut each strip in half (Inner Borders)

From the blue, cut:

◆ Three 2½-inch crosswise strips; cut one strip in half (Side Outer Borders) and leave the other two full length (Top and Bottom Outer Borders)

Attaching the Borders

STEP 1. Measure through the center of your quilt vertically. Cut two gold inner border strips to this exact measurement.

STEP 2. Attach these strips to the sides of your quilt top. Press the seam allowances toward the border.

STEP 3. Measure across the center of the quilt horizontally. Include the side borders in your measurement. Cut the remaining two inner border strips to this exact measurement.

STEP 4. Attach these strips to the top and bottom of your quilt top. Press the seam allowances toward the border.

STEP 5. Repeat Steps 1 through 4 for the blue outer borders.

QUILTING

STEP 1. Press the finished quilt top. Mark the quilting design, using one of your own or following these suggestions.

■ Quilt around each star.

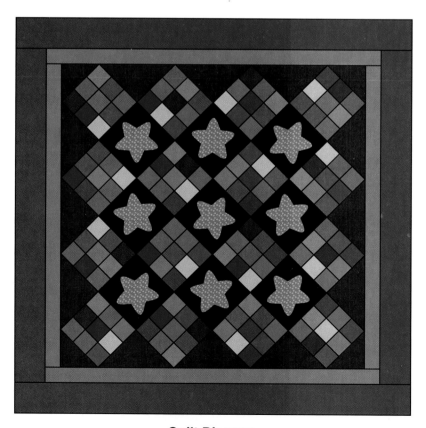

Quilt Diagram

- Sew an X across each Nine Patch.
- Quilt ¼ inch inside the edges of the setting triangles.
- Stitch in the ditch between the borders.
- Quilt through the center of the outer border.

STEP 2. Layer the quilt top, batting, and backing. Baste the layers together.

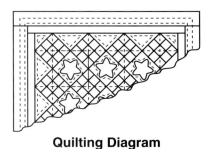

Quilting Diagram

STEP 3. Quilt by hand or machine.

STEP 4. Trim the batting and backing even with the quilt top. Remove the basting.

BINDING

STEP 1. Cut three 1½-inch crosswise strips to prepare 105 total inches of single-fold straight-grain binding.

STEP 2. Join the strips end to end with diagonal seams. Fold in half lengthwise with wrong sides together and press. Attach the binding to the quilt, following the instructions on page 242.

Make It FUN

To "age" your quilt, the designers suggest a tea bath. Shorten the dyeing time in the following recipe for a lighter effect.

1 large bowl
2 quarts hot tap water
6–8 tea bags

Directions: Steep the bags in the hot water for 15 minutes. Remove the bags. Add the quilt and soak it for 30 minutes. Rinse the quilt in cool water. Squeeze. Lay flat to dry. Press. ■

Star

For machine and fusible appliqué,
cut pattern piece as shown. For hand appliqué,
add ⅛" to ¼" to pattern piece.

Stars and Scraps Forever

Judith Hughes Marte, *Around the Block Quilt Designs*

*T*hese asymmetrical stars dance and twinkle and stand upright at attention, creating a lively lap-size quilt. Although at first glance these star blocks might look complicated, they're really quite simple. By first piecing mini-sections, then joining those together, you create the star shape with easy straight seams and no tricky set-in angles. Cutting the pieces is a breeze, thanks to a handy technique that lets you use templates together with your rotary cutter and ruler.

SIZE

Finished quilt is 51 × 59 inches
Finished block is 8 inches square

FABRICS and SUPPLIES

Yardage based on 44-inch-wide fabric
- 1⅓ yards *total* of one or more light plaids or prints for star backgrounds
- 1⅛ yards black print for inner border, corner squares, and binding
- ½ yard red print for sashing strips
- ⅛ yard *each* of 24 different medium to dark plaids for stars and pieced outer border
- 3½ yards for backing
- Batting, larger than 51 × 59 inches
- Template plastic
- Rotary cutter, ruler, and mat

GETTING READY

COLOR and FABRIC TIPS:

A rainbow-bright array of plaids in all sizes gives this quilt a cheerful country look. For a less scrappy feel, consider making each star out of one fabric instead of six different ones. Or, you could vary the plaids within the stars, but limit the background to only one or two fabrics. Once you start looking through your fabric collection, you'll find that this quilt design lends itself to a wide range of fabric and color variations. For extra interest, think about using a directional print for the sashing. You could cut some pieces with the fabric pattern running horizontally, some vertically, and some diagonally. If you want to try this, allow some extra yardage for the sashing.

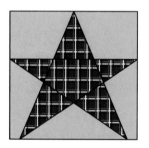

Example of one fabric per star

- Wash, damp dry, and press all fabrics before using.
- All seam allowances are ¼ inch and should be pressed to one side, unless otherwise indicated.
- Trace pattern pieces **A, B, C, D, E, F,** and **G** on pages 70–71 onto template plastic and cut them out. The pattern pieces include ¼-inch seam allowances.
- This quilt includes some templates (**B, C, E,** and **F**) that must be used both right side up and reversed. This is always specified in the instructions, and is denoted on the pattern pieces with (r) following the pattern letter name. Mark these templates so you can tell easily which side is the reverse.
- In preparation for rotary cutting, trim the selvages off the red print and black print fabrics and square off one crosswise edge of each fabric, as described on page 236.
- Cutting directions for each part of the quilt are provided in the sections indicated by the yellow rotary cutters. This format allows you to cut what you need as you get ready to assemble each part of the quilt. If you prefer to cut all the pieces at once, skip ahead, looking for the yellow rotary cutters, and cut all the pieces before starting to sew.

ASSEMBLING the BLOCKS

Cutting for Blocks (make 24)

From the 24 different plaids, cut:

- One 4 × 14-inch strip off the end of *each* of the 24 fabrics; set aside

for the borders. (Do this before cutting the star block pieces.)

- 24 *each* of A, B, B Reverse, C, C Reverse, and D

From the background fabric, cut:

- 24 *each* of E, E Reverse, F, F Reverse, and G

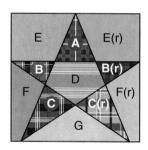

Block Diagram

Make It FAST

Use your rotary cutter with the star templates for fast and accurate cutting. Layer four star fabrics at a time on your cutting mat. Draw around the star templates, leaving ¼ to ½ inch between templates. Lay your quilter's ruler along the drawn lines as a guide and cut through all the layers with your rotary cutter. As you cut, put the pieces in piles in a star arrangement to keep them in their proper places (refer to the Block Diagram). Be especially careful not to mix up pieces B and C with their reverse pieces. Use the same marking and cutting technique for the light background pieces, adding them to the piles as you go. ■

Piecing the Blocks

STEP 1. Keep your pieces in piles in the star block arrangement, but mix up pieces *within* each pile so the color combinations vary from star to star. (Omit this step if you want to make each star out of a single fabric.)

STEP 2. Referring to **Diagram 1**, join pieces into subsections. The piecing goes much faster if you make all 24 of each subsection at once, rather than piecing an entire block at a time. It's a good idea to complete at least one block first to double-check the pattern pieces and your seam allowances.

- Sew *all* B and F pieces together.
- Sew *all* C and D pieces together.
- Sew *all* G and C Reverse pieces together.
- Sew *all* B Reverse and F Reverse pieces together.
- Sew *all* E, A, and E Reverse pieces together.

Star Subsections

Diagram 1

STEP 3. Using **Diagram 2** for reference, join subsections together as follows:

- Sew Subsection B/F to Subsection C/D.

- Add Subsection G/C Reverse to the B/F/C/D unit.
- Add Subsection B Reverse/F Reverse.
- Add Subsection E/A/E Reverse to the top to complete the block.

ASSEMBLING the CENTER

Cutting  for Setting Pieces

From the red print, cut:

- ◆Twenty-four 8½ × 2½-inch sashing pieces

Piecing the Center

STEP 1. Make six horizontal rows by joining four star blocks with four sashing strips, as shown in **Diagram 3**. Turn the blocks in different directions, either randomly or in a coordinated arrangement. Press seam allowances toward the sashing strips.

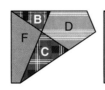
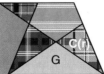
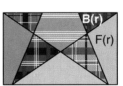
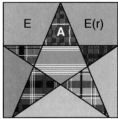

Diagram 2

Diagram 3

Make It EASY

You may want to mark sewing lines on the fabric pieces. Without them, it can be difficult to know how to match the asymmetrical parts of the star and background. To mark, simply lay your rotary ruler with the ¼-inch mark along the edge of the piece and draw along the edge of the ruler, as shown in **A**. To save time, try doing this just the first time you join each set of two pieces (B and F, for example). After seeing how a set matches up, as shown in **B**, you may be able to do the rest without marking them. ∎

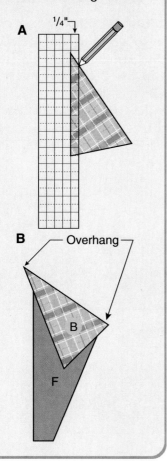

A

B

STEP 2. Referring to the **Assembly Diagram**, lay out the rows. Note that they are staggered; the first row has a star on the left end, the second a sashing strip, and so on all the way along the six horizontal rows. Join the rows. Press.

BORDERS

Cutting for Borders

From the black print, cut:

◆ Five 2-inch crosswise strips; cut one strip in half and join the halves to two other strips (Inner Borders)

◆ Four 4-inch squares (Corner Squares)

From the star fabrics set aside earlier, cut:

◆ *Approximately* 144 strips, each 4 inches long and varying in width from 1¼ to 2½ inches (Pieced Outer Border)

Attaching the Borders

STEP 1. Measure through the center of the quilt vertically. Cut the two long pieced inner border strips to this exact measurement. Set aside the leftovers.

STEP 2. Attach these strips to the sides of your quilt top. Press toward the border.

STEP 3. Measure across the center of the quilt horizontally, including the side borders in

Assembly Diagram

your measurement. Cut the remaining two inner border strips to this exact measurement. (If the strips are not long enough, attach the leftover pieces you set aside.) Attach to the top and bottom of your quilt top. Press toward the border.

STEP 4. To make the pieced outer borders, measure through the center of the quilt top horizontally (for top and bottom borders) and vertically (for side borders). Include the inner borders in these measurements. Join strips of star fabrics along the 4-inch

sides to make four 4-inch-wide borders to these exact measurements (you may need to cut more strips from the star fabrics). Be sure to alternate fabrics in a pleasing arrangement. Take in or let out a few seams as needed to achieve a perfect fit.

STEP 5. Add a black print corner square to each end of the top and bottom borders. Press the seams toward corner squares.

STEP 6. Sew a pieced border to each side of the quilt top, as shown in the **Quilt Diagram**.

Press toward the border. Sew pieced borders to the top and bottom of the quilt top, taking care to align the corner square seams with the seams joining the side borders. Press toward the border.

QUILTING

STEP 1. To prepare the backing, cut the backing fabric in half crosswise into two 1¾-yard pieces. Cut off the selvages and then sew the two pieces together side by side to make a backing piece approximately 84 × 63 inches.

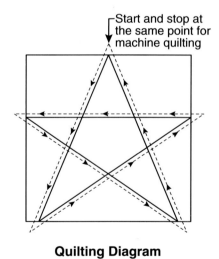

Quilting Diagram

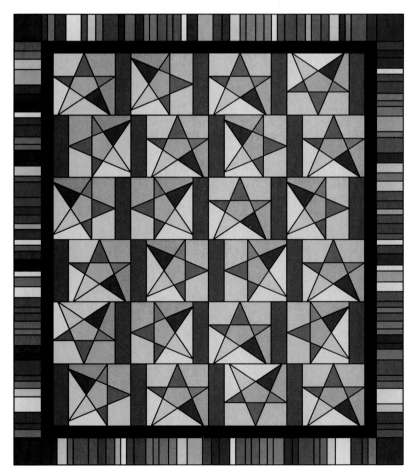

Quilt Diagram

STEP 2. Press the finished quilt top. Mark the quilting design, using one of your own or following these suggestions.

■ Machine quilt around each star in one continuous line.

■ Sew ¼ inch from the seam between the inner and outer pieced border.

■ Quilt ¼ inch from both seams in each sashing strip.

STEP 3. Layer the quilt top, batting, and backing. Baste the layers together.

STEP 4. Quilt by hand or machine.

STEP 5. Trim the backing and batting even with the quilt top. Remove the basting.

BINDING

STEP 1. Cut the binding fabric into seven 2½-inch crosswise strips to make approximately 250 inches of continuous straight-grain double-fold binding.

STEP 2. Join the strips end to end with diagonal seams. Fold in half lengthwise with wrong sides together and press. Attach the binding to the quilt, following the instructions on page 242.

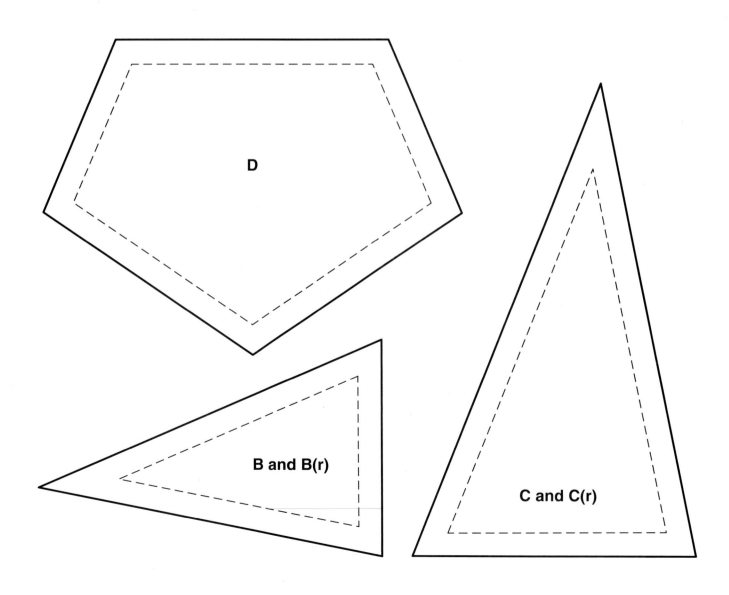

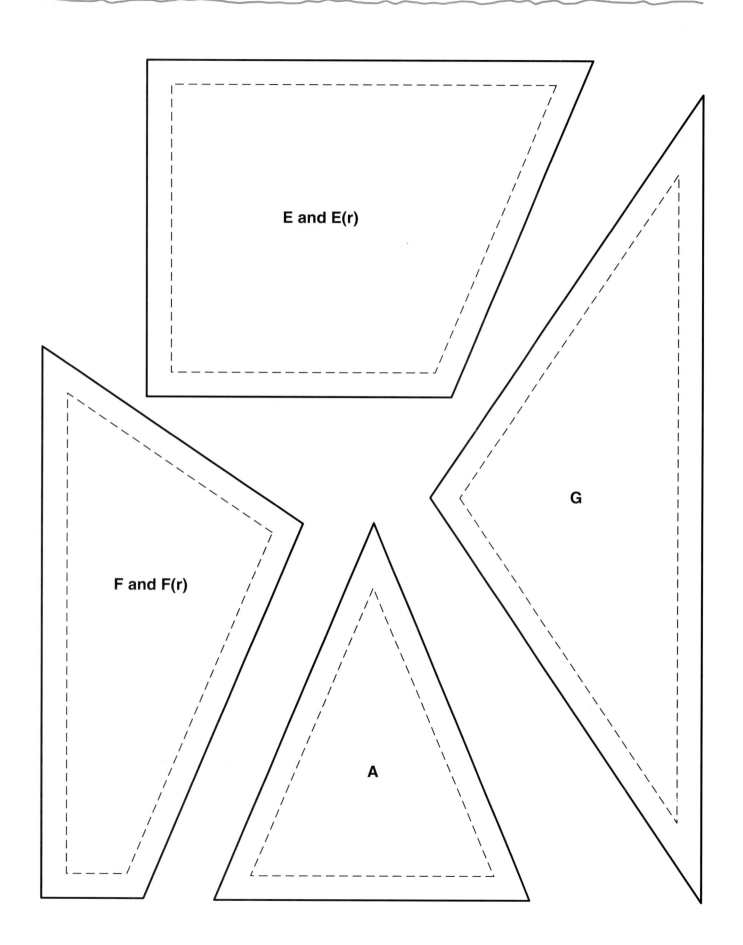

Christmas Cheer

These Guys Don't Melt
❄
Homespun Stars Tree Skirt
❄
Saint Nicholas
❄
Father Christmas
❄
Christmas Angel
❄
Gingerbread Cookies

These Guys Don't Melt

Toni Phillips and Juanita Simonich, *Fabric Expressions*

*H*ere's a winter wonderland like you've never seen it before! Superquick fusible appliqué and an ingenious piecing shortcut for the Snowball blocks guarantee that you'll be done with this wall quilt long before the spring thaw.

SIZE

Finished quilt is 36 × 41 inches

FABRICS and SUPPLIES

Yardage based on 44-inch-wide fabric

- ½ yard teal plaid for backgrounds
- ½ yard red-and-blue plaid for borders and blocks
- ½ yard light plum check for sashing
- ½ yard dark teal for corner squares and binding
- ⅓ yard teal print for backgrounds
- ⅓ yard teal-on-teal print for backgrounds
- ¼ yard ivory for snow
- ⅛ yard light red plaid*

- ⅛ yard *each* of two green plaids for trees*
- ⅛ yard (or 4½ × 28-inch scrap) black check for tall snowman*
- Batting, larger than 36 × 41 inches (low-loft polyester or needlepunch cotton)
- 1⅛ yards for backing
- Gold embroidery floss or perle cotton thread
- Twenty-seven ¼- to ⅜-inch buttons for eyes and mouths
- Fusible web for appliqué
- Rotary cutter, ruler, and mat

*Some fabric shops will not cut ⅛-yard pieces. Purchase ¼ yard and save the extra for other projects, or check your scrap bag to see if you have any suitable leftovers. Check the size of the scrap against the size of the pieces to be cut to confirm you have enough fabric.

GETTING READY

COLOR and FABRIC TIPS:

This quilt is a veritable plaid extravaganza. One of the keys to success when working with many plaids is to keep a sense of scale in mind. Plaids, like prints, come in small, medium, and large. A pleasing mix of all sizes creates visual interest.

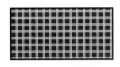

Varying Scales of Plaid

- Wash, damp dry, and press all fabrics before using.

- All seam allowances are ¼ inch and should be pressed to one side, unless otherwise indicated.

- In preparation for rotary cutting, trim the selvages off the background, sashing, border, and binding fabrics and square up one crosswise edge of each fabric, as described on page 236.

- To make complete pattern pieces, join the sections of Blocks **A, B,** and **E** as indicated on the patterns, matching the dots to complete the patterns.

- Reverse pattern pieces **A1** through **H4,** then trace them onto fusible web, following the directions on page 238. Be sure to transfer the piece numbers. Make two of each piece in Block A. Note that **A1** has two different sizes marked; prepare one of each size.

- Cutting directions for each section of the quilt are provided in the sections indicated by the yellow rotary cutters. This format allows you to cut what you need as you get ready to assemble each part of the quilt. If you prefer to cut all the pieces at once, skip ahead, looking for the yellow rotary cutters, and cut all the pieces before starting to sew.

Make It EASY

Here's a quick size guide for the appliqué pieces of the quilt. This gives you a way to check whether the size scrap you want to use is large enough. The amounts indicated are minimum sizes. ■

- Teal star print: 2 × 22 inches for snowball blocks

- Light ivory-and-tan print: 7 × 2 inches

- Medium ivory-and-tan print: 10 × 4 inches

- One or more light plaids: 3 inches square each (need a total of three) for snowball blocks

- Dark red plaid: 4 × 6 inches

- One or more medium plaids: 3 inches square each (need a total of two) for snowball blocks

- Blue: 3 × 6 inches

- Navy plaid: 4 × 7 inches

- Light gold-and-red plaid: 4 × 2 inches

- Black plaid: 3 × 4 inches

- Orange check: 3 × 5 inches

- Black-and-orange plaid: 4 × 12 inches

- Gold plaid: 3 × 5 inches

- Green check: 2 × 1 inches

- Brown-and-orange plaid: 5 inches square

- Brown-and-red plaid: 5 inches square

- Purple: 4 × 5 inches

- Light gold-and-brown plaid: 5 × 6 inches

ASSEMBLING the BACKGROUND

Refer to the **Assembly Diagram** while cutting and sewing the background.

Cutting for Block A (make 2)

From the teal plaid, cut:

♦ Two 4½ × 20½-inch pieces

Cutting for Block B (make 1)

From the teal print, cut:

♦ One 20½ × 4½-inch piece

Cutting for Block C (make 1)

From teal-on-teal print, cut:

♦ One 10½ × 7½-inch piece

Cutting for Block D (make 1)

From the teal-on-teal print, cut:

♦ One 10½ × 9½-inch piece

Cutting for Block E (make 1)

From the teal plaid, cut:

♦ One 6½ × 32½-inch piece

Cutting for Blocks F, G, and H (make 1 of each)

From the teal print, cut:

♦ Three 6½-inch squares

Cutting for Sashing

From the light plum, cut seven 1½-inch crosswise strips; from these strips cut the following:

♦ Two 6½-inch pieces
♦ Two 10½-inch pieces
♦ Four 20½-inch pieces
♦ Two 29½-inch pieces
♦ Three 32½-inch pieces

Cutting for Snowball Blocks (make 5)

From teal star print, cut:

♦ Twenty 1-inch squares (Y)

From one or more light plaids, cut:

♦ Three 2½-inch squares (X)

From one or more medium plaids, cut:

♦ Two 2½-inch squares (X)

Piecing the Snowball Blocks

STEP 1. Use a ruler and pencil to draw diagonal lines across four Y squares on the wrong side of the fabric, as shown in Diagram 1.

Make 4

Diagram 1

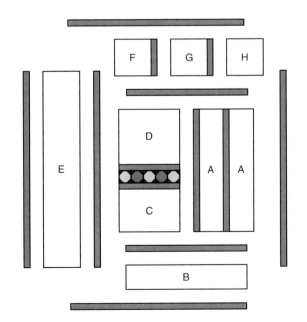

Assembly Diagram

STEP 2. Lay a Y on each corner of X with right sides together and the drawn lines positioned as shown in **Diagram 2.**

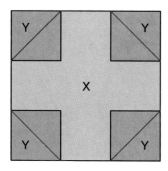

Diagram 2

STEP 3. Stitch along the drawn lines. Trim the seam allowances to ¼ inch, as shown in **Diagram 3.** Press. Repeat to make a total of three light and two medium snowballs.

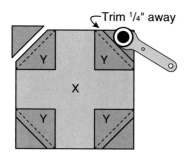

Trim ¼" away

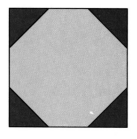

Diagram 3

Piecing the Background

STEP 1. For this step and the ones that follow, refer to the **Assembly Diagram** on page 77. Sew a 20½-inch sashing strip to the left edge of each Block A (tree). In this step and the ones that follow, press seams toward the sashing pieces. Join the two units. Press.

STEP 2. To make the snowball section, join the five pieced snowball blocks, alternating light and medium blocks. Refer to the photograph on page 74 for color placement. Press.

STEP 3. Sew 10½-inch sashing strips to the top and bottom of the snowball section. Join Block C and Block D to this unit. Press. Sew this unit to the left side of the tree unit from Step 1. Press.

STEP 4. Sew a 20½-inch sashing strip to the upper edge of Block B (hills). Press.

STEP 5. To make the snowman section, join Blocks F, G, and H with two 6½-inch sashing strips. Press.

STEP 6. Sew a 20½-inch sashing strip to the lower edge of the snowman section. Press.

STEP 7. Join the B section to the snowman section and tree section. Press.

STEP 8. Sew a 32½-inch sashing strip between the assembled unit from Step 7 and Block E. Press. Add a 32½-inch sashing strip to each side of this unit. Add 29½-inch sashing strips to the top and bottom of this unit to complete the center. Press.

Make It EASY

For all of the blocks in this quilt, refer to the **Appliqué Diagram** and the pattern pieces for placement guides. All the pieces have been numbered, so you can simply add pieces in numerical order (A1 before A2, G3 before G4). ■

APPLIQUÉING THE BLOCKS

Using the pattern pieces traced onto fusible web and the fabrics listed, prepare the blocks (directions for fusible appliqué are on page 238).

Preparing Block A

◆ 2 A1 (snow) from the ivory

◆ 2 A2 (tree trunk) from brown plaid

◆ 1 A3 (tree) from *each* of the two green plaids

For the tree blocks, fuse pieces A1, A2, and A3 onto the teal plaid background pieces. Remember that the size of A1, the snow, is different in each tree block.

Preparing Block B

◆ 1 B3 (left hill) from ivory

◆ 1 B1 (middle hill) from light ivory-and-tan print

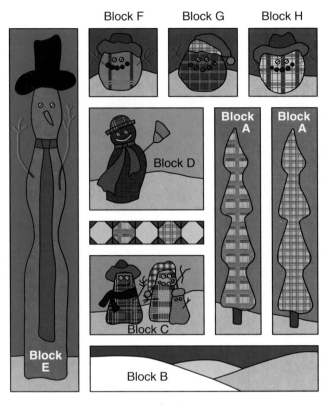

Block F   Block G   Block H

Appliqué Diagram

Make It FUN

Using gold embroidery floss, satin stitch two eyes onto Block D. With a stem stitch, create a smile and add a satin stitch circle at each end. Chain stitch the broom handle.

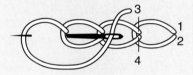

Chain Stitch

Add faces and waving arms to your snowpeople. Use small buttons for eyes on the mom and dad. For the dad's mouth, use a stem stitch and add a french knot at each end. For the mom, use small round buttons to put a smile on her face. Satin stitch eyes on Junior. Use a stem stitch for the arms. See the pattern pieces for placement for these extra touches. ■

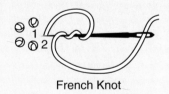

French Knot

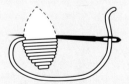

Satin Stitch

For stem stitch, see page 157 in Farmer's Market

◆ 1 B2 (right hill) from medium ivory-and-tan print

For the hills, fuse pieces B1, B2, and B3 onto the teal print background piece.

Preparing Block C

◆ 1 C1 (snow) from ivory

◆ 1 C2 (father's hat) from dark red plaid

◆ 1 C3 (father's hat brim) from light red plaid

◆ 1 C4 (father) from red-and-blue plaid

◆ 1 each of C5 and C6 (scarf) from blue

◆ 1 C7 (mother) from purple

◆ 1 C8 (mother's hat) from black plaid

◆ 1 C9 (mother's hat ball) from orange check

◆ 1 C10 (child) from gold plaid

◆ 1 C11 (child's hat) from green check

For the family, fuse pieces C1 through C11 onto the teal-on-teal print background piece.

Preparing Block D

◆ 1 D1 (snow) from ivory

◆ 1 D2 (body) from navy plaid

◆ 1 each of D3, D4, and D9 (scarf) from light red plaid

◆ 1 each of D5 and D6 (hat) from red-and-blue plaid

◆ 1 D7 (broom base) from orange check

◆ 1 D8 (broom bristles) from gold plaid

◆ 1 D10 (scarf knot) from dark red plaid

For the broom snowman, fuse pieces D1 through D10 onto the teal-on-teal print background piece.

Preparing Block E

◆ 1 E1 (snow) from ivory

◆ 1 E2 (body) from black check

◆ 1 each of E3, E4, and E5 (tie) from light red plaid

◆ 1 each of E6 and E7 (hat) from black-and-orange plaid

◆ 1 E8 (nose) from orange check

For the tall snowman, fuse pieces E1 through E8 onto the teal plaid background piece. Pick out two buttons for the snowman's eyes, and use a stem stitch to embroider his arms.

Preparing Blocks F, G, and H

◆ 1 each of F1, G1, and H1 (snow) from ivory

◆ 1 each of F4 and H4 (hat brims) from light red plaid

◆ 1 each of F3, G4, and H3 (hats) from dark red plaid

◆ 1 G5 (hat ball) from orange check

◆ 1 G3 (hat cuff) from light gold-and-red plaid

◆ 1 F2 (head) from brown-and-orange plaid

◆ 1 G2 (head) from brown-and-red plaid

◆ 1 H2 (head) from light gold-and-brown plaid

Assembling Blocks F, G, and H

For the round snowmen, fuse pieces F1 through F4 (left snowman), G1 through G5 (middle snowman), and H1 through H4 (right snowman) onto the teal print background squares. Embroider the arms on each snowman with a stem stitch, and add buttons for their eyes and mouths.

BORDERS

Cutting for Borders

From the red-and-blue plaid, cut:

◆ Two 4 × 34½-inch pieces (Side Borders)

◆ Two 4 × 29½-inch pieces (Top and Bottom Borders)

From the dark teal, cut:

◆ Four 4-inch squares (Corner Squares)

Attaching the Borders

STEP 1. Attach the 34½-inch strips to the sides of the quilt top. Press toward the border.

STEP 2. Sew teal corner squares to each end of the top and bottom border strips. Press the seams toward the border.

STEP 3. Attach these strips to the top and bottom of your quilt top, taking care to align the corner square seam with the side border seam. Press toward the border.

QUILTING

STEP 1. Press the finished quilt top. Mark the quilting design, using one of your own or following these suggestions.

■ Outline all appliqué shapes.

■ Stitch in the ditch between all blocks and sashing.

■ Quilt ¼ inch from the seams inside the snowball blocks.

■ Echo quilt inside the trees.

■ Quilt random stars into the block backgrounds.

■ Fill the snow patches with meandering squiggly lines (stipple quilting).

■ Channel quilt with parallel lines spaced 1 inch apart in the borders.

STEP 2. Layer the quilt top, batting, and backing. Baste the layers together.

STEP 3. Quilt by hand or machine.

STEP 4. Trim the batting and backing even with the quilt top. Remove the basting.

BINDING

STEP 1. Cut four 2¼-inch crosswise strips of binding fabric to make 166 total inches of double-fold straight-grain binding.

STEP 2. Join the strips end to end with diagonal seams. Fold in half lengthwise with wrong sides together and press. Attach the binding to the quilt, following the instructions on page 242.

Make It FAST

If your quilt has a lot of different-colored fabrics in it, machine quilting with clear monofilament thread is the quickest answer to the perennial question, "What color quilting thread should I use?". Clear thread is best for a predominately light-colored quilt; smoke for a dark-colored one. Using this kind of "invisible" thread saves time since you won't have to change thread colors as you quilt in different sections. ■

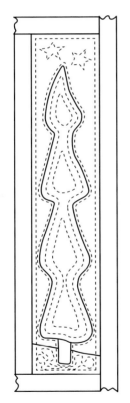

Quilting Diagram

Quilt Diagram

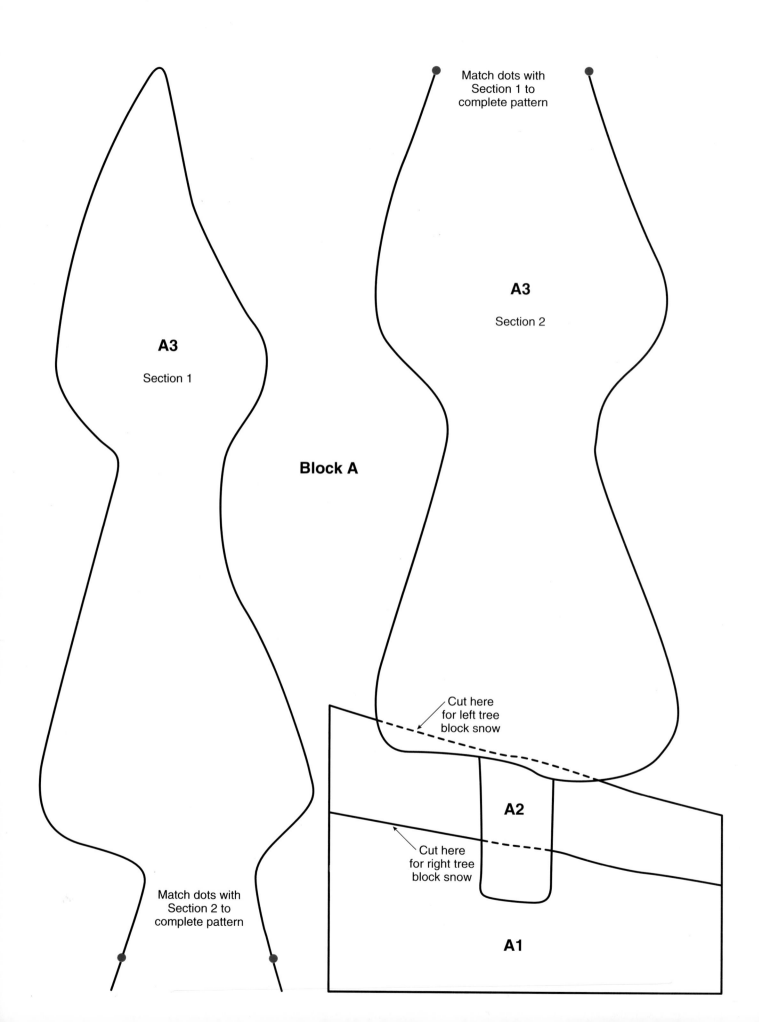

A3

Section 1

Block A

A3

Section 2

Match dots with
Section 1 to
complete pattern

Match dots with
Section 2 to
complete pattern

Cut here
for left tree
block snow

A2

Cut here
for right tree
block snow

A1

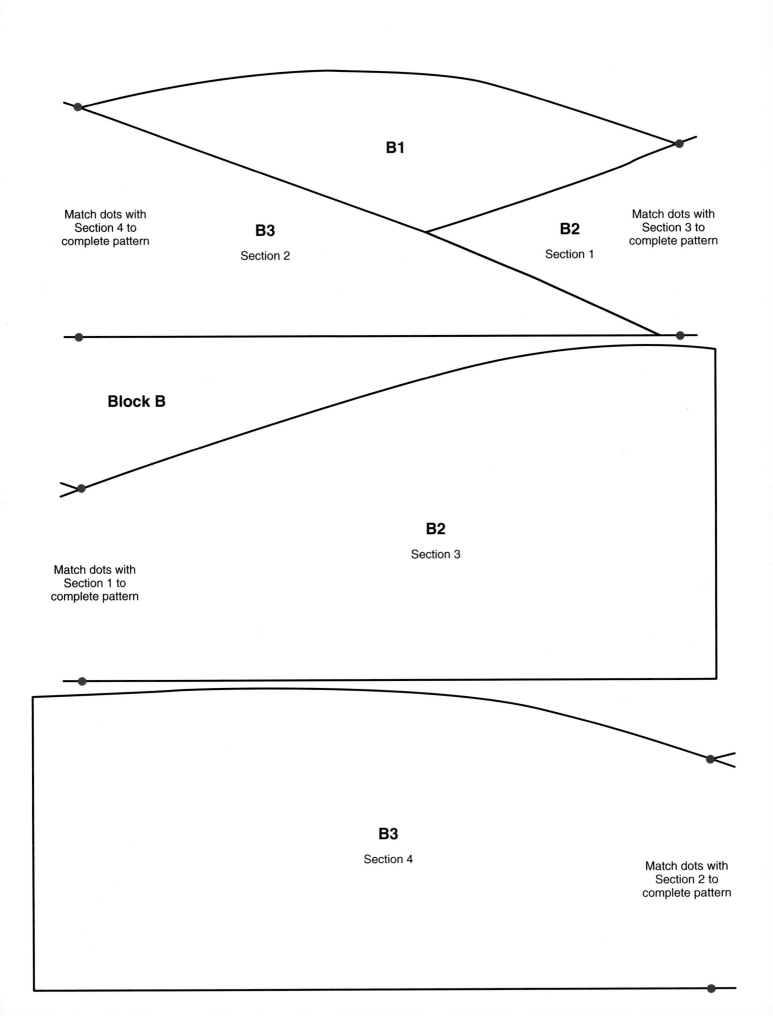

B1

Match dots with
Section 4 to
complete pattern

B3

Section 2

B2

Match dots with
Section 3 to
complete pattern

Section 1

Block B

Match dots with
Section 1 to
complete pattern

B2

Section 3

B3

Section 4

Match dots with
Section 2 to
complete pattern

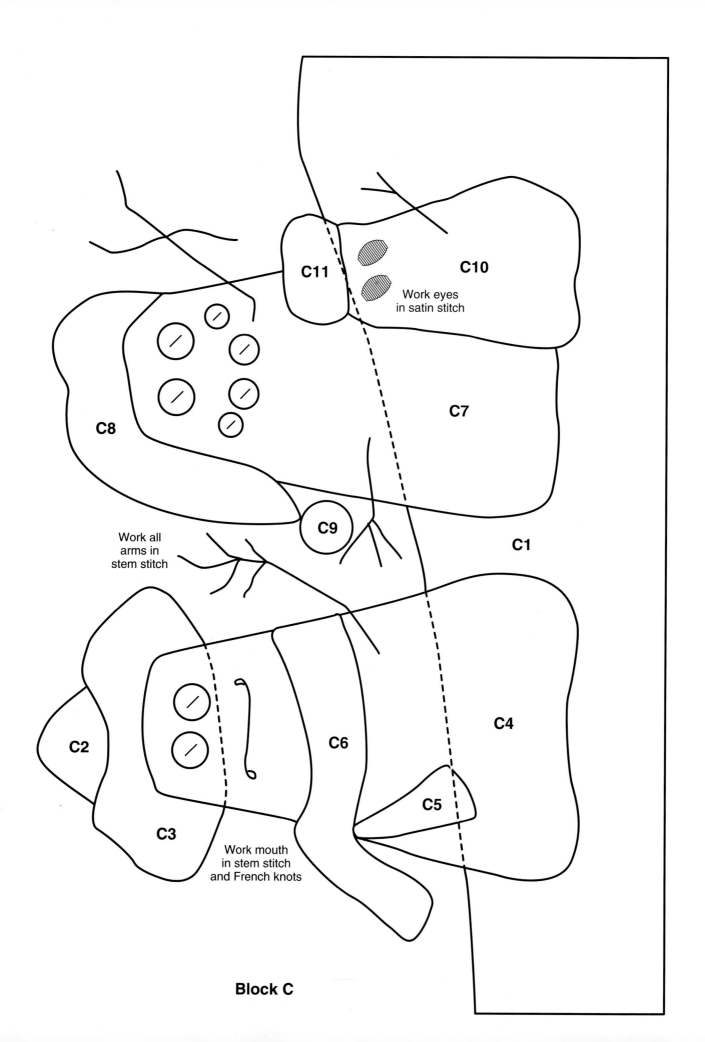

C11

C10

Work eyes
in satin stitch

C7

C8

C9

C1

Work all
arms in
stem stitch

C2

C6

C4

C3

C5

Work mouth
in stem stitch
and French knots

Block C

Block D

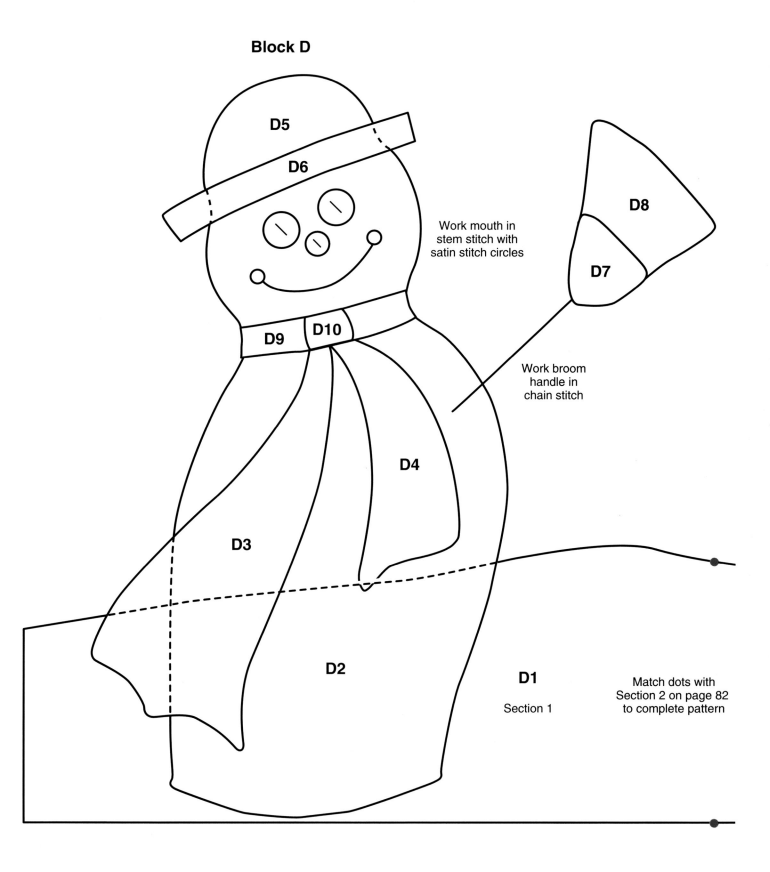

D5

D6

D8

Work mouth in
stem stitch with
satin stitch circles

D7

D9   D10

Work broom
handle in
chain stitch

D4

D3

D2

D1

Section 1

Match dots with
Section 2 on page 82
to complete pattern

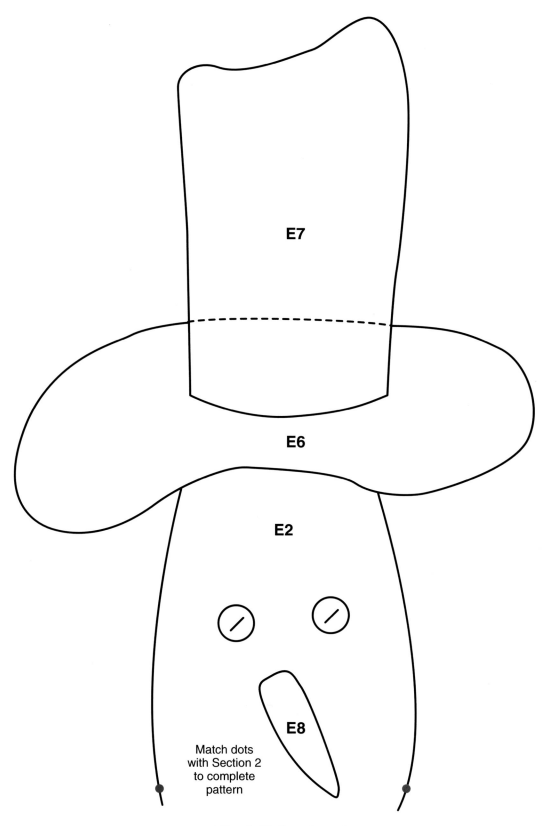

E7

E6

E2

E8

Match dots
with Section 2
to complete
pattern

Block E Section 1

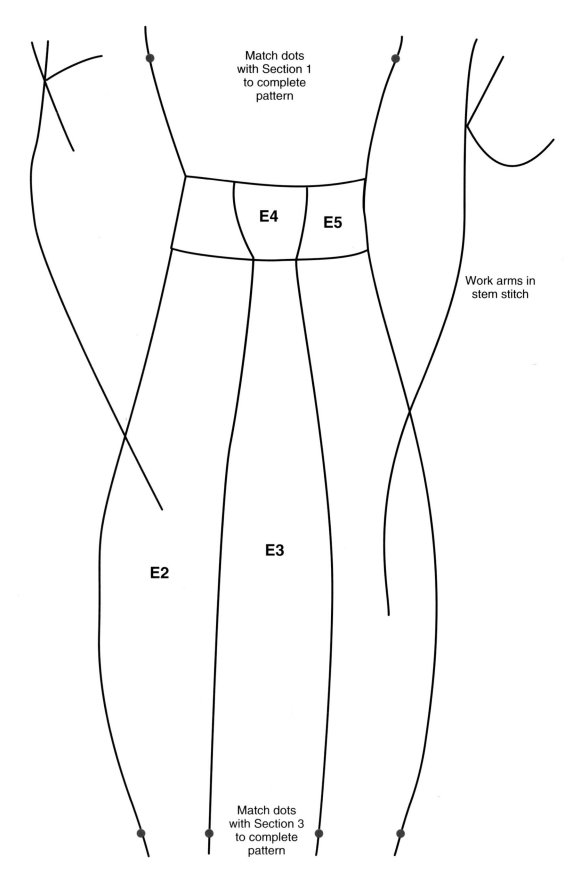

Match dots with Section 1 to complete pattern

Work arms in stem stitch

E4

E5

E2

E3

Match dots with Section 3 to complete pattern

Block E Section 2

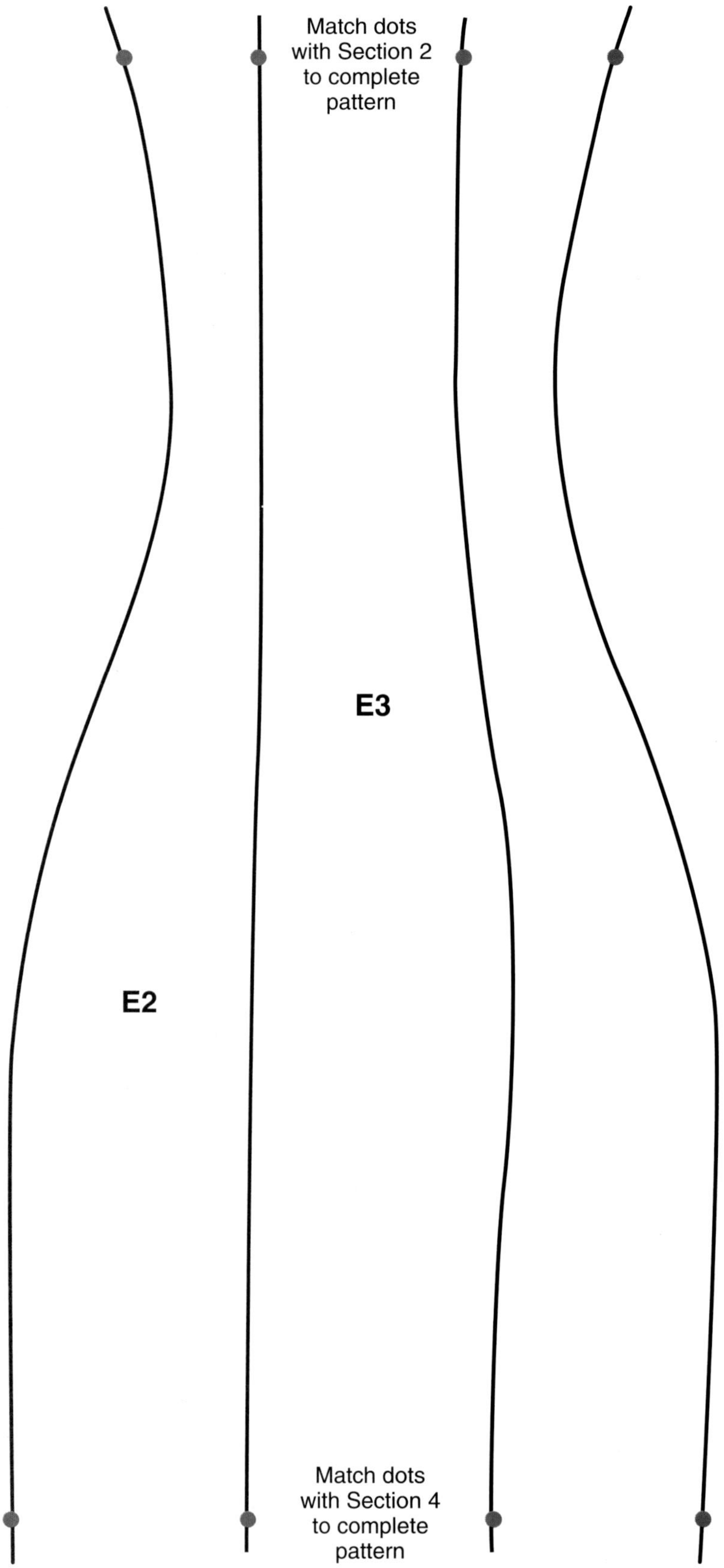

Match dots
with Section 2
to complete
pattern

E3

E2

Match dots
with Section 4
to complete
pattern

Block E Section 3

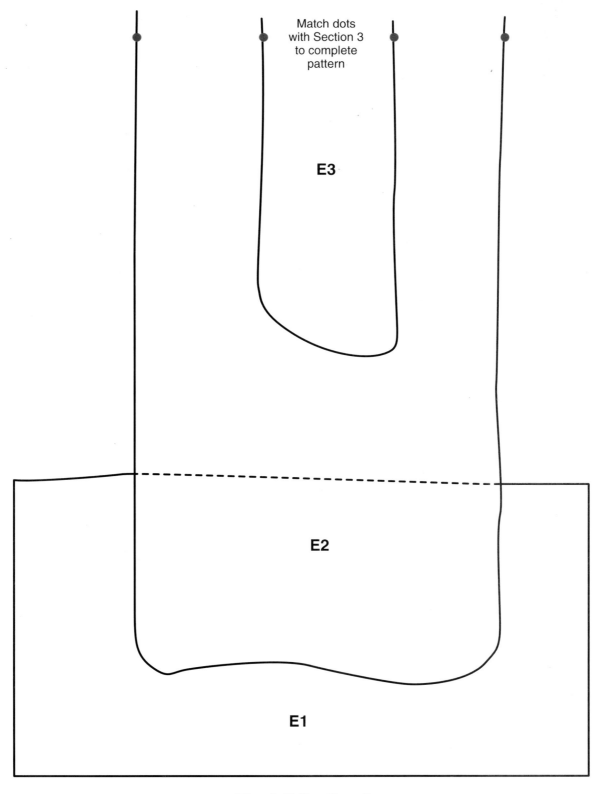

Match dots with Section 3 to complete pattern

E3

E2

E1

Block E Section 4

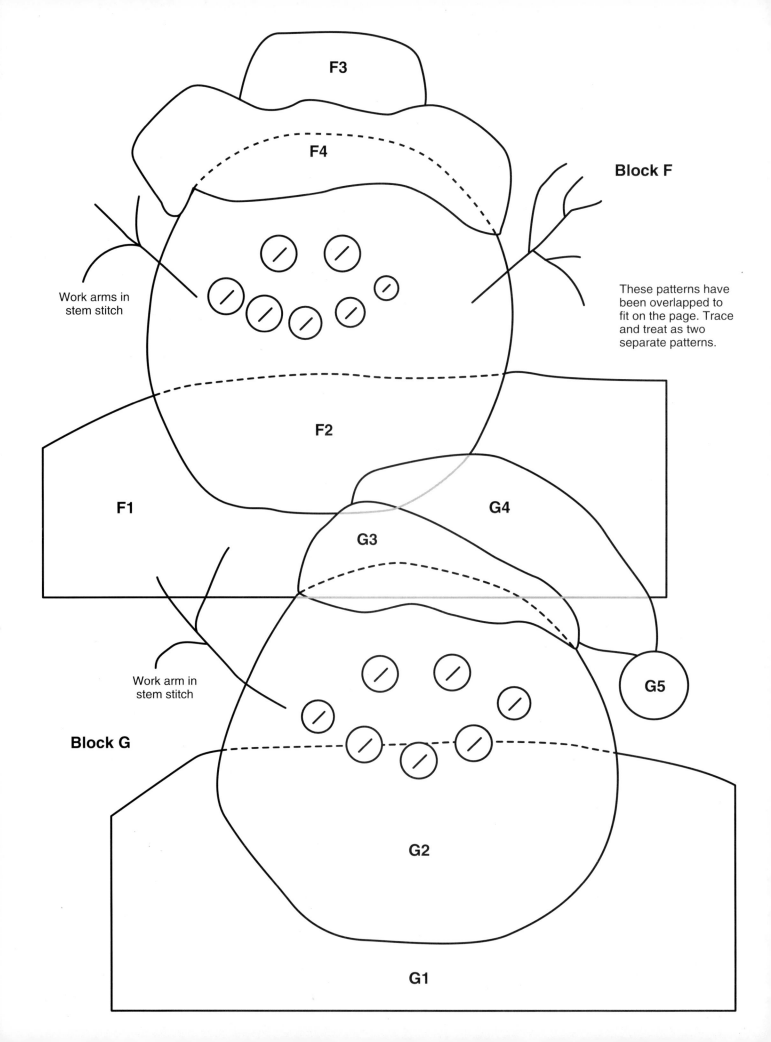

F3

F4

Block F

Work arms in
stem stitch

These patterns have
been overlapped to
fit on the page. Trace
and treat as two
separate patterns.

F2

F1

G4

G3

Work arm in
stem stitch

G5

Block G

G2

G1

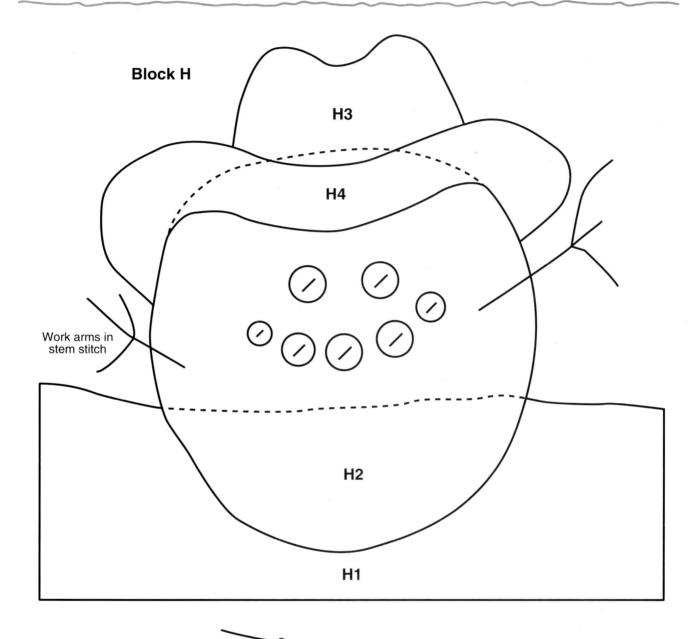

Block H

H3

H4

H2

H1

Work arms in
stem stitch

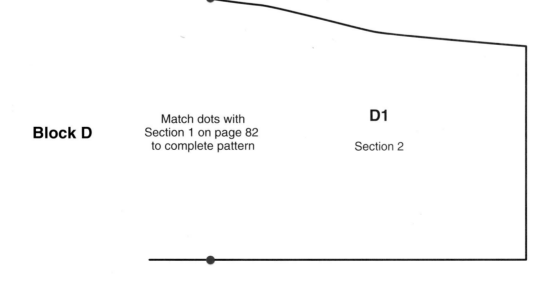

Block D

Match dots with
Section 1 on page 82
to complete pattern

D1

Section 2

thimbleberries

Homespun Stars Tree Skirt

Lynette Jensen, *Thimbleberries*

*J*ust a couple of hours at the sewing machine, and you'll have a charming tree skirt to enjoy year after year. This project goes together so quickly you can easily make some as last-minute gifts (holiday procrastinators take note!). Tailor your fabric choices to match the room decor, or pick from the wonderful assortment of Christmas prints that are available every year.

SIZE

Finished skirt is 52 inches in diameter

FABRICS and SUPPLIES

Yardage based on 44-inch-wide fabric
- 2 yards taupe check for skirt background

- 1¾ yards green print for ruffle and sash
- 1½ yards red print for ruffle and sash
- ½ yard gold solid for stars
- 2½ yards for backing
- Batting, larger than 52 inches square
- Contrasting embroidery floss for buttonhole stitching (optional)
- Template plastic or fusible web, depending on appliqué technique
- Rotary cutter, ruler, and mat

GETTING READY

COLOR and FABRIC TIPS:

Small prints in reds, greens, and golds emphasize the old-fashioned look of the skirt. Another option for a homespun feel is to combine richly colored plaids with prints. You could also use large-scale Christmas prints for a more contemporary look. Just be sure there is enough contrast between the background fabric and the star fabric so that the stars stand out nicely.

Classic Christmas colors
are still favorites

- Wash, damp dry, and press all fabrics before using.

- All seam allowances are ¼ inch and should be pressed to one side, unless otherwise indicated.

- See "Appliqué Basics" on page 238 and choose a method. Then, trace the **Star** pattern on page 97 onto template plastic or fusible web, depending on the method you've chosen.

- Cutting directions for each part of the quilt are provided in the sections indicated by the yellow rotary cutters. This format allows you to cut what you need as you get ready to assemble each part of the quilt. If you prefer to cut all the pieces at once, skip ahead, looking for the yellow rotary cutters, and cut all the pieces before starting to sew.

SKIRT ASSEMBLY

Making the Gore Pattern

To make a full-size **Gore Pattern**, follow the steps below, and refer to the diagram.

STEP 1. Create a 25-inch paper square. Fold the square in half diagonally and crease well. Unfold.

STEP 2. Trace the shape of **Pattern A** on page 97 into the bottom corner, between the edge of the paper and the diagonal crease line.

STEP 3. Measure 17¾ inches from the wide part of A along edge of the paper and diagonal fold line, and make a mark.

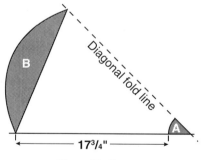

Gore Pattern

STEP 4. Trace **Half-Pattern B** on page 97 onto a folded piece of paper to make a complete B.

STEP 5. Place one end of the straight side of B at the mark you made in Step 3. Position the other end of piece B to meet the diagonal crease mark. Tape B in place. With a dark marker, trace along the outside curve of B, along the diagonal crease, and

along the curve of A. This creates the completed **Gore Pattern**.

Cutting for the Skirt

From the taupe background fabric, cut:

♦ 8 gores, using your completed Gore Pattern. Place one long straight edge along the straight grain of the fabric. (If you are using a directional print, place the pattern piece whatever way looks best to you. Depending on your pattern placement, you may end up needing more fabric.)

From the gold, cut:

♦ 24 Stars, following the directions for the appliqué method you have chosen

Assembling the Skirt

STEP 1. Referring to the photograph on page 92 for placement, fuse or appliqué three stars to each gore. Vary the stars on each skirt gore by turning them so they don't all point in the same direction. Embroider around the edges of each star using a buttonhole stitch, if desired. Instructions for the buttonhole stitch are on page 61.

Make It FUN

Try using a variety of "crazy quilt" stitches along the edges of the stars, making each one different. You could also embellish the stars with French knots, tiny bells, or buttons. ■

STEP 2. Join the eight gores together, leaving the last seam open, as shown in **Diagram 1.** Press.

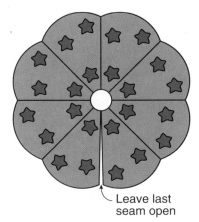

Leave last seam open

Diagram 1

QUILTING

STEP 1. To prepare the backing, cut two 16-inch-wide crosswise strips from the backing fabric. Sew these strips together end to end to form one long strip, approximately 16 × 84 inches. Press the seam open. Referring to **Diagram 2,** lay this strip along one side of the remaining piece of backing fabric, matching the seam with the approximate center point of the side. (The strip will extend beyond the large piece on both ends.) Sew the 16-inch strip to the large piece. Press the seam allowances open. Trim the strip even with the large piece. The resulting backing should measure approximately 58 inches square.

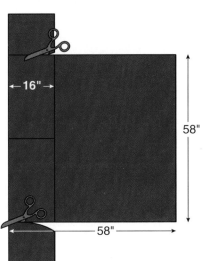

←16"→

58"

58"

Diagram 2

STEP 2. Press the skirt top. Layer the skirt, batting, and backing. Baste the layers together.

STEP 3. Mark the quilting design. Quilt by hand or machine, using your own

design or following these suggestions.

- Fill the areas around the stars with an all-over meander pattern (large random puzzle-piece shapes). Keep these meander quilting lines about ¼ inch away from the stars.

- Stitch inside the stars, approximately ¼ inch from the end of the buttonhole stitches.

STEP 4. Baste around the outside through all the layers ¼ inch from all edges. Trim the excess batting and backing even with the skirt top, as shown in **Diagram 3.**

Baste ¼" from edge

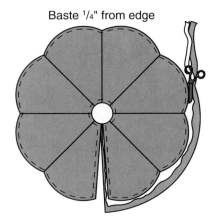

Diagram 3

Make It FAST

For a speedy finish, tie the layered tree skirt instead of quilting it. Use perle cotton in a color that complements those in your tree skirt. ■

BINDING

STEP 1. The two short edges of the tree skirt must be bound before the ruffle is added. To prepare the binding, cut two 3 × 20-inch strips of skirt background fabric.

STEP 2. Fold each strip in half lengthwise with wrong sides together. Lay the binding on the right side of the skirt along each open edge, with raw edges even and the folded edge of the binding toward the body of the skirt, as shown in **Diagram 4**. Stitch. Fold to the wrong side and stitch in place by hand or machine.

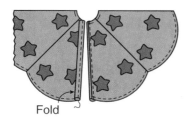

Diagram 4

RUFFLE

Cutting  for Ruffle

From the green, cut:

◆ Seven 6½-inch crosswise strips

From the red, cut:

◆ Seven 4½-inch crosswise strips

Making the Ruffle

STEP 1. Remove the selvages from the ruffle strips. Sew all seven green strips together end to end to form one long strip. Press. Repeat with the red strips.

STEP 2. With right sides together, sew the red strip to the green strip along one long edge. Press. (Don't worry if these long pieced strips are not exactly the same length; simply trim any excess.)

STEP 3. Fold the joined strip in half lengthwise with wrong sides together. Press. You will notice that some green fabric appears on the red side of the ruffle, giving the appearance of a double ruffle, as shown in **Diagram 5**.

Diagram 5

STEP 4. Fold in about ½ inch on each end and edge stitch the openings shut, as shown in Diagram 6.

Diagram 6

STEP 5. Fold this long ruffle in half crosswise and mark the midpoint with a pin. Fold in half again (into quarters) and mark the fold lines with pins.

STEP 6. Stitch a double row of gathering stitches within ¼ inch of the raw edges.

STEP 7. Place the ruffle on the skirt with right sides together and raw edges even. Gather the ruffle by pulling the thread ends. Distribute the fullness, matching pins with every other gore seam,

as shown in **Diagram 7**. Stitch. Lightly press toward the skirt. Zigzag or overcast stitch along the edges of this seam.

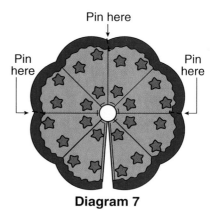

Diagram 7

ASSEMBLING the SASH

Cutting for Sash

From each of the ruffle fabrics, cut:

◆ 4½-inch-wide *bias* strips, totaling 90 inches in length

Assembling and Attaching the Sash

STEP 1. Sew the green strips together end to end to make one long strip. Press. Repeat with the red strips.

STEP 2. With right sides together, join the long strips along the long edge, leaving an 18-inch opening in the center of one side and tapering the ends to form points. See **Diagram 8**. Trim the points, clip the corners, turn right side out, and press.

←— 18" —→

Diagram 8

STEP 3. Stitch one side of the sash opening to the right side of the inner tree skirt opening, as shown in **Diagram 9.** Turn under ¼ inch on the remaining side of the sash opening and hand stitch in place, covering the seam allowances as you would with a binding.

Diagram 9

Make It EASY

When gathering the ruffle, stitch only half the ruffle length, stop, cut the thread, then continue. That way you will need to gather only half the ruffle at a time. ■

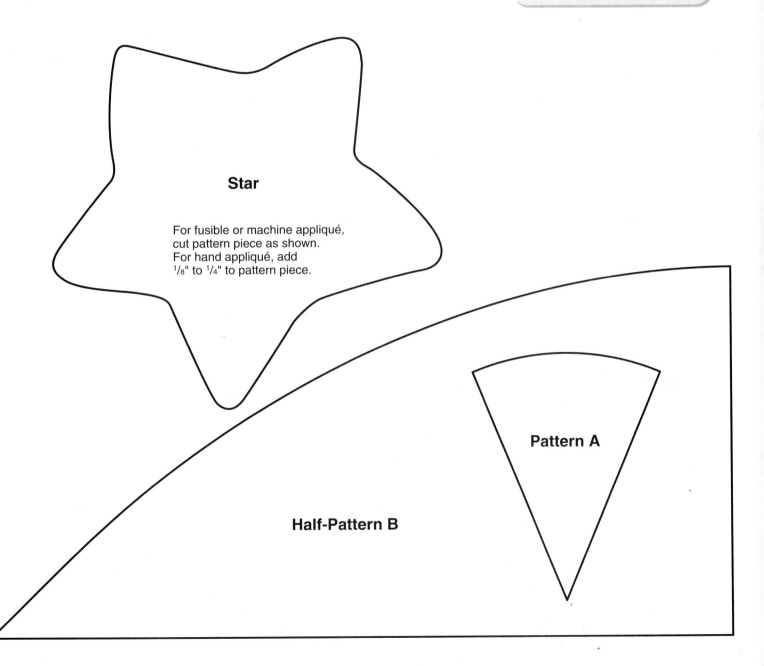

Star

For fusible or machine appliqué, cut pattern piece as shown. For hand appliqué, add ⅛" to ¼" to pattern piece.

Pattern A

Half-Pattern B

KATRINKA
DESIGNS

Saint Nicholas

Kathy Boudreau, *Katrinka Designs*

*A*n elegant addition to your holiday home decor or a great gift, this miniature wall-hanging is so easy that you really can get it done by Christmas—even if you've procrastinated until the last minute to get started! You may even find, once you're seated at the sewing machine, that it's quick and easy to make several of these snappy St. Nicks at the same time.

SIZE

Finished quilt is 14½ × 18 inches

FABRICS and SUPPLIES

Yardage based on 44-inch-wide fabric
- ½ yard brown print for borders
- ⅓ yard black print for upper background
- ⅛ yard tan print for lower background
- ⅛ yard off-white plaid for upper robe
- ⅛ yard black solid for binding
- Scraps for lower robe, hat, beard, face, hands, and fur trim
- ½ yard for backing
- ½ yard ribbon or jute for belt (optional)
- Several star sequins (optional)
- Black, fine-point, permanent felt-tip pen
- Blusher or red pencil
- Batting, larger than 14½ × 18 inches
- Template plastic or fusible web, depending on appliqué method chosen

GETTING READY

COLOR and FABRIC TIPS:
Note that this Santa is not in his traditional red suit, yet there's no mistaking who he is. If you switch to red fabrics for his robes, make sure you pick a background that gives enough contrast so St. Nick still stands out. If you go with a light Santa on a dark background, as in the quilt shown in the photograph, you may need to back light-colored fabrics with interfacing to prevent shadowing.

St. Nicholas in red

- Wash, damp dry, and press all fabrics before using. If using metallic fabrics, use a press cloth to prevent melting.

- All seam allowances are ¼ inch and should be pressed to one side, unless otherwise indicated.

- See "Appliqué Basics" on page 238 and choose a method. Then, trace the pattern pieces for Saint Nicholas' **Right Hand, Left Hand, Lower Robe, Left Upper Robe, Right Upper Robe, Hat, Face, Beard, Hat Trim,** and **Hat Ball** on pages 102–103 onto template plastic or fusible web, depending on the method you've chosen. Since this project is especially well suited to fusible appliqué, the pattern pieces have already been reversed. If you are using hand or machine appliqué, you will need to reverse the pattern pieces if you want your St. Nick to face in the same direction as the one shown on the quilt.

- Cutting directions for each part of the quilt are provided in the sections indicated by the yellow rotary cutters. This format allows you to cut what you need as you get ready to assemble each part of the quilt. If you prefer to cut all the pieces at once, skip ahead, looking for the yellow rotary cutters, and cut all the pieces before starting to sew.

ASSEMBLING the CENTER SECTION

Cutting for the Center Section

From the various scraps:

◆ Cut out the pieces for Saint Nicholas, following the directions for the appliqué method you have chosen.

From the upper background fabric, cut:

◆ One 10½ × 12½-inch piece

From the lower background fabric, cut:

◆ One 10½ × 2-inch piece

Piecing and Appliquéing the Center Section

STEP 1. Sew the two background pieces together along the 10½-inch sides. Press toward the darker fabric.

STEP 2. Lay all the pieces of St. Nicholas in the center of the background, with the lower edge of his robe approximately ½ inch below the seam. Pieces are numbered in the order in which they must be appliquéd. Use the photograph and the **Placement Guide** on the opposite page to help position the pieces properly. NOTE: If you choose to add a jute or ribbon belt, add it before you appliqué the pieces down.

STEP 3. Appliqué, using your favorite technique.

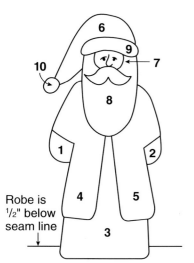

Robe is
1/2" below
seam line

Numbers on placement guide
indicate order of fusing or stitching.

Placement Guide

Attaching the Borders

STEP 1. Attach a side border to each side of the central motif. Press the seam allowances toward the border.

STEP 2. Attach the top and bottom borders. Press toward the border.

Make It FAST

With a small quilt, pin basting is the quickest way to go, whether you'll be quilting by hand or by machine. If you've used fusible appliqué, don't put safety pins through the St. Nick portion of the quilt. Instead, pin around the appliqué and out to the borders, spacing pins every 3 inches or so. If you're hand quilting in a hoop, just move any pins out of the way of the hoop. ■

Make It EASY

A light box would be a big help with this project. Use it to trace the pieces for appliqué and to transfer the face details from the pattern onto your quilt. A lamp placed underneath a glass-top table gives you an easy and inexpensive light box. ■

BORDERS

Cutting for Borders

From the border fabric, cut:

◆ Two 2½ × 14-inch pieces (Side Borders)

◆ Two 2½ × 14½-inch pieces (Top and Bottom Borders)

Quilt Diagram

QUILTING

STEP 1. Press the finished quilt top. Mark the quilting design, using one of your own or following these suggestions; see the **Quilt Diagram** on page 101 for details.

■ Outline quilt around Saint Nicholas.

■ Quilt ¼ inch on each side of the border seams.

STEP 2. Layer the quilt top, batting, and backing. Baste the layers together.

STEP 3. Quilt by hand or machine.

STEP 4. Trim the batting and backing even with the quilt top. Remove the basting.

BINDING

STEP 1. Cut two crosswise strips to prepare 80 total inches of straight-grain binding. Cut the strips 2 inches wide for double-fold binding.

STEP 2. Join the strips end to end with diagonal seams. Fold in half lengthwise with wrong sides together and press. Attach the binding to the quilt, following the instructions on page 242.

Make It FUN

Using the pen, draw in the mustache and facial details. (See the photograph on page 98 and the **Placement Guide** on page 101.) Use the blusher or red pencil to color in his cheeks. Sew a star sequin to the hat brim and scatter several more across the upper border, if desired. ■

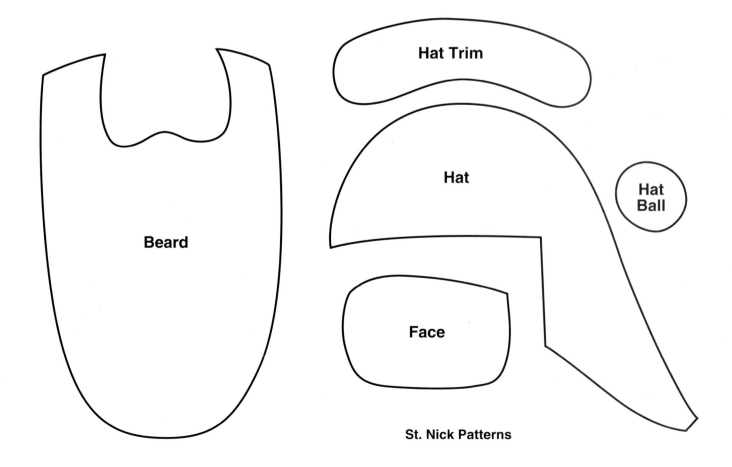

Beard

Hat Trim

Hat

Hat Ball

Face

St. Nick Patterns

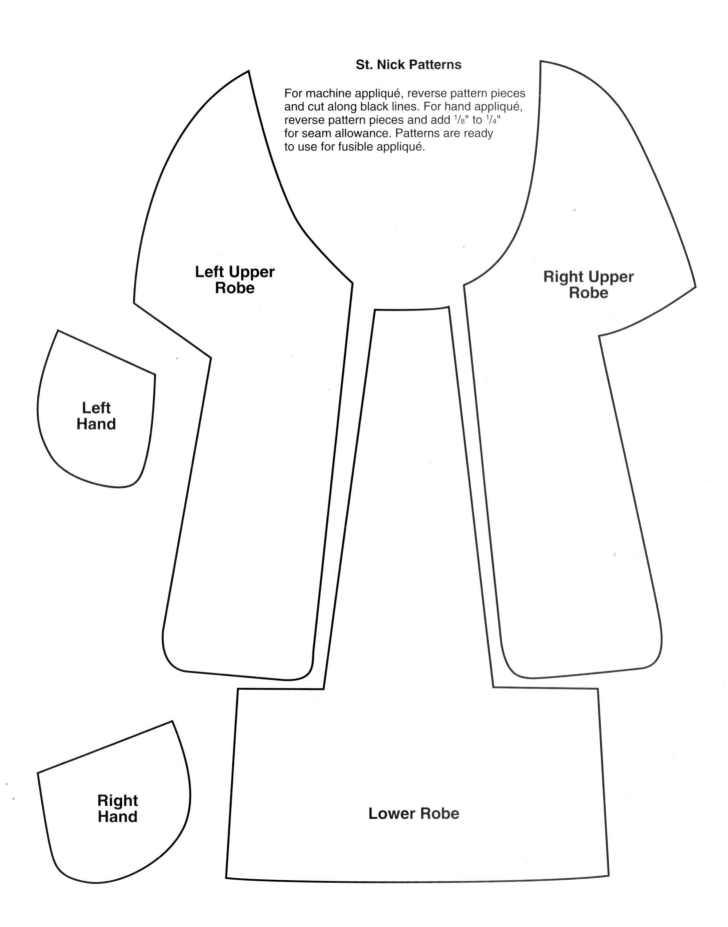

St. Nick Patterns

For machine appliqué, reverse pattern pieces and cut along black lines. For hand appliqué, reverse pattern pieces and add $1/8$" to $1/4$" for seam allowance. Patterns are ready to use for fusible appliqué.

Left Upper Robe

Right Upper Robe

Left Hand

Right Hand

Lower Robe

COUNTRY
THREADS

Father Christmas

Connie Tesene and Mary Tendall, *Country Threads*

A quartet of Santas come bearing gifts and other traditional Christmas trappings. This wall quilt looks terrific above a mantel, where it can become the focal point of your holiday decorating. This project is so much fun to put together, you might want to invite some friends over for an afternoon of Santa-making. Ask everyone to bring red and green fabric to swap and share, put on a pot of coffee, set out a plate of Christmas cookies, and have some fun!

SIZE

Finished quilt is 29 × 43 inches
Finished block is 8½ × 15½ inches

FABRICS and SUPPLIES

Yardage based on 44-inch wide fabric

- ⅜ yard red check for outer border
- ⅓ yard *each* of four assorted lights for backgrounds
- ¼ yard *each* of four assorted reds for coats and hats
- ¼ yard of white for beards and trim
- ⅜ yard green plaid for sashing and inner border
- ¼ yard red for center square and binding
- ⅛ yard green for tree and wreath
- ⅛ yard tan for hands and face
- ⅛ yard blue for bag
- 1 yard for backing
- Batting, larger than 29 × 43 inches
- Tan and black embroidery floss (optional)
- Black, extra-fine point, permanent felt-tip pen
- Template plastic or fusible web, depending on appliqué method
- Rotary cutter, ruler, and mat

GETTING READY

COLOR and FABRIC TIPS:

A quilt filled with Santas cries out for red and green with accents of white. To keep the mix of colors spicy and not predictable, pick different kinds of reds, like a deep burgundy, bright tomato red, maroon, and country barn red. Contrary to popular belief, different reds do work together well.

Mix and match different reds.

- Wash, damp dry, and press all fabrics before using.
- All seam allowances are ¼ inch and should be pressed to one side, unless otherwise indicated.
- In preparation for rotary cutting, trim the selvages off the background, border, and binding fabrics and square off one crosswise edge of each fabric, as described on page 236.
- See "Appliqué Basics" on page 238 and choose a method. Then, trace the patterns on pages 109–111 onto template plastic or fusible web, depending on the method you've chosen. For hand or machine appliqué, *reverse* the patterns first before making templates for Santas that exactly match those shown in the quilt. If you don't want to bother reversing the patterns, the arm positions and what they are holding will be reversed from the quilt shown.
- Cutting directions for each part of the quilt are provided in the sections indicated by the yellow rotary cutters. This format allows you to cut what you need as you get ready to assemble each part of the quilt. If you prefer to cut all the pieces at once, skip ahead, looking for the yellow rotary cutters, and cut all the pieces before starting to sew.

ASSEMBLING the BLOCKS

Cutting for Blocks (make 4)

From the assorted lights, cut:

♦ Four 9 × 16-inch pieces (Background)

Follow the directions for the appliqué method you have chosen when cutting the following.

From the white, cut:

♦ 4 Hat Trims

♦ 4 Coat Trims

♦ 4 Beards

From the assorted reds, cut:

♦ 4 Bodies

♦ 4 Left Sleeves

♦ 4 Right Sleeves

♦ 1 Gift

♦ 1 Bow

From the tan, cut:

♦ 8 Hands

♦ 4 Faces

From the green, cut:

♦ 1 Tree

♦ 1 Wreath

From the blue, cut:

♦ 1 Bag

Appliquéing the Blocks

STEP 1. Arrange the pieces for each Santa on a background block. Take care to position all the Santas in approximately the same spot on each block. Position the red body first, then follow the **Body Pattern and Placement Guide** on page 110–111 when adding the other pieces. Do a trial run before fusing or appliquéing for good. Remember to do the underneath pieces first. For help in determining the order of adding the pieces, see the **Appliqué Guide**. Repeat to make a total of four blocks, using the tree, wreath, gift, and bag.

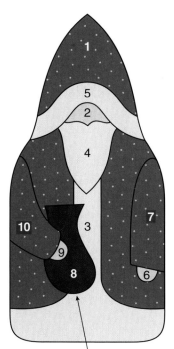

Tree and gift done in same order.
Add wreath *last,* after hand and sleeve.

Appliqué Guide

STEP 2. Embroider around all the appliqué shapes with black embroidery floss, using a buttonhole stitch (see page 61). With the black pen, draw two closely spaced eyes on each Santa.

Make It FUN

Glue or stitch teddy bear and star buttons with a tiny sprig of artificial greenery to the open edge of the bag. With the tan embroidery floss, stitch along the line marked on the appliqué pattern to create a drawstring. Also stitch along the lines on the gift to make a ribbon and bow. ■

ASSEMBLING the CENTER

Cutting for the Center

From the green plaid, cut:

◆ Two 2 × 16-inch pieces (Vertical Sashing Strip)

◆ Two 2 × 9-inch pieces (Horizontal Sashing Strip)

From the red, cut:

◆ One 2-inch center square

Piecing the Center

STEP 1. Refer to the **Quilt Diagram** when reading these directions. Sew a Father Christmas block to each side of a 2 × 16-inch sashing strip. Press toward the sashing. Repeat with the other two blocks and sashing strip.

Make It EASY

If you plan to do the buttonhole embroidery by hand, use lightweight or sewable fusible web. This thinner web makes it much easier to get the needle through. If you will be doing the buttonhole stitch with your machine, you can use either heavy or lightweight fusible web. ■

Quilt Diagram

STEP 2. Sew a 9-inch sashing strip to each side of the red center square. Press toward the sashing.

STEP 3. Join the block rows to the sashing and center square row to complete the quilt center. Press.

BORDERS

Cutting for Borders

From the green plaid, cut:

◆ Two 2 × 19-inch pieces (Top and Bottom Inner Borders)

◆ Two 2 × 36-inch pieces (Side Inner Borders)

From the red check, cut:

◆ Two 4 × 22-inch pieces (Top and Bottom Outer Borders)

◆ Two 4 × 43-inch pieces (Side Outer Borders)

Attaching the Borders

STEP 1. Attach inner border pieces to the top and bottom of the quilt top. Press toward the border. Attach inner borders to the sides and press.

STEP 2. Attach outer border pieces to the top and bottom of the quilt top. Press toward the border. Attach outer borders to the sides and press.

QUILTING

STEP 1. Press the finished quilt top. Mark the quilting design, using one of your own or following these suggestions.

■ Quilt ¼ inch from the edges of the hat trim.

■ Quilt along the lines of the beard and sleeves.

■ Quilt in the ditch around each Santa's body.

■ Stitch a 1¾-inch diagonal grid through the block backgrounds, sashing, and inner and outer borders.

STEP 2. To make the 1 yard of fabric work for the quilt back, it will need to be pieced. Cut a 3-inch strip from one long selvage side. Trim this to 36 inches and sew it to one of the 36-inch long sides of the backing piece. Press the seam open.

STEP 3. Layer the quilt top, batting, and backing. Baste all the layers together.

Quilting Diagram

Make It FAST

For marking a large background grid, like the one used in this quilt, try a hera for quick and easy marking. Move the narrow edge of this palm-size, hard plastic tool along the side of your rotary ruler and use the resulting indentations in the fabric as your quilting guides. If you need to erase, just dab the lines in the fabric with water and they'll disappear like magic. After quilting, you'll never even know the marks were there. Heras are available in most quilt shops or mail-order catalogs. ■

STEP 4. Quilt by hand or machine.

STEP 5. Trim the batting and backing even with the quilt top. Remove the basting.

BINDING

STEP 1. Cut four 1½-inch crosswise strips to prepare 160 inches of single-fold straight-grain binding.

STEP 2. Join the strips end to end with diagonal seams. Fold in half lengthwise with wrong sides together and press. Attach the binding to the quilt, following the instructions on page 242.

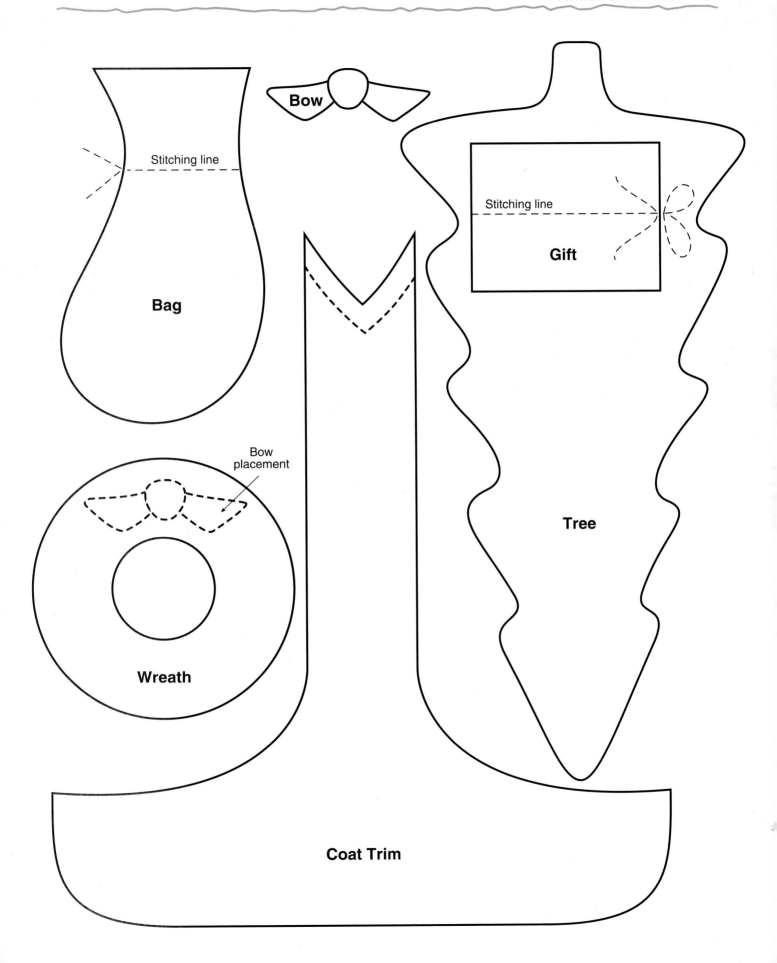

Stitching line

Bow

Stitching line

Gift

Bag

Bow placement

Tree

Wreath

Coat Trim

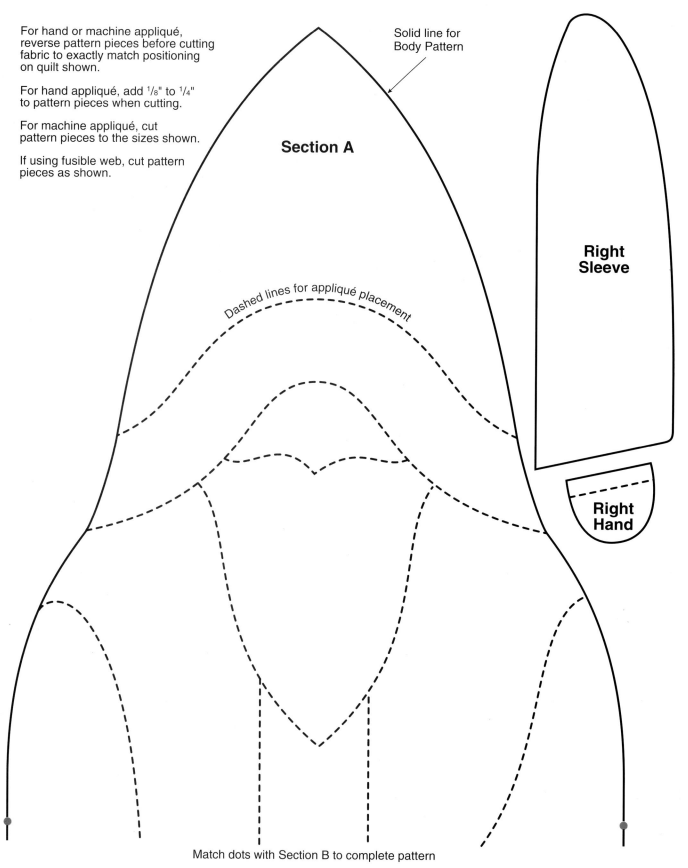

For hand or machine appliqué, reverse pattern pieces before cutting fabric to exactly match positioning on quilt shown.

For hand appliqué, add 1/8" to 1/4" to pattern pieces when cutting.

For machine appliqué, cut pattern pieces to the sizes shown.

If using fusible web, cut pattern pieces as shown.

Solid line for Body Pattern

Section A

Dashed lines for appliqué placement

Right Sleeve

Right Hand

Match dots with Section B to complete pattern

Body Pattern and Placement Guide

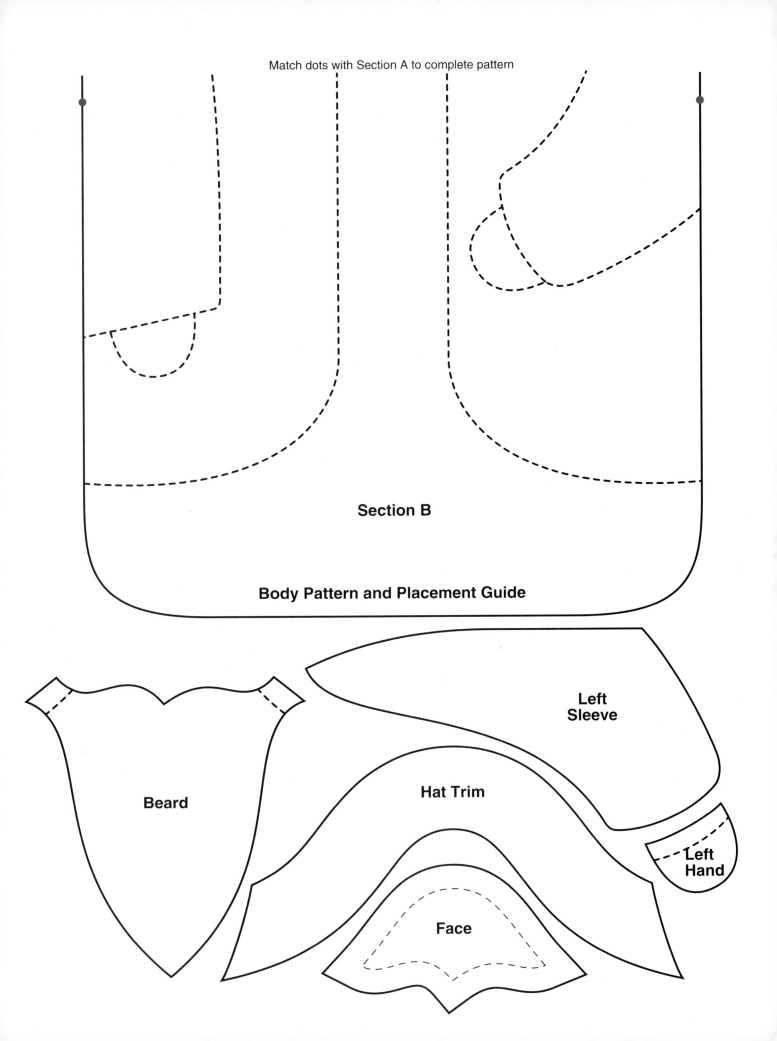

Match dots with Section A to complete pattern

Section B

Body Pattern and Placement Guide

Left Sleeve

Beard

Hat Trim

Left Hand

Face

Christmas Angel

Sandy Gervais, *Pieces from My Heart*

*T*his tiny angel hovering above the treetops is a tender symbol of the holiday spirit. An easy afternoon project, this little quilt would make a wonderful surprise rolled up in someone's stocking on Christmas morning. Or, treat it like an oversize gift tag and attach it to the ribbon on a wrapped package. Your extra handmade gesture is sure to be appreciated.

SIZE

Finished quilt is 10 inches square

FABRICS and SUPPLIES

Yardage based on 44-inch-wide fabric
- ¼ yard dark blue for sky
- Scraps of a variety of reds, blues, greens, golds, and dark tans for angel and border
- Scrap of muslin for angel
- ⅜ yard for backing (or one 11½-inch-square scrap)
- Batting, 11½ inches square
- Gold embroidery floss
- Black embroidery floss
- Fusible web for appliqué
- Powdered blush
- Raw umber acrylic paint

GETTING READY

COLOR and FABRIC TIPS:
This little angel looks just heavenly floating against a dark indigo sky. To stay with this mood, look for a deep navy or black fabric, perhaps even one with tiny stars printed on it. Make sure the angel's body and wings contrast with whatever background you choose. The same thing applies to the hearts and stars on the border—make sure there's sufficient contrast so the little appliqué shapes don't get lost.

- Wash, damp dry, and press all fabrics before using.

- All seam allowances are ¼ inch and should be pressed to one side, unless otherwise indicated.

- Trace the patterns on pages 116–117 for the **Angel, Trees, Stars,** and **Hearts** onto fusible web, following the directions on page 238 and reversing the patterns. Note that the stars and hearts are all different—each will need its own pattern.

- Cutting directions for each part of the quilt are provided in the sections indicated by the yellow rotary cutters. This format allows you to cut what you need as you get ready to assemble each part of the quilt. If you prefer to cut all the pieces at once, skip ahead, looking for the yellow rotary cutters, and cut all the pieces before starting to sew.

Strong Contrast   Low Contrast

ASSEMBLING the CENTER

Cutting for the Center

From the dark blue, cut:

- One 7½-inch square (background)

Using the pattern pieces traced onto fusible web and the fabric scraps listed below, press the fusible web onto the wrong side of the fabric for the following pieces:

- 1 dress from a red scrap

- 1 of each wing and 1 tiny star (for the corner of the dress) from a gold scrap

- 1 face and 2 legs from the muslin

- 1 each large, medium, and small tree from different green scraps

Appliquéing the Center

Referring to the **Quilt Diagram** for placement, fuse the dress to the background, then add the wings, face, legs, and star. Fuse the three trees to the background.

BORDERS

Cutting for Borders

From the scraps, cut:

- Twenty to thirty 2-inch-wide pieces varying in length from 1 to 2½ inches

Using the pattern pieces traced onto fusible web and the fabric scraps listed below, press the fusible web onto the wrong side of the fabric for the following pieces:

- 11 different stars from gold scraps

- 4 different hearts from red scraps

Make It FAST

A small cutting mat and ruler set to the left of your sewing machine allow you to cut the scrap pieces for the border as you sew. Selecting the color and width one piece at a time lets you get just the right combination of colors and fabrics for a pleasing scrap border. ■

Preparing the Borders

STEP 1. Join the pieces along the 2-inch sides to make one long strip, approximately 2 × 40 inches, as shown in **Diagram 1**. Press.

2"

Diagram 1

STEP 2. From this strip, cut two 7½-inch pieces. Attach them to the top and bottom of the quilt top. Press toward the border.

STEP 3. From the remaining pieced strip, cut two 10½-inch pieces. Attach them to the sides of the quilt top. Press toward the border.

Appliquéing the Borders

Fuse the stars and hearts onto the border. You can use the photograph on page 112 for place-ment ideas, but feel free to put the stars and hearts wherever they work best on your particular scrap border.

ASSEMBLING the QUILT

STEP 1. Smooth out the batting on your work surface. Lay the backing right side *up* on top of it. Lay your quilt top right side *down* on the backing. Pin baste the layers together.

STEP 2. Stitch ¼ inch from the edges of the quilt top, leaving a 2-inch opening for turning. Trim the backing and batting even with the quilt top.

STEP 3. Turn the quilt right side out and press. Whipstitch the opening shut.

Make It FUN

To make the angel's eyes, dip a very sharp pencil tip in the brown paint and dot it on the face, referring to the **Angel Appliqué Pattern** and the photograph for placement. For her rosy cheeks, dip a cotton swab in the powdered blush and dab it on the muslin face. To make the hair, take a piece of embroidery floss (six strands thick) and form two loops (about 1½ inches long). Tack these loops on top of the angel's head with more gold embroidery floss. ■

1½"

Quilt Diagram

QUILTING

Using the embroidery floss, quilt your own design or follow these suggestions. Large, chunky stitches add to the homespun, folk-art feel of this project, so don't spend a lot of time trying for tiny, perfect stitches.

■ Highlight the stars and angel by stitching around them with two strands of gold embroidery floss.

■ Stitch around the trees and hearts with two strands of black embroidery floss.

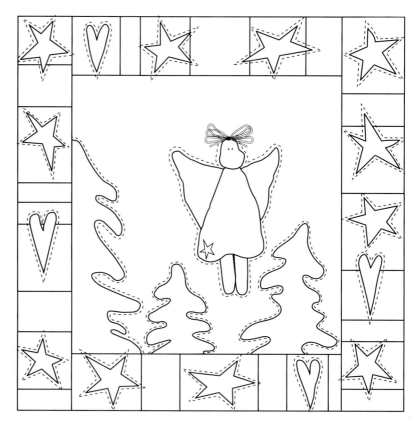

Quilting Diagram

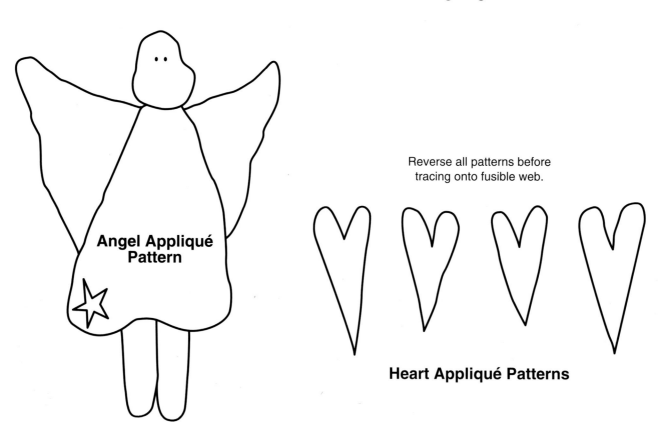

Angel Appliqué Pattern

Reverse all patterns before tracing onto fusible web.

Heart Appliqué Patterns

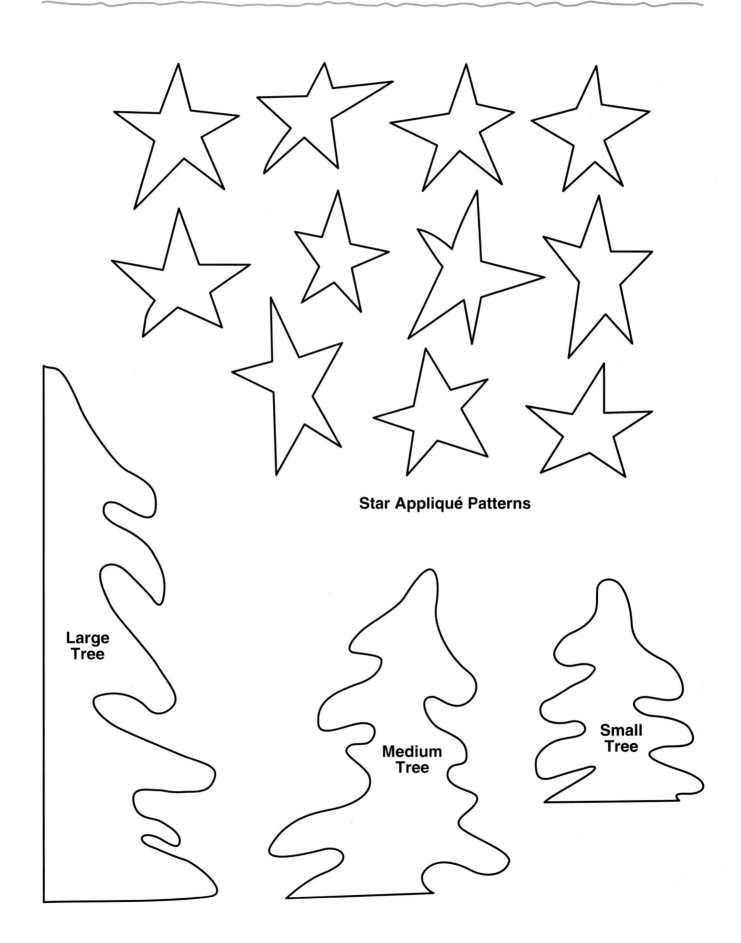

Star Appliqué Patterns

Large Tree

Medium Tree

Small Tree

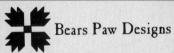
Bears Paw Designs

Gingerbread Cookies

Jill Kemp, *Bears Paw Designs*

*T*ake a break from baking cookies in the kitchen and spend a little while at your sewing machine whipping up a batch of jolly gingerbread kids. Boys and girls skip across the surface of this scrap quilt, winding their way through pine trees and cozy red cottages. In traditional red and green, this wall quilt could become part of your holiday decorations. Or, made in colors to match your kitchen, it could be kept on display all year round.

SIZE

Finished quilt is 35 × 40 inches
Finished blocks are 6 × 8, 3 × 8, and 3 × 4 inches

FABRICS and SUPPLIES

Yardage based on 44-inch-wide fabric

- ½ yard gold for outer border
- ¼ yard red for binding
- ¼ yard red-and-green plaid for inner border
- Scraps of assorted greens for trees, holly leaves, and block backgrounds
- ¼ yard brown for gingerbread boy and tree trunks
- Scraps of assorted light and medium tans for block backgrounds and gingerbread cookies
- Scraps of assorted golds for gingerbread cookies and stars
- Scraps of assorted reds for block backgrounds, houses, and heart and berry appliqués
- 1⅓ yards for backing
- Batting, larger than 35 × 40 inches
- Template plastic or fusible web, depending on appliqué method
- Rotary cutter, ruler, and mat
- Tan dye or tea for dyeing (optional)

119

GETTING READY

COLOR and FABRIC TIPS:

This scrap bag quilt gives you plenty of opportunities to combine bits and pieces of fabrics left over from other projects. The quilt in the photo sticks to a traditional Christmas color theme of red and green, with some tans, golds, and browns used as neutrals. Change the look by using rich navy blue in place of the red. Lots of plaids are used here to enhance the homespun charm, but small prints or tone-on-tone muslins would be equally effective.

Try navy in place of red.

■ Wash, damp dry, and press all fabrics before using.

■ All seam allowances are ¼ inch and should be pressed to one side, unless otherwise indicated.

■ In preparation for rotary cutting, trim the selvages off the border and binding fabrics and square off one crosswise edge of each, as described on page 236.

■ See "Appliqué Basics" on page 238 and choose a method. Then, trace the patterns for the **Heart, Star, Ginger Girl, Ginger Boy, Holly Leaf,** and **Holly Berry** on pages 124–125 onto template plastic or fusible web, depending on the method you've chosen.

■ Trace pattern pieces **A, B,** and **F** onto template plastic and cut them out. See the rotary/template cutting method described in "Make It Fast" on page 121.

■ This quilt includes some templates that must be used both right side up and reversed. This is always specified in the instructions, and is denoted on the pattern pieces with (r) following the pattern letter name.

■ Cutting directions for each part of the quilt are provided in the sections indicated by the yellow rotary cutters. This format allows you to cut what you need as you get ready to assemble each part of the quilt. If you prefer to cut all the pieces at once, skip ahead, looking for the yellow rotary cutters, and cut all the pieces before starting to sew.

Make It EASY

Here's a quick size reference guide for different parts of the quilt. This gives you an easy way to check whether the size scrap you want to use is large enough. The sizes given are for one block. ■

■ Green for trees: 4 × 8 inches

■ Tree background: 4 × 10½ inches

■ House background: 6 × 7 inches

■ Gingerbread Cookie background: 7 × 9 inches

■ Heart and Star background: 4 × 5 inches

■ Gingerbread Cookie appliqué shapes: 5½ × 8 inches

■ Heart and Star appliqué: 3 inches square (each)

■ Holly Leaf appliqué: 2½ × 3½ inches

■ Holly Berry appliqué: 1 inch square

ASSEMBLING the BLOCKS

Cutting the Tree Block (make 11)

From assorted light background fabrics, cut:

◆ 11 A and 11 A Reverse

◆ Twenty-two 1¾ × 2-inch pieces (C)

From assorted green fabrics, cut:

◆ 11 B

From assorted brown fabrics, cut:

◆ Eleven 1 × 2-inch pieces (D)

Make 11

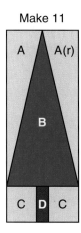

Tree Block

Piecing the Tree Block

STEP 1. Sew A and A reverse to each side of B, as shown in **Diagram 1**, to make the top of the tree. Press.

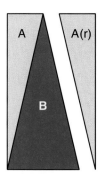

Diagram 1

STEP 2. Sew a C to each side of D to make the trunk unit, as shown in **Diagram 2**. Press.

Diagram 2

STEP 3. Join the trunk unit to the tree unit to complete the block. Press. Repeat to make a total of 11 blocks.

Make It FAST

To save time and cut more accurately, use your rotary cutter with templates A, B, and F. Trace around the plastic templates onto the right sides of the fabric. To get the A Reverse pieces, place two layers of fabric wrong sides together before you trace on the top. When you cut the piece out of these two layers, the piece underneath will automatically be the reverse. Align the edge of a rotary ruler exactly along the lines you've drawn and cut. For better accuracy, use a mechanical pencil to draw the cutting lines. ■

Cutting  the House Block (make 3)

Select three background fabrics; from each fabric, cut:

◆ Two 1 × 5½-inch pieces (G)

◆ One 2 × 5½-inch piece (I)

◆ One 3⅞-inch square; cut the square in half diagonally to make two triangles (E and E Reverse)

Select three house fabrics; from each fabric, cut:

◆ Two 2¼ × 5½-inch pieces (H)

◆ 1 F

Piecing the House Block

STEP 1. Sew E and E Reverse to each side of F, as shown in **Diagram 3**, to complete the roof. Press.

Make 3

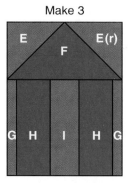

House Block

Diagram 3

STEP 2. Sew an H to each side of I, as shown in **Diagram 4A**, then sew a G to each side of this unit, as shown in **4B**. This completes the bottom of the house. Press.

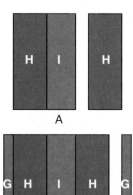

Diagram 4

STEP 3. Join the roof unit to the house unit to complete the block. Press. Repeat to make a total of three blocks.

Cutting the Gingerbread Cookie Blocks (make 6 Boys and 3 Girls)

From assorted red, green, and tan fabrics, cut:

◆ Nine 6½ × 8½-inch pieces (Background)

From brown, tan, and gold scraps, cut the following pieces, using the directions for the appliqué method you have chosen:

◆ 6 Ginger Boys

◆ 3 Ginger Girls

Make 6　　Make 3

Gingerbread Cookie Blocks

Appliquéing the Gingerbread Cookie Blocks

Appliqué the cookie shapes to the backgrounds, following the instructions for the appliqué method you have chosen. Follow the lead of the gingerbread kids in the quilt and don't position every one exactly straight. Part of the charm of this quilt comes from the fact that some of the kids are tilted to one side or the other. Repeat to make a total of six Boy blocks and three Girl blocks.

Cutting for Heart and Star Blocks (make 1 of each)

From each of two different tan fabrics, cut:

◆ One 3½ × 4½-inch piece (Background)

From the fabric scraps listed below, cut the following shapes, using the directions for the appliqué method you have chosen:

◆ 2 Stars from gold (save one for the border)

◆ 2 Hearts from two different reds (save one for the border)

Make 1　　Make 1

Heart and Star Blocks

Make It FUN

Add some fun accents to your gingerbread kids. Glue or stitch tiny buttons for eyes. Add buttons down the front of the boys and narrow ribbon or rickrack trim to the bottom of the girls' skirts. On a few of the tree blocks, add a gold star button. ■

Appliquéing the Heart and Star Blocks

Appliqué the stars and hearts to the backgrounds, following the instructions for the appliqué method you have chosen.

ASSEMBLING the CENTER

STEP 1. Referring to the **Quilt Diagram**, assemble the blocks into four horizontal rows. Pay attention to the order in which the Tree, Gingerbread Cookie, and House Blocks are arranged. Press, alternating the direction of the seam allowances from row to row.

STEP 2. Join the rows to complete the quilt top. Press.

BORDERS

Cutting for Borders

From the red-and-green plaid, cut:

◆ Four 1½-inch crosswise strips (Inner Border)

From the gold, cut:

◆ Four 3½-inch crosswise strips (Outer Border)

From the fabric scraps listed below, cut the following shapes, using the directions for the appliqué method you have chosen:

◆ 2 Holly Leaves from one or more green fabrics

◆ 3 Holly Berries from one or more red fabrics

Attaching the Borders

STEP 1. Measure through the center of your quilt vertically. Cut two red-and-green inner border strips to this exact measurement.

STEP 2. Attach these strips to the sides of your quilt top. Press toward the border.

STEP 3. Measure across the center of the quilt horizontally. Include the side borders in your measurement. Cut the remaining two inner border strips to this exact measurement.

STEP 4. Attach these strips to the top and bottom of your quilt top. Press toward the border.

STEP 5. Repeat Steps 1 through 4 for the gold outer borders.

STEP 6. Appliqué the holly leaves and berries and the star and heart set aside earlier onto the lower right corner of the quilt. Follow the directions for the appliqué method you have chosen.

QUILTING

STEP 1. Press the finished quilt top. Mark the quilting design, using one of your own or following these suggestions.

■ Quilt ¼ inch outside the appliqué pieces.

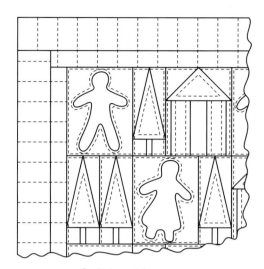

Quilting Diagram

■ Quilt ¼ inch inside the trees and houses.

■ Stitch in the ditch along the sides of blocks.

■ Fill the borders with straight lines of quilting spaced 2 inches apart.

STEP 2. Layer the quilt top, batting, and backing. Baste the layers together.

STEP 3. Quilt by hand or machine.

STEP 4. Trim the batting and backing even with the quilt top. Remove the basting.

BINDING

STEP 1. Cut four 2-inch crosswise strips to prepare 168 inches of double-fold straight-grain binding.

STEP 2. Join the strips end to end with diagonal seams. Fold in half lengthwise with wrong sides together and press. Attach the binding to the quilt, following the instructions on page 242.

Quilt Diagram

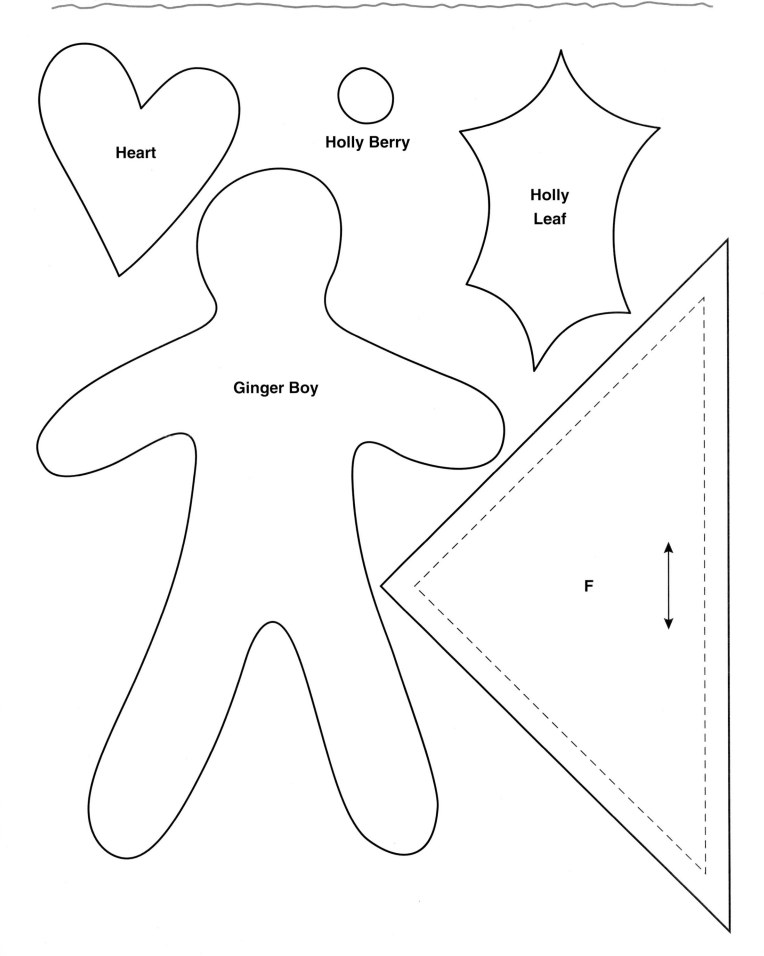

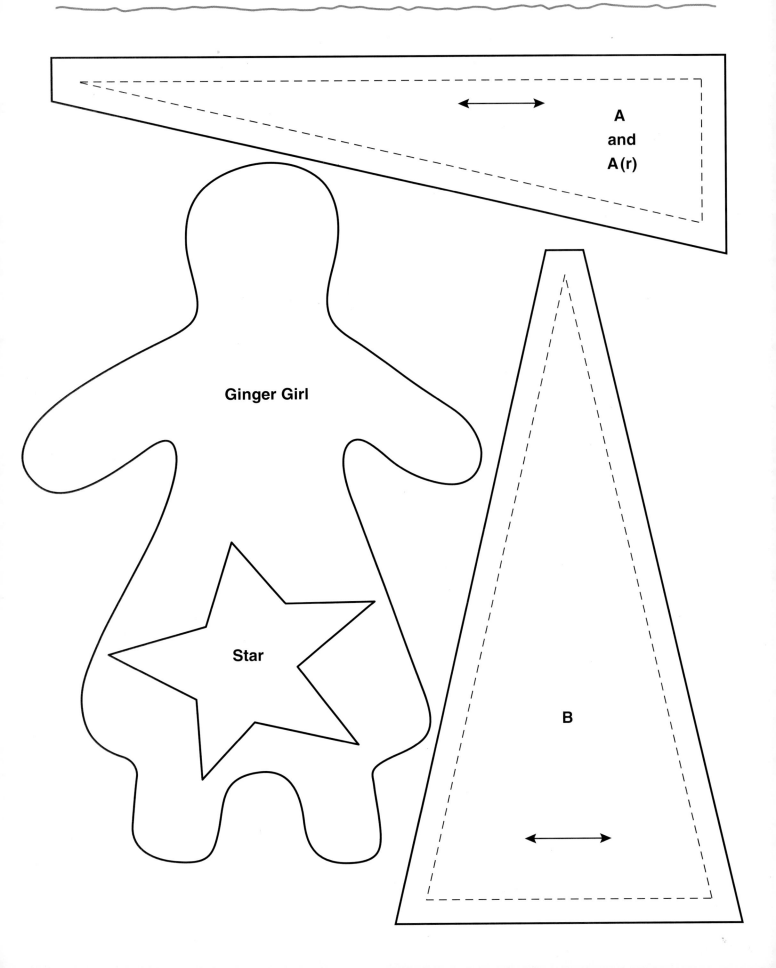

Heart to Heart

Heart and Hand

♥

Homestead Hearts

♥

Hearts

♥

Hearts and Spools

Heart and Hand

Sandy Gervais, *Pieces from My Heart*

*H*eart and hands working in unison is a natural combination for quiltmakers. This little quilt would make a loving gift or token of appreciation for someone near and dear to your heart. Check your scrap bag for bits and pieces of favorite fabrics, and check the button box for just the right finishing touches.

SIZE

Finished quilt is 9 × 12½ inches

FABRICS and SUPPLIES

Yardage based on 44-inch-wide fabric
- ¼ yard of black-on-brown print for background (or one 8 × 11-inch scrap)
- ⅛ yard of red print for heart (or one 5 × 8-inch scrap)
- Scrap of gold print for hand (at least 3 × 5 inches)
- Scraps of a variety of different reds, golds, and browns for pieced border, hearts, and cuff
- ⅜ yard for backing (or one 10½ × 14-inch scrap)
- Batting, 10½ × 14 inches
- Eight ⅝- to ¾-inch buttons
- Gold embroidery floss
- Black embroidery floss
- Fusible web for appliqué
- White dressmaker's tracing paper
- Regular tracing paper

GETTING READY

COLOR and FABRIC TIPS:
Picture changing the red, gold, and brown color palette of this quilt to blue, gold, and tan. Any other color trio of your choosing would work equally well—the key is to think about three main colors. Substitute a plaid for the heart background (just make sure there is good contrast between the heart and the background). The border is the perfect place for using up leftover bits of favorite fabrics.

- Wash, damp dry, and press all fabrics before using.

- All seam allowances are ¼ inch and should be pressed to one side, unless otherwise indicated.

- Trace the patterns for the **Large Heart, Small Heart, Hand,** and **Cuff** on page 132 onto fusible web, following the directions on page 238.

- Cutting directions for each part of the quilt are provided in the sections indicated by the yellow rotary cutters. This format allows you to cut what you need as you get ready to assemble each part of the quilt. If you prefer to cut all the pieces at once, skip ahead, looking for the yellow rotary cutters, and cut all the pieces before starting to sew.

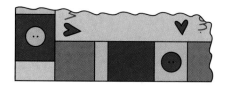

Blue Palette

ASSEMBLING the CENTER

Cutting for the Center

From the brown, cut:

- One 6½ × 10-inch piece (Background)

Using the pattern pieces traced onto fusible web and the fabric scraps listed below, prepare the following (directions for fusible appliqué are on page 238).

- 1 Large Heart from the red
- 1 Hand from the gold
- 1 Cuff from one of the scraps
- 2 Small Hearts from a second scrap

Appliquéing the Center

Referring to the **Quilt Diagram** for placement, fuse the Large Heart onto the background. Add the Hand and then the Cuff.

Quilt Diagram

BORDERS

Cutting for Borders

From the scraps, cut:

- ◆ Twenty to thirty 2-inch-wide pieces, varying in length from 1 to 3¼ inches

Preparing the Borders

STEP 1. Join the pieces along the 2-inch sides to make one long strip, approximately 2 × 45 inches, as shown in **Diagram 1.** Press all the seams in the same direction.

2"

Diagram 1

STEP 2. From this strip, cut two 6½-inch pieces. Attach them to the top and bottom of the quilt top. Press toward the border.

STEP 3. From the remaining pieced strip, cut two 13-inch pieces. Attach them to the sides of the quilt top. Press toward the border.

LETTERING

STEP 1. Trace the **Lettering Guide** on page 133 onto a piece of regular tracing paper. To transfer the lettering onto the background fabric, lay your quilt top on a hard surface. Lay the dressmaker's tracing paper on top of it, shiny side down. Lay the tracing paper with the lettering on top of the dress-makers' tracing paper, aligning it with the quilt top. Use a pencil to trace the letters with firm, steady pressure.

STEP 2. Thread your needle with three strands of gold floss and embroider the letters with a backstitch, as shown in **Diagram 2.**

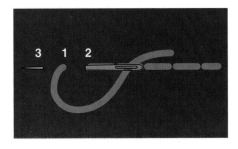

Backstitch
Diagram 2

STEP 3. Fuse the two small hearts in place, referring to the **Quilt Diagram** for placement.

Make It FAST

If you have trouble threading the floss through the eye of the needle you normally use for quilting, try a sharp with a larger eye. Cut the ends of the floss at an angle and pinch them between two moistened fingers to flatten them out, making it easier to insert them through the eye. If those tricks don't work, get out the needle threader! ■

ASSEMBLING the QUILT

STEP 1. Smooth the batting out on your work surface. Lay the backing right side *up* on top of it. Lay your quilt top right side *down* on the backing. Pin baste the layers together.

STEP 2. Stitch ¼ inch from the edges of the quilt top, leaving a 2½-inch opening along the bottom for turning. Trim the backing and batting even with the quilt top.

STEP 3. Turn right side out and press. Whipstitch the opening shut.

STEP 4. Sew on buttons, using the **Quilt Diagram** for placement suggestions.

Make It FUN

This quilt is the perfect place to highlight any antique buttons you might have in your collection. Or, in place of vintage buttons, tiny red or pewter heart-shaped buttons would make a nice finishing touch. ∎

QUILTING

Using embroidery floss, quilt your own design or follow these suggestions. Because of the homespun, folk-art look of this quilt, large chunky stitches are perfectly acceptable. Don't worry about making tiny, perfectly spaced quilting stitches.

■ Outline the large heart with three strands of gold embroidery floss.

■ Stitch around the hand and cuff with three strands of black floss.

■ Quilt around the little hearts with one strand of black floss.

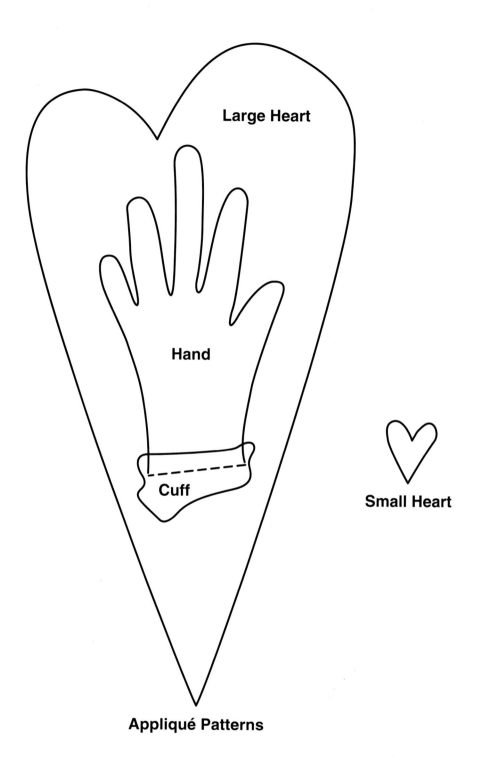

Large Heart

Hand

Cuff

Small Heart

Appliqué Patterns

whatsoever the hand finds to do, the heart should go forth in unison.

Lettering Guide

KATRINKA
DESIGNS

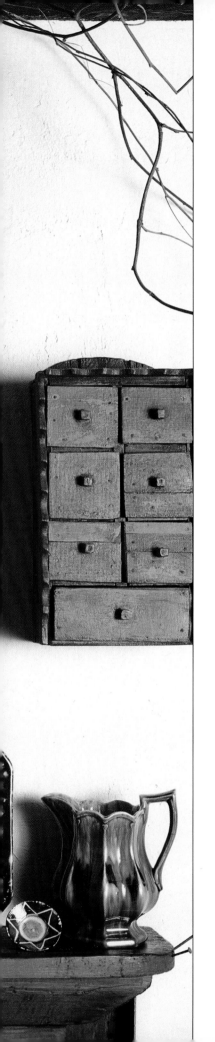

Homestead Hearts

Kathy Boudreau, *Katrinka Designs*

*T*raditional block patterns get a time-saving boost from today's quick and easy techniques. Instead of having to piece the house blocks and appliqué the heart-in-hand blocks with needle and thread, you can fuse or machine appliqué in a fraction of the time. This handsome wall quilt has a clever added touch—interlocking prairie points that form a colorful accent between the blocks and the border.

SIZE

Finished quilt is 28 inches square
Finished block is 6 inches square

FABRICS and SUPPLIES

Yardage based on 44-inch-wide fabric
- ⅜ yard dark gray plaid for top and bottom borders
- ¼ yard different dark gray plaid for side borders
- ¼ yard red for binding
- ⅛ yard light gray plaid for roofs
- Scraps of a variety of lights for background (each at least 8 inches square)

- Scraps of five different red prints for houses (each at least 5 × 6 inches)
- Scraps of four additional grays for hands (each at least 4 × 6 inches)
- Scraps of four different gold prints for sashing (each at least 6 × 8 inches)
- Scraps of a variety of grays, golds, and reds for prairie points, hearts, and sashing squares (each at least 4 inches square)
- 1 yard for backing
- Batting, larger than 28 inches square
- Template plastic or fusible web, depending on appliqué method
- Rotary cutter, ruler, and mat
- 8 buttons (optional)

135

GETTING READY

COLOR and FABRIC TIPS:

Red, gray, and gold form the basic color trio in this scrap-based quilt. If you want to work in different colors, follow this lead and pick three main color families, then look for varied scraps within those groups. When using directional prints like plaids or stripes for the backgrounds, vary the way they will run in the quilt. In the quilt shown you'll notice some run horizontally, while others run vertically.

Other Color Trio Options

- Wash, damp dry, and press all fabrics before using.
- All seam allowances are ¼ inch and should be pressed to one side, unless otherwise indicated.
- In preparation for rotary cutting, trim the selvages off the border and binding fabrics and square up one crosswise edge of each fabric, as described on page 236.
- See "Appliqué Basics" on page 238 and choose a method. Then, trace the patterns for the **House, Roof, Hand,** and **Heart** on page 139 onto template plastic or fusible web, depending on the method you've chosen. If you are using fusible web, remember to *reverse* the pattern pieces for the House, Roof, and Hand first before tracing onto the web.
- Cutting directions for each part of the quilt are provided in the sections indicated by the yellow rotary cutters. This format allows you to cut what you need as you get ready to assemble each part of the quilt. If you prefer to cut all the pieces at once, skip ahead, looking for the yellow rotary cutters, and cut all the pieces before starting to sew.

ASSEMBLING the BLOCKS

Cutting for Blocks (make 9)

From the light scraps, cut:

- ◆ Nine 6½-inch squares (Background)

Using the directions for the appliqué method you have chosen, cut the following:

- ◆ 5 Houses from the various reds
- ◆ 5 Roofs from the light gray
- ◆ 4 Hands from the various grays
- ◆ 4 Hearts from the red scraps

Appliquéing the Blocks

Referring to the **Appliqué Guide** and the photograph on page 134 for placement, and following the directions for the method you're using, appliqué Houses, Roofs, Hands, and Hearts to the background squares. For hand appliqué, apply a Heart to each Hand *before* sewing the hand on the background square.

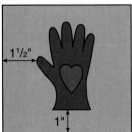

Match center of hand with center of block

Appliqué Guide

ASSEMBLING the CENTER

Cutting for the Center

From each of the four gold scraps, cut:

♦ Three 1½ × 6½-inch pieces

From the red scraps, cut:

♦ Four 1½-inch squares

Piecing the Center

STEP 1. Arrange the blocks and 6½-inch sashing pieces in three rows of three blocks each. Join the blocks into rows, as shown in **Diagram 1**. Press the seam allowances toward the sashing.

STEP 2. Join the remaining sashing pieces to the red sashing squares, as shown in **Diagram 2**. Press toward the gold sashing pieces. Repeat to make a second sashing row.

Diagram 1

Make 2

Diagram 2

STEP 3. Join the sashing and the block rows, as shown in **Diagram 3**. Press.

Diagram 3

BORDERS

Cutting for Borders

From the various scraps, cut:

♦ Forty 3-inch squares (Prairie Points)

From one of the dark gray plaids, cut:

♦ Two 4½ × 20½-inch pieces (Side Borders)

From the other dark gray, cut:

♦ Two 4½ × 28½-inch pieces (Top and Bottom Borders)

Attaching the Borders

STEP 1. To make prairie points, fold each 3-inch square in half with wrong sides together and press. With the folded edge facing away from you, bring the corners in to the center of the

lower raw edge, as shown in **Diagram 4**. Press. Baste in place a scant ¼ inch from the raw edge. Repeat to make a total of 40 prairie points.

Make 40

Diagram 4

Make It FAST

To make the basting step go faster, set your machine for a basting stitch and feed all the folded prairie points through in a long chain, without stopping between units. After they've all been basted, clip the threads to separate them. ■

STEP 2. Position 10 prairie points on the right and left sides of the quilt top, as shown in **Diagram 5** on page 138. Flaps should face up and points face in, with raw edges aligning with the edge of the quilt. Baste in place a scant ¼ inch from the edge.

Diagram 5

STEP 3. Sew 20½-inch border strips to the sides. Press so that the prairie points face outward.

STEP 4. Repeat Steps 2 and 3 with the remaining prairie points and 28½-inch border strips on the top and bottom of the quilt top.

QUILTING

STEP 1. Press the finished quilt top. Mark the quilting design, using one of your own or following these suggestions.

■ Outline quilt all the appliqué shapes.

■ Quilt in the ditch between the blocks and sashing.

■ Within each border, stitch diagonal lines spaced 1¼ inches apart. Change the direction of the lines from border to border, as shown in the **Quilting Diagram.**

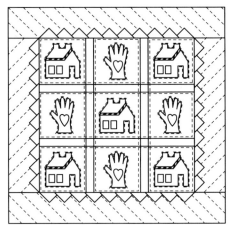

Quilting Diagram

STEP 2. Layer the quilt top, batting, and backing. Baste the layers together.

STEP 3. Quilt by hand or machine.

STEP 4. Trim the batting and backing even with the quilt top. Remove the basting.

Quilt Diagram

Make It FUN

Add a button for embellishment to each red corner square in the sashing, and to the red heart in each hand. ■

BINDING

STEP 1. Cut three 2-inch cross-wise strips from the red binding fabric to prepare 120 inches of double-fold straight-grain binding.

STEP 2. Join the strips end to end with diagonal seams. Fold in half lengthwise with wrong sides together and press. Attach the binding to the quilt, following the instructions on page 242.

Make It EASY

A walking foot or even-feed attachment can make adding the binding easy. This special foot feeds all the layers through at the same time, reducing the chance of puckers or tucks in the binding or backing. ■

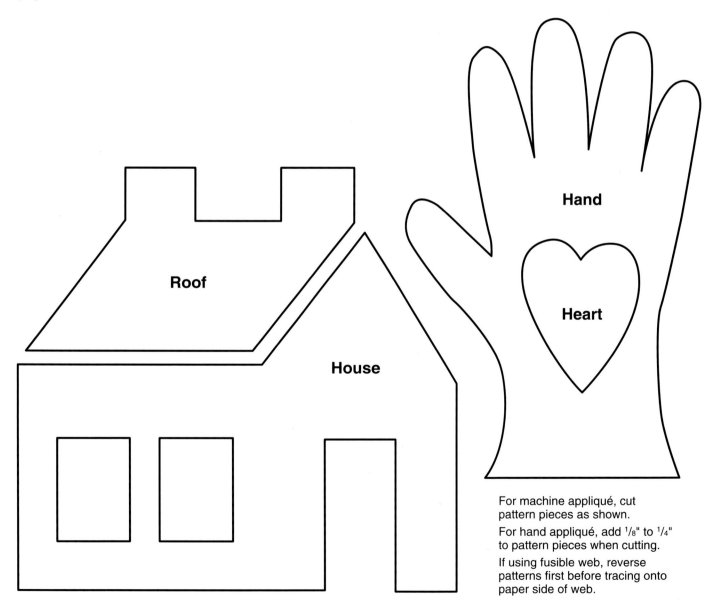

Roof

House

Hand

Heart

For machine appliqué, cut pattern pieces as shown.

For hand appliqué, add ¹/₈" to ¹/₄" to pattern pieces when cutting.

If using fusible web, reverse patterns first before tracing onto paper side of web.

PLUM CREEK PATCHWORK

Hearts

Johanna Wilson, *Plum Creek Patchwork*

*S*end your special valentine a token of your affection with a quilter's touch. The smallest of these little quilts could easily fit inside an envelope, onto which you can fuse a few extra red hearts. What a lovely way to say you care enough to make it yourself! The wall quilt goes together in a jiffy and makes a lovely heartfelt gift any day of the year.

SIZE

Finished wall quilt is 21 × 18 inches
Finished mini quilts range from 6 × 5 to 7½ × 16½ inches

FABRICS and SUPPLIES for WALL QUILT

Yardage based on 44-inch-wide fabric

- ⅝ yard cream-and-red stripe for background and backing
- ¼ yard *total* of various fabrics for hearts
- ¼ yard red stripe for sashing and binding
- ¼ yard black-and-red check for borders
- Batting, larger than 21 × 18 inches
- Buttons, bows, ribbon, and lace (optional)
- Template plastic, fusible web, and/or freezer paper, depending on appliqué method
- Rotary cutter, ruler, and mat

GETTING READY

COLOR and FABRIC TIPS:

Although an assortment of reds is a natural choice for this heart-themed quilt, don't let your color scheming stop there. Consider an array of rainbow colors for the hearts, set against a sparkling white background. Or how about solid Amish colors with a dramatic black background? If you're using plaids and checks, let the lines run diagonally on the hearts for more interest.

Hearts in rainbow colors

- Wash, damp dry, and press all fabrics before using.
- All seam allowances are ¼ inch and should be pressed to one side, unless other-wise indicated. When adding sashing, always press toward the sashing strip.
- In preparation for rotary cutting, trim the selvages off the backing, binding, and border fabrics and square off one crosswise edge of each fabric, as described on page 236.
- See "Appliqué Basics" on page 238 and choose a method. Then, trace the **Appliqué Patterns** on page 145 onto template plastic or fusible web, depending on the method you've chosen.
- Cutting directions for each part of the quilt are provided in the sections indicated by the yellow rotary cutters. This format allows you to cut what you need as you get ready to assemble each part of the quilt. If you prefer to cut all the pieces at once, skip ahead, looking for the yellow rotary cutters, and cut all the pieces before starting to sew.

ASSEMBLING the BACKGROUND

Cutting for the Background

NOTE: Refer to the **Background Diagram** as you cut.

From the cream-and-red stripe, cut:

- One 23 × 20-inch piece (Backing—cut first)
- One 11 × 5-inch piece (A)

- One 5 × 8-inch piece (B)
- One 5 × 14-inch piece (C)
- Two 5 × 3¾-inch pieces (D)

From the red stripe for the sashing, cut:

- One 2 × 8-inch piece
- One 11 × 2-inch piece
- One 2 × 14-inch piece
- One 5 × 1½-inch piece

Piecing the Background

STEP 1. Refer to the **Background Diagram** as you read these directions. Sew a D to each long edge of the 5 × 1½-inch sashing strip. Press.

STEP 2. Sew the 2 × 8-inch sash-ing strip to one long edge of B. Press toward the sashing.

Make It FAST

You can take a shortcut and rotary cut the background and sashing pieces from crosswise strips. Use 5-inch strips for the background and 2-inch strips for the sashing. However, pay attention if you are using a directional print and want it to run the same way in every background panel (as shown in the photograph on page 140). Since background A is set in the quilt horizontally, you would need to cut that piece separately so the stripes run in the right direction. The red stripe used for the sashing is subtle, without much contrast, so having the lines run in different directions is not distracting. ■

STEP 3. Sew the 11 × 2-inch sashing strip to one long edge of A. Press.

STEP 4. Sew the 2 × 14-inch sashing strip to one long edge of C. Press.

STEP 5. Join the D unit to the B unit, as shown in **Diagram 1**. Press.

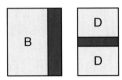

Diagram 1

STEP 6. Sew the A unit to the top of this unit, as shown in **Diagram 2**. Press.

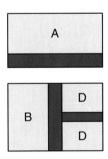

Diagram 2

STEP 7. Sew the C unit to the right side of this unit to complete the background, as shown in **Diagram 3**. Press.

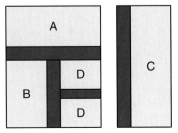

Diagram 3

APPLIQUÉ

Cutting for Appliqué

From the various heart fabrics, cut the following pieces, using the directions for the appliqué method you have chosen:

- ◆ 5 Large Hearts
- ◆ 10 Medium Hearts
- ◆ 11 Small Hearts

Appliquéing

Referring to the photograph on page 140 and following the directions for your method, appliqué the hearts to the background. Overlap them in places, and save a few to apply after you have attached the borders.

BORDERS

Cutting for Borders

From the black-and-red check for the borders, cut:

- ◆ Two 2½-inch crosswise strips; from these strips, cut two 17-inch pieces (Top and Bottom) and two 18-inch pieces (Sides)

Attaching the Borders

STEP 1. Refer to the **Quilt Diagram** on page 144 as you read these directions. Attach the 17-inch border strips to the top and bottom of the quilt top. Press toward the border.

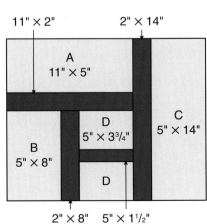

11" × 2"   2" × 14"

A
11" × 5"

D
5" × 3¾"

C
5" × 14"

B
5" × 8"

D

2" × 8"   5" × 1½"

Dimensions are cut sizes,
not finished sizes

Background Diagram

Quilt Diagram

STEP 2. Attach the 18-inch border strips to the sides of the quilt top. Press toward the border.

STEP 3. Take any hearts you had set aside and appliqué them to your top now, overlapping the borders.

STEP 3. Quilt by hand or machine.

STEP 4. Trim the batting and backing even with the quilt top. Remove the basting.

BINDING

STEP 1. From the red, cut two 2-inch crosswise strips to prepare 90 inches of double-fold straight-grain binding. (Cut and add another short strip if necessary.)

STEP 2. Join the strips end to end with diagonal seams. Fold in half lengthwise with wrong sides together and press. Attach the binding to the quilt, following the instructions on page 242.

Make It FUN

Don't hold back! Have a good time embellishing your quilt with buttons, ribbons, bows, or lace. Turn your mini quilt into a treasured keepsake by incorporating special touches like buttons and lace from your wedding gown, tiny satin hair bows worn by a favorite little girl when she was a baby, or vintage lace or antique buttons from a relative's attic. ■

QUILTING

STEP 1. Press the finished quilt top. Mark the quilting design, using one of your own or following these suggestions. Since there's so little quilting needed on this project, this makes a manageable learn-to-quilt project for a beginner.

■ Stitch in the ditch between the background panels and the sashing strips.

■ Outline the hearts, stitching either right along the edges or ¼ inch away.

STEP 2. Layer the quilt top, batting, and backing. Baste the layers together.

Make It EASY

Before you bind your quilt, consider adding a hanging sleeve. Cut a fabric strip 4 × 20 inches. Hem the ends with ¼-inch seams. Fold in half lengthwise, wrong sides together. Press. With raw edges even, machine baste the sleeve to the back of the quilt along the upper edge. Hand stitch the fold to the quilt back. The binding will cover the raw edges. ■

FABRICS and SUPPLIES for MINI QUILTS (to make all five mini quilts pictured)

■ ⅝ yard cream-and-red stripe for backgrounds and backings

■ ⅜ yard *total* of various fabrics for borders

■ ¼ yard *total* of various fabrics for hearts

■ Scraps of batting, approximately 18 × 36 inches total

■ Buttons, bows, ribbon, and lace (optional)

■ Template plastic, fusible web, and/or freezer paper, depending on appliqué method

■ Rotary cutter, ruler, and mat

ASSEMBLING the MINI QUILTS

Read "Getting Ready" on page 142 to prepare the fabrics and appliqué templates. Cut backgrounds A through D as for the wall quilt. Cut and add 1¾-inch borders to A, B, and C. Cut and add 1-inch borders to D. Cut out and appliqué hearts, following the directions for the method you've chosen.

Cut backing and batting pieces 1 inch larger than each mini quilt top. Lay the backing right side *up* on the batting. Place the quilt top right side *down* on the backing, as shown in **Diagram 4**. Sew ¼ inch from the edge all the way around the quilt top, leaving an opening along the bottom edge for turning, as shown. Trim the backing and batting even with the edge of the quilt top. Clip the corners. Turn. Press gently from the back and hand stitch the bottom edge closed. Quilt. Embellish as desired.

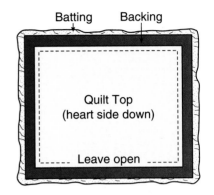

Diagram 4

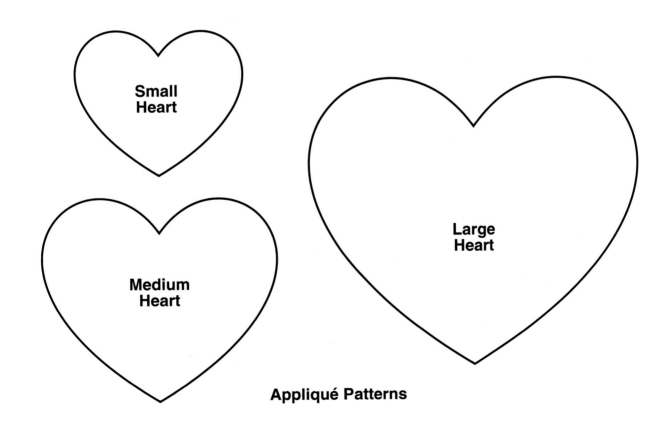

Appliqué Patterns

Hearts and Spools

Connie Tesene and Mary Tendall, *Country Threads*

*I*f you have a friend who's as serious about quilting as you are, why not make this quilt as a gift to show her that she's "sew special" to you? Equally at home on a wall in the sewing room or the family room, this quilt gives you the perfect opportunity to showcase your collection of fabrics. Little bits of a lot of different fabrics give this quilt its scrappy, spunky charm.

SIZE

Finished quilt is 24 × 28 inches
Finished block is 4½ inches
   square

FABRICS and SUPPLIES

Yardage based on 44-inch-wide fabric

- ⅜ yard navy for outer border
- ¼ yard medium tan plaid for inner border
- ¼ yard small brown check for middle border
- ¼ yard large brown check for binding
- ⅛ yard *each* 12 assorted lights for block backgrounds
- ⅛ yard *each* 12 assorted darks for spools and hearts
- 1 yard for backing
- Batting, larger than 24 × 28 inches
- Rotary cutter, ruler, and mat

GETTING READY

COLOR and FABRIC TIPS:
If you look closely at this quilt, you'll notice that the brown check fabric is used in both the middle border and the binding. The only difference is that the binding is a larger-scale check. Repeating a similar fabric in two different scales is a fun element to work into a quilt. Also notice how the dark navy outer border serves as an effective frame for the interior of the quilt.

- Wash, damp dry, and press all fabrics before using.

- All seam allowances are ¼ inch and should be pressed to one side, unless otherwise indicated.

- In preparation for rotary cutting, trim the selvages off the border fabrics and square up one crosswise edge of each fabric, as described on page 236.

- Cutting directions for each part of the quilt are provided in the sections indicated by the yellow rotary cutters. This format allows you to cut what you need as you get ready to assemble each part of the quilt. If you prefer to cut all the pieces at once, skip ahead, looking for the yellow rotary cutters, and cut all the pieces before starting to sew.

Two scales are better than one

ASSEMBLING the BLOCKS

Cutting for Blocks (make 12)

The following instructions are for *one* block. Repeat to make 12 blocks. Mix and match heart, spool, and background colors from block to block.

From the assorted darks, cut:

◆ Two 2 × 3½-inch pieces (Heart Piece 1)

◆ Two 2-inch squares (Spool Piece 2)

◆ Four 1-inch squares (Spool Piece 3)

◆ Two 3½ × 1¼-inch pieces (Spool Piece 4)

◆ Four 1¼-inch squares (Spool Piece 5)

From the assorted lights, cut:

◆ Two 1¼ × 5-inch pieces (Background Piece 6)

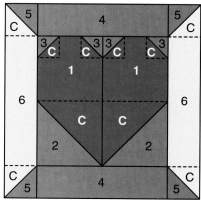

C=connector squares

Block Diagram

Make It EASY

The blocks are pieced using a technique borrowed from Mary Ellen Hopkins. She uses pieces called "connector squares" to add triangles to rectangles or large squares.

To use a connector square, place it on the background block, right sides together, in the desired corner. Sew across the square diagonally, stitching from corner to corner (you may want to mark this line first), as shown in **A.** Trim off the outside corner of the connector square, as shown in **B.** Do not cut the corner off the background block. Fold the corner square back over the seam and press, as shown in **C.** ■

Stitch

Trim square only

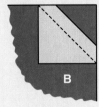

Press

Piecing the Blocks

STEP 1. Lay Pieces 2 and 3 on Piece 1 with right sides together, as shown in **Diagram 1.** Prepare two of these units, using the same color fabrics for both.

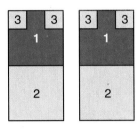

Diagram 1

STEP 2. Following **Diagram 2**, stitch in a continuous line in the direction of the arrows without taking the fabric out of the machine. Trim Pieces 2 and 3 only, leaving a ¼-inch seam allowance. Refer to "Make It Easy" on this page for details on trimming. Press.

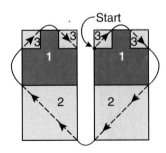

Diagram 2

STEP 3. Create the heart unit by placing the two pieces from Step 2 right sides together and sewing the center seam. Press.

STEP 4. Sew a Piece 4 to the top and bottom of the heart unit. Press.

STEP 5. Lay a Piece 5 on each end of Piece 6. Stitch diagonal-

ly in the directions shown in **Diagram 3.** Trim and press.

Make 2

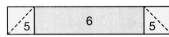

Diagram 3

STEP 6. Create the spool by sewing a Step 5 unit to each side of the heart unit, as shown in **Diagram 4.** Press. Repeat to make a total of 12 blocks.

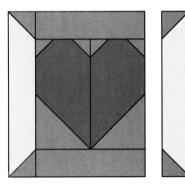

Diagram 4

Make It FAST

In a quilt like this one, with lots of quick sewing tricks, you don't want to let an empty bobbin slow you down. Prefill several extra bobbins with a neutral thread like a medium gray or medium tan. These colors will blend well with nearly every fabric color, which is especially helpful in a scrappy quilt like this one. ■

ASSEMBLING the CENTER

Lay the blocks out in a pleasing arrangement of four rows of three blocks each. Join the blocks into horizontal rows. Press, alternating the direction of the seam allowances from row to row. Join the rows. Press.

BORDERS

Cutting for Borders

From the medium tan plaid, cut:

◆ Two 2 × 14-inch strips

◆ Two 2 × 21½-inch strips

From the small brown check, cut:

◆ Two 1 × 17-inch strips

◆ Two 1 × 22½-inch strips

From the navy, cut:

◆ Two 3½ × 18-inch strips

◆ Two 3½ × 28½-inch strips

Attaching the Borders

STEP 1. Sew the two 14-inch medium tan strips to the top and bottom of the quilt. Press toward the border. Sew the 21½-inch medium tan strips to the sides. Press.

STEP 2. Sew the brown check strips to the quilt, adding the top and bottom borders first, then the sides. Press toward the borders.

Make It FUN

Don't be in a hurry to stitch all your blocks together. Take the time to play with different arrangements to make sure the colors and fabrics are balanced throughout. For a quick and easy temporary design surface, tack a flannel pillowcase to the wall in your sewing room. The pillowcase will be just the right size to hold these 12 blocks as you adjust the block placement. ■

STEP 3. Sew the navy strips to the quilt, adding the top and bottom borders first, then the sides. Press toward the borders.

QUILTING

STEP 1. Press the finished quilt top. Mark the quilting design, using one of your own or following these suggestions.

■ Stitch ¼ inch inside and outside the spools.

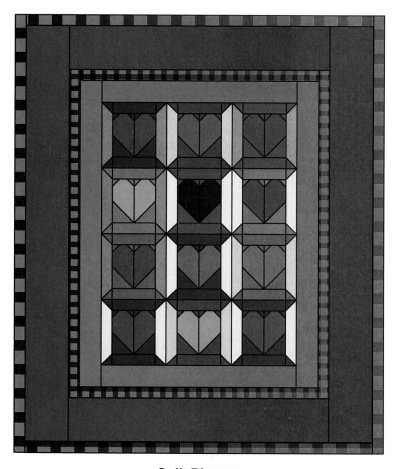

Quilt Diagram

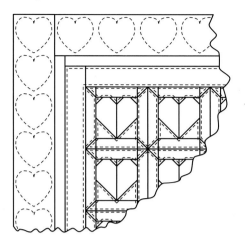

Quilting Diagram

- Outline the curves and points of the hearts.

- Stitch in the ditch between the blocks.

- Quilt ¼ inch from both edges of the inner border.

- Add quilted hearts to the outer border.

- Trace the pieced heart shape from the center of the quilt and use that to create the stencil for the hearts in the border.

STEP 2. Layer the quilt top, batting, and backing. Baste the layers together.

STEP 3. Quilt by hand or machine.

STEP 4. Trim the batting and backing even with the quilt top. Remove the basting.

BINDING

STEP 1. Cut three 1¼-inch crosswise strips to prepare 125 inches of single-fold straight-grain binding.

STEP 2. Join the strips end to end with diagonal seams. Fold in half lengthwise with wrong sides together and press. Attach the binding to the quilt, following the instructions on page 242.

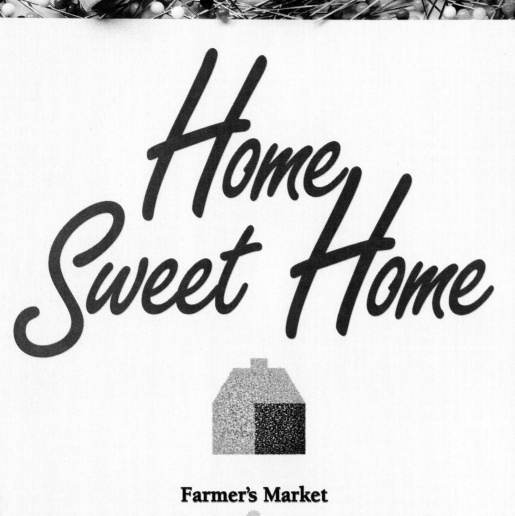

Home Sweet Home

Farmer's Market

Toni Phillips and Juanita Simonich, *Fabric Expressions*

*T*hese veggies look farm fresh, thanks to inspired fabric selections that capture the color and texture of ripe tomatoes, velvety eggplants, and ruddy carrots. The perfect complement to your kitchen or breakfast nook, this wall quilt also looks at home as a table runner. If your other hobby is gardening, fill a wooden bowl or rustic bushel basket with some of midsummer's colorful harvest and place it on the table along with this quilt to create a fun tabletop display. (If you don't happen to be a gardener, take a cue from the photo and use fun fabric fakes for the garden vegetables.)

SIZE

Finished quilt is 12 × 38 inches
Finished block is 8 × 10 inches

FABRICS and SUPPLIES

Yardage based on 44-inch-wide fabric

- ⅜ yard dark green print for block borders and binding
- ⅜ yard purple plaid for sashing and border
- ¼ yard ticking for inner blocks
- ¼ yard light gold for block backgrounds
- Scraps of three different reds for tomatoes
- Scraps of two different purples for eggplant
- Scraps of two different oranges for carrots
- Scraps of three different greens for leaves
- ½ yard for backing
- Batting, larger than 12 × 38 inches
- Fusible web
- Rotary cutter, ruler, and mat
- Purple floss or #5 Pearl cotton

GETTING READY

COLOR and FABRIC TIPS:
In the cutting information, dimensions of pieces are given width × height. If you want to use directional prints like stripes and plaids, buy extra fabric and cut some pieces out lengthwise to keep the stripes running in the same direction in the sashing and border.

Notice that the large purple plaid in the borders of the quilt in the photograph on page 154 was cut deliberately so that the dark stripe runs down the center. You may need extra fabric to do this, as well.

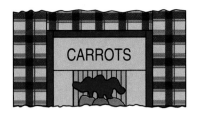

Precisely placed plaids
create special effects

■ Wash, damp dry, and press all fabrics before using.

■ All seam allowances are ¼ inch and should be pressed to one side, unless otherwise indicated.

■ In preparation for rotary cutting, trim the selvages off the dark green, light gold, and purple plaid fabrics, and square off one crosswise edge of each fabric, as described on page 236.

■ This project is designed especially for fusible appliqué. Remember to *reverse* the patterns first before tracing onto the web, as described on page 238.

■ Cutting directions for each part of the quilt are provided in the sections indicated by the yellow rotary cutters. This format allows you to cut what you need as you get ready to assemble each part of the quilt. If you prefer to cut all the pieces at once, skip ahead, looking for the yellow rotary cutters, and cut all the pieces before starting to sew.

ASSEMBLING the BLOCKS

Cutting for Block Backgrounds (make 3)

Refer to the **Block Diagram** for guidance as you cut the following pieces.

From the ticking, cut:

◆ Three 4½ × 5-inch pieces (A)

From the gold, cut:

◆ One 2-inch crosswise strip; cut this strip into six 2 × 5-inch pieces (B)

◆ One 3-inch crosswise strip; cut this strip into three 7½ × 3-inch pieces (C)

◆ One 2½-inch crosswise strip; cut this strip into three 7½ × 2½-inch pieces (D)

From the dark green, cut:

◆ Three 1-inch crosswise strips; from these strips, cut six 7½ × 1-inch pieces (E) and six 1 × 10½-inch pieces (F)

Piecing the Backgrounds

STEP 1. Sew a B to each 5-inch side of A, as shown in **Diagram 1**. Press.

STEP 2. Sew C to the top of this unit and D to the bottom, as shown in **Diagram 2**. Press.

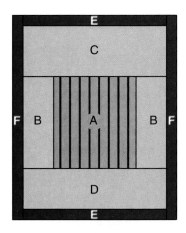

Block Diagram

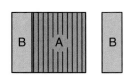

Diagram 1

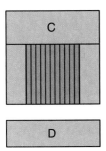

Diagram 2

STEP 3. Referring to the **Block Diagram**, sew E pieces to the top and bottom of the unit and an F to each side. Press. Repeat to make a total of three block backgrounds.

STEP 4. To transfer the lettering onto C, trace the lettering on page 158 onto a piece of paper and redraw over the letters with a dark marker. Position each block over the lettering and trace lightly onto the fabric with a soft pencil.

Make It EASY

If you have a light table, tracing the letters from the paper onto the fabric blocks is a snap. But not everyone has a light table on hand. For a simple substitute, tape the paper with the lettering onto a window. Then, tape the fabric block over this paper, positioning the lettering correctly. The sunlight shining through the paper and fabric will make tracing easy. ■

STEP 5. Embroider the letters, using the stem stitch and three strands of floss. See **Diagram 3**.

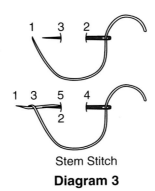

Stem Stitch
Diagram 3

Cutting for Appliqué

From the red, purple, orange, and green scraps, cut out the appliqué shapes on page 159, following the directions for fusible appliqué, and referring to the photograph on page 154 for color selection.

Appliquéing the Blocks

Referring to the photograph on page 154 for placement, fuse vegetables to the block backgrounds. Note that the eggplants and carrots extend below the center ticking square and a tomato peeks out to the left.

ASSEMBLING the CENTER

Cutting for Sashing

From the purple plaid, cut:

◆ Two 8½ × 2½-inch pieces

Make It FAST

If your sewing machine has a buttonhole or blanket stitch, try that as a decorative way to machine appliqué the shapes in place. If you've fused the shapes to the background, the buttonhole stitch is a nice way to add a finishing touch to the raw edges of the fabric. ■

Piecing the Center

Referring to the **Quilt Diagram** on page 158, join the three vegetable blocks with the two sashing strips to make one long row. Press.

BORDERS

Cutting for Borders

From the purple plaid, cut:

◆ Two 2½ × 34½-inch pieces (Side Borders)

◆ Two 12½ × 2½-inch pieces (Top and Bottom Borders)

Attaching the Borders

STEP 1. Attach the side border strips to the quilt top. Press toward the borders.

STEP 2. Attach the top and bottom border strips to the quilt top. Press toward the borders.

QUILTING

STEP 1. Press the finished quilt top. Mark the quilting design, using one of your own or following these suggestions. This wall quilt was quilted by machine using clear monofilament thread that blends well with all the assorted fabrics.

■ Quilt in the ditch between the backgrounds and the green borders.

■ Quilt in the ditch between the purple plaid and the green borders.

■ For an extra touch of class with very little effort, machine stipple quilt in the ticking background around the appliqué shapes.

STEP 2. Layer the quilt top, batting, and backing. Baste all the layers together.

STEP 3. Quilt by hand or machine.

STEP 4. Trim the batting and backing even with the quilt top. Remove the basting.

BINDING

STEP 1. Cut three 2½-inch crosswise strips to prepare 120 inches of double-fold straight-grain binding.

STEP 2. Join the strips end to end with diagonal seams. Fold in half lengthwise with wrong sides together and press. Attach the binding to the quilt, following the instructions on page 242.

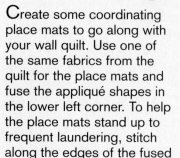

Make It FUN

Create some coordinating place mats to go along with your wall quilt. Use one of the same fabrics from the quilt for the place mats and fuse the appliqué shapes in the lower left corner. To help the place mats stand up to frequent laundering, stitch along the edges of the fused appliqué shapes. ■

Quilt Diagram

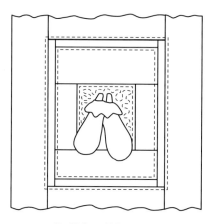

Quilting Diagram

CARROTS EGGPLANT TOMATOES

Lettering Guide (Enlarge 150%)

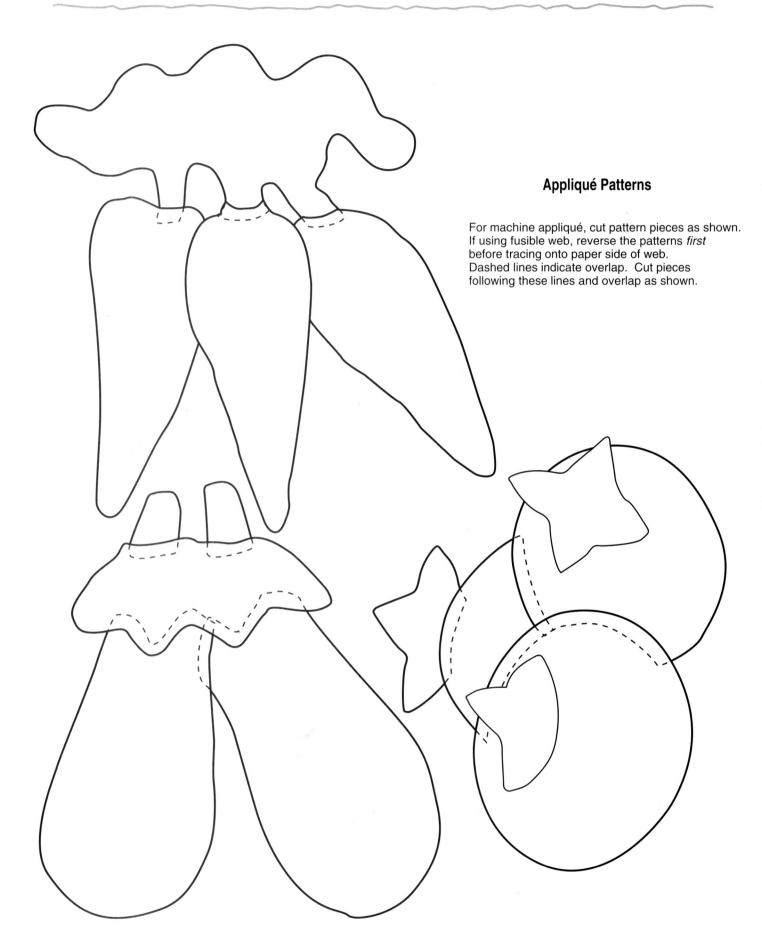

Appliqué Patterns

For machine appliqué, cut pattern pieces as shown.
If using fusible web, reverse the patterns *first*
before tracing onto paper side of web.
Dashed lines indicate overlap. Cut pieces
following these lines and overlap as shown.

Bears Paw Designs

Birdhouse Alley

Jill Kemp, *Bears Paw Designs*

*H*ere's a quilt to capture any bird lover's flight of fancy. If you look closely, you'll recognize there are only three basic styles of birdhouse block stitched from different fabrics creating the look of an eclectic neighborhood. The feathered friends that peek out from doors or sit proudly on the roofs are a cinch to appliqué using the quick-fuse method. A neat cutting trick that pairs the rotary cutter with templates makes short work of cutting all the pieces, leaving plenty of time to grab your binoculars and do some bird watching outside the sewing room.

SIZE

Finished quilt is 32½ × 38½ inches
Finished large block is 12 × 17 inches
Finished small blocks are 5½ × 7 inches

FABRICS and SUPPLIES

Yardage based on 44-inch-wide fabric
- 1 yard blue plaid for background
- ½ yard brown plaid for borders
- ½ yard brown print for perches and binding

- ¼ yard *each* of 13 different house fabrics (or one 8 × 10-inch scrap of each)
- ⅛ yard *each* of 13 different roof fabrics (or one 4 × 12-inch scrap of each)
- Scrap of red print for birds (approximately 6 × 8 inches)
- Scrap of black print for entrances (approximately 9 inches square)
- Scrap of blue print for bird heads
- 1⅛ yards for backing
- Batting, larger than 32½ × 38½ inches
- Template plastic
- Fusible web (optional)
- Rotary cutter, ruler, and mat

GETTING READY

COLOR and FABRIC TIPS:
Note that the roof fabrics are darker than the building fabrics. If you use directional prints like plaids and stripes, pay attention to how you cut them out if you want all the pieces in a particular block to run the same way. (See the birdhouse second from the top on the left side of the quilt in the photograph for an example.) The quilt shown uses a different building fabric and a different roof fabric for each birdhouse. If you want a less scrappy look, you can repeat some or all of the fabrics.

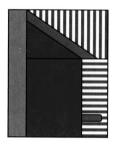

Beware of
directional fabrics

- Wash, damp dry, and press all fabrics before using.
- All seam allowances are ¼ inch and should be pressed to one side, unless otherwise indicated.
- In preparation for rotary cutting, trim the selvages off the blue plaid and brown plaid fabrics and square off one crosswise edge of each fabric, as described on page 236.
- Trace pattern pieces **A, B, C, D, E, F, G, J, K, L, P,** and **Q,** found on pages 168–169, onto template plastic and cut them out. Use the rotary cutter and template method described on page 163 to speed up cutting out these pattern pieces.
- This quilt includes some templates that must be used both right side up and reversed. This is always specified in the instructions, and is denoted on the pattern pieces with (r) following the pattern letter name.
- See "Appliqué Basics" on page 238 and choose a method. Then, trace the patterns for the **Bird, Bird Head, Perch, Large Entrance,** and **Small Entrance,** found on pages 168–169, onto template plastic or fusible web and cut them out. If you are using fusible web, be sure to reverse the pattern pieces.
- Cutting directions for each part of the quilt are provided in the sections indicated by the yellow rotary cutters. This format allows you to cut what you need as you get ready to assemble each part of the quilt. If you prefer to cut all the pieces at once, skip ahead, looking for the yellow rotary cutters, and cut all the pieces before starting to sew.

ASSEMBLING the BLOCKS

Cutting for Blocks

Block 1 (make 4)
From the blue plaid, cut:
- 4 A and 4 A Reverse
- 4 E and 4 E Reverse

Select 4 roof fabrics; from each, cut:
- 1 B
- 1 C

Select 4 house fabrics; from each, cut:
- 1 D

From the black print, cut:
- 4 Large Entrances, following the directions for the appliqué method you have chosen

Block 2 (make 4)
From the blue plaid, cut:
- 4 F and 4 F Reverse
- One 1-inch crosswise strip; from this strip, cut eight 1 × 5-inch pieces (piece I)

Select 4 roof fabrics; from each, cut:
- 1 G

Select 4 house fabrics; from each, cut:
- One 5-inch square (piece H)

From the black print, cut:
- 4 Small Entrances, following the directions for the appliqué method you have chosen

Block 3 (make 4)
From the blue plaid, cut:
- 2 J and 2 J Reverse

- One 2 × 20-inch strip; from this strip, cut four 2 × 4⅞-inch pieces (piece M)

Select 4 roof fabrics; from these, cut:

- 2 K and 2 K Reverse

Select 4 building fabrics; from these, cut:

- 2 L and 2 L Reverse
- One 3½ × 4⅞-inch piece (piece N)

From the blue print, cut:

- 1 Bird Head and 1 Bird Head Reverse, following the directions for the appliqué method you have chosen

From the brown print, cut:

- One 1½-inch crosswise strip; from this strip, cut four 1½ × 7½-inch pieces (piece O)
- 4 Perches, following the directions for the appliqué method you have chosen

Block 4 (make 1)

From the blue plaid, cut:

- 1 P and 1 P Reverse
- One 4 × 12½-inch piece (piece R)
- Two 1 × 10-inch pieces (piece S)
- Two 1½ × 7-inch pieces (piece T)

Select a roof fabric; from it, cut:

- 1 Q

Select a building fabric; from it, cut:

- One 9½ × 7-inch piece (piece U)

From the black print, cut:

- 6 Large Entrances, following the directions for the appliqué method you have chosen

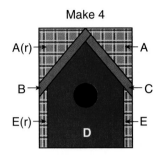

Make 4

Block 1

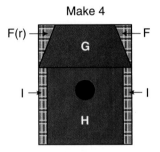

Make 4

Block 2

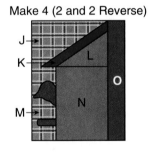

Make 4 (2 and 2 Reverse)

Block 3

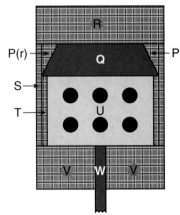

Make 1

Block 4

Rotary Cutting with Templates

Stack all the fabrics to be cut using the same pattern right side up on a rotary mat. Trace around the plastic template onto the right side of the top fabric. Align the edge of a rotary ruler exactly along the lines you've drawn and cut with the rotary cutter. For more accurate pieces, use the thin lead of a mechanical pencil to draw the cutting lines.

Piecing the Blocks

Block 1 (birdhouse with peaked roof)

STEP 1. Sew E and E Reverse to D, as shown in **Diagram 1**. Press.

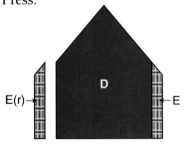

Diagram 1

STEP 2. Attach C and then B, as shown in **Diagram 2**. Press.

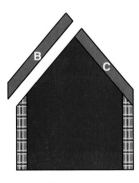

Diagram 2

STEP 3. Attach A and A Reverse to the sides, as shown in **Diagram 3**. Press.

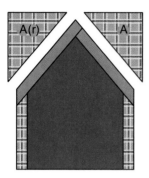

Diagram 3

STEP 4. Appliqué a Large Entrance, using pattern piece D as a placement guide. Repeat to make a total of four blocks.

Block 2
(birdhouse with flat roof)

STEP 1. Sew an I to each side of H, as shown in **Diagram 4**. Press.

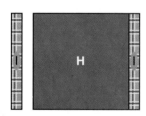

Diagram 4

STEP 2. Sew F and F Reverse to G, as shown in **Diagram 5**. Press.

Diagram 5

STEP 3. Join the roof unit to the house unit. Press.

STEP 4. Appliqué a Small Entrance, centering it from side to side and placing the top edge of the entrance ¾ inch from the bottom edge of the roof. Repeat to make a total of four blocks.

Block 3
(side view birdhouse)

STEP 1. Join J (or J Reverse), K (or K Reverse), and L (or L Reverse), as shown in **Diagram 6**. Press. (Note that two units are reverse units.)

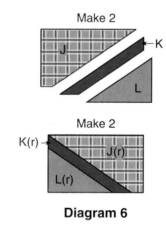

Diagram 6

STEP 2. Sew M to N, as shown in **Diagram 7**. Press.

Diagram 7

STEP 3. Join the roof unit to the building unit with piece L over piece N, press, and then sew piece O to the correct side, as shown in **Diagram 8**. Press. Repeat to make a total of four blocks (two reverse).

STEP 4. Appliqué Perches to all four blocks. Appliqué Bird Heads to two of the blocks. (See the photograph on page 160.)

Block 4 (large birdhouse)

STEP 1. Sew a T to each side of U, as shown in **Diagram 9**, to complete the house unit.

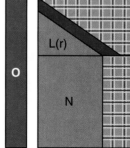

Diagram 9

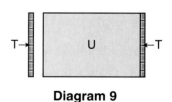

Diagram 8

Make It FAST

Note that several blocks have pieces that must be reversed. Save time by not making separate patterns for reverse pieces. Instead, just make a single plastic template for those pieces that are to be cut both right side and reversed. To get the reverse pieces, simply lay some of the fabrics (as many as you need reversed pattern pieces for) wrong side up in your rotary cutting stack. As you trace and cut out the patterns, you will automatically create reverse pieces from these "flopped" pieces of fabric. ■

STEP 2. Sew P and P Reverse to Q, as shown in **Diagram 10**, to complete the roof unit.

Diagram 10

STEP 3. Join the roof unit to the house unit, and then sew an S to each side, as shown in **Diagram 11**.

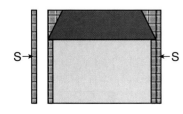

Diagram 11

STEP 4. Sew R to the top of this unit.

STEP 5. Appliqué six Large Entrances, referring to the photograph on page 160 for placement. Position four outer entrances ⅞ inch from the top, 1¼ inches from the bottom, and set in 1 inch from the sides. Center the middle two entrances between these.

ASSEMBLING the CENTER

Cutting for Setting Pieces

From the blue plaid, cut:

◆ Two 6 × 4½-inch pieces (piece V)

◆ Six 1½-inch crosswise strips; from these strips, cut:

  ◆ One 7½-inch piece (Vertical Sashing Strip)

  ◆ Six 6-inch pieces (Horizontal Sashing Strips)

  ◆ Four 31½-inch pieces (Vertical Sashing Strips)

  ◆ Two 27½-inch pieces (Horizontal Sashing Strips)

From the red print, cut:

◆ 1 Bird and 1 Bird Reverse, following the directions for the appliqué method you have chosen

From the brown print, cut:

◆ One 1½ × 11½-inch piece (piece W)

Piecing the Center

STEP 1. Sew the V pieces to the top of one Block 1 birdhouse and one Block 2 birdhouse, as shown in **Diagram 12**. Press.

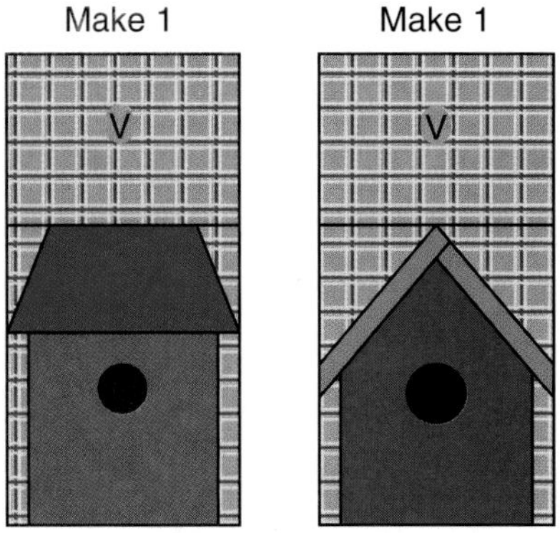

Make 1   Make 1

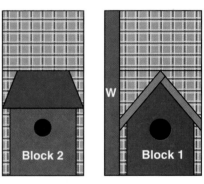

Diagram 12

STEP 2. Sew W between these units, as shown in **Diagram 13**. Press.

Diagram 13

STEP 3. Join this unit to the bottom of the large birdhouse. Press.

STEP 4. Join a small birdhouse to each side of the 7½-inch sashing strip, as shown in **Diagram 14**. Press.

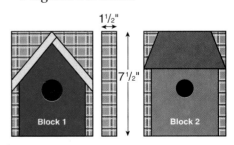

Diagram 14

STEP 5. Attach this unit to the top of the large birdhouse. Press.

STEP 6. Join the eight remaining small birdhouses and the six 6-inch sashing strips into two vertical rows, as shown in **Diagram 15**. Press.

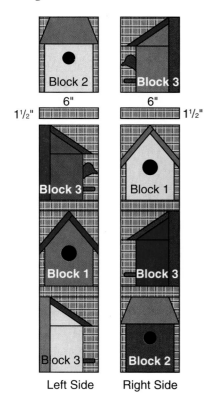

Diagram 15

STEP 7. Join the three vertical birdhouse rows and the four 31½-inch sashing strips, as shown in **Diagram 16**. Press. Add 27½-inch sashing strips to the top and bottom of this unit to complete the center. Press.

STEP 8. Appliqué red Birds, referring to the photograph on page 160 for help in placement.

BORDERS

Cutting for Borders

From the brown plaid, cut:

◆ Four 3-inch crosswise strips

Attaching the Borders

STEP 1. Measure through the center of your quilt vertically. Cut two border strips to this exact measurement.

STEP 2. Attach these strips to the sides of your quilt top. Press toward the border.

STEP 3. Measure across the center of the quilt horizontally. Include the side borders in your measurement. Cut the remaining two border strips to this exact measurement.

STEP 4. Attach these strips to the top and bottom of your quilt top. Press toward the border.

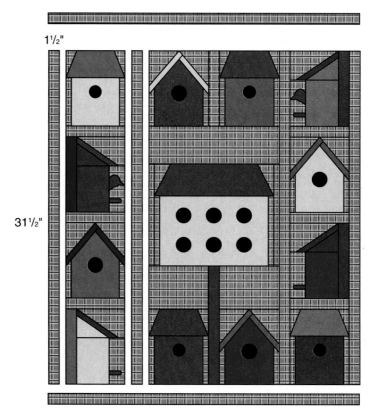

Diagram 16

Make It FUN

Since the birdhouse blocks are all the same size, you can combine them in any order. You might even want to see how you like having the blocks with the birds peeking out facing toward the outside edges of the quilt instead of facing toward the center. ■

Make It EASY

To gently round the corners of your quilt to look like the one in the photograph, place a small glass or saucer at the corner, as shown in the diagram. Trace around it and cut along the drawn line. Attach the binding as you normally would, rounding each corner as you get to it. Clip the curves as necessary when turning the binding over to the back and finish as usual. ■

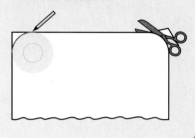

QUILTING

STEP 1. Press the finished quilt top. Mark the quilting design, using one of your own or following these suggestions.

■ Stitch in the ditch along all seams in the house blocks.

■ Quilt ⅛ to ¼ inch along the edge of each house entrance and bird.

■ Quilt "boards" on the houses and "shingles" on the roofs.

STEP 2. Layer the quilt top, batting, and backing. Baste all the layers together.

STEP 3. Quilt by hand or machine.

STEP 4. Trim the batting and backing even with the quilt top. Remove the basting.

BINDING

STEP 1. Cut four 2-inch bias strips to prepare 160 inches of double-fold bias binding.

STEP 2. Join the strips end to end with diagonal seams. Fold in half lengthwise with wrong sides together and press. Attach the binding to the quilt following the instructions on page 242.

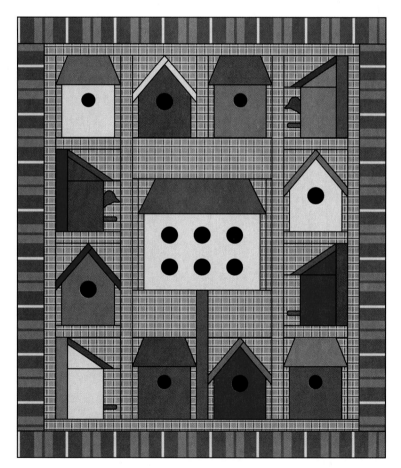

Quilt Diagram

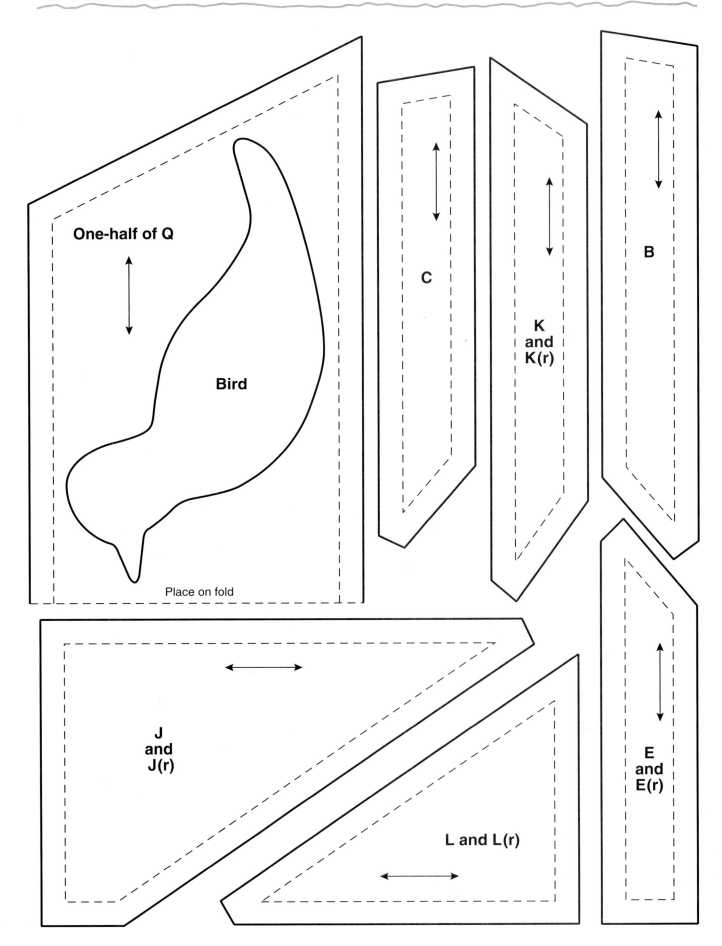

One-half of Q

Bird

Place on fold

C

K and K(r)

B

J and J(r)

L and L(r)

E and E(r)

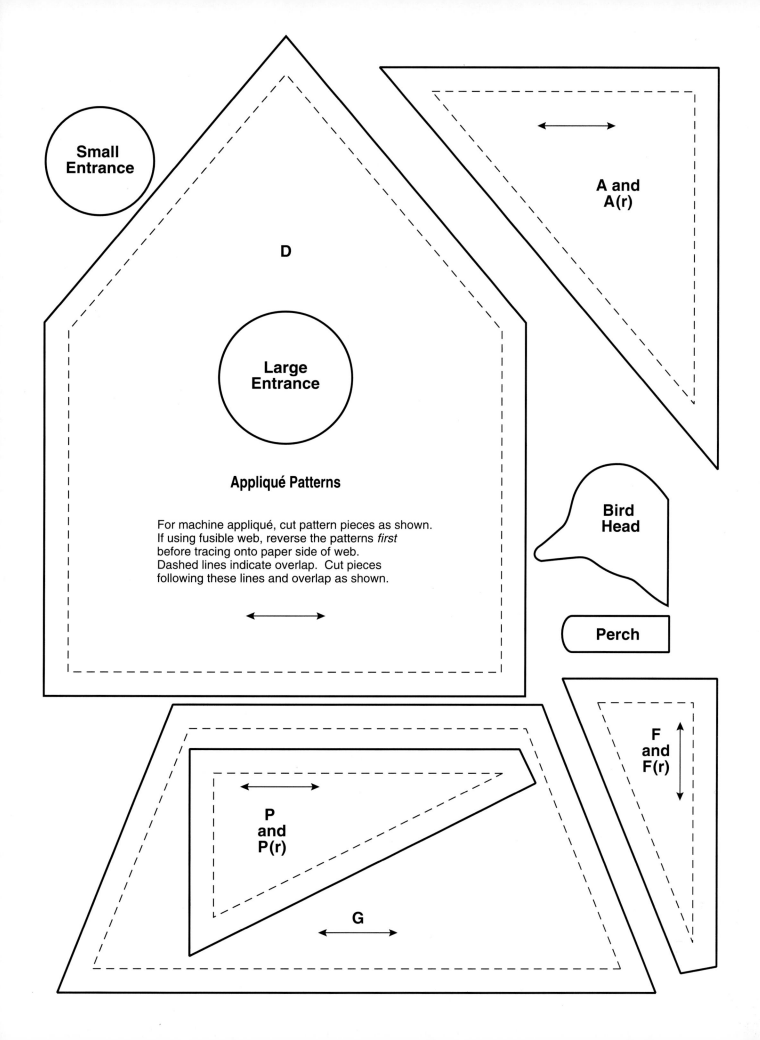

Small Entrance

A and A(r)

D

Large Entrance

Appliqué Patterns

For machine appliqué, cut pattern pieces as shown.
If using fusible web, reverse the patterns *first*
before tracing onto paper side of web.
Dashed lines indicate overlap. Cut pieces
following these lines and overlap as shown.

Bird Head

Perch

F and F(r)

P and P(r)

G

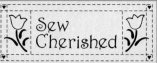

Summer Camp

Retta Warehime, *Sew Cherished*

The heavenly scent of pine trees, the peace of sleeping under star-filled skies, and the rustic charm of a log cabin are all brought together in this quilt that celebrates the pleasures of summer vacations. Making this quilt can be just as relaxing as the mood it evokes—there are no templates, so cutting all the pieces is a breeze with the help of your rotary cutter and ruler.

SIZE

Finished quilt is 20 × 33 inches
Finished block is $3\frac{1}{2} \times 5\frac{3}{4}$ inches

FABRICS and SUPPLIES

Yardage based on 44-inch-wide fabric
- $\frac{1}{2}$ yard tan print for background
- $\frac{3}{8}$ yard brown check for outer border
- $\frac{1}{4}$ yard rust print for sashing
- $\frac{1}{4}$ yard dark red print for binding
- $\frac{1}{8}$ yard green print for inner border*
- $\frac{1}{8}$ yard black print for roofs*
- $\frac{1}{8}$ yard gold print for corner squares*

- Scrap of gold print for stars (at least 3 × 12 inches)
- 1-inch crosswise strips of 3 reds, 3 blues, 3 golds, and 3 greens for houses (12 strips total)
- Two $\frac{3}{4}$-inch crosswise strips *each* of 4 different green fabrics for trees (8 strips total)
- Scrap of an additional brown fabric for tree trunks (at least 2 × 8 inches)
- $\frac{3}{4}$ yard for backing
- Batting, larger than 20 × 33 inches
- Rotary cutter, ruler, and mat

* Some fabric shops will not cut $\frac{1}{8}$-yard pieces. Purchase $\frac{1}{4}$ yard and save the extra for other projects, or check your scrap bag to see if you have any suitable leftovers. Check the size of the scrap against the size of the pieces that need to be cut to confirm that you have enough fabric.

GETTING READY

COLOR and FABRIC TIPS:
Rustic hues of rust, brown, green, and gold help create the feel of the outdoors. When you're piecing the cabin blocks, keep in mind that color placement can be either as suggested in the directions or random. And there's no rule that says all the houses have to match!

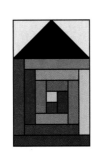

Place colors randomly

- Wash, damp dry, and press all fabrics before using.
- All seam allowances are ¼ inch and should be pressed to one side, unless otherwise indicated.
- In preparation for rotary cutting, trim the selvages off each of the fabrics and square off one crosswise edge, as described on page 236.
- Cutting directions for each part of the quilt are provided in the sections indicated by the yellow rotary cutters. This format allows you to cut what you need as you get ready to assemble each part of the quilt. If you prefer to cut all the pieces at once, skip ahead, looking for the yellow rotary cutters, and cut all the pieces before starting to sew.

ASSEMBLING the BLOCKS

Cutting for Cabin Block (make 5)

From the tan, cut:

- One 2¼-inch crosswise strip; from this strip, cut 10 squares

From the black print, cut:

- One 2¼ × 20-inch piece; from this piece, cut five 2¼ × 4-inch pieces (Roof)

From the gold print, cut:

- Five 1-inch squares (Cabin Centers)

If you haven't done so already, from each of the red, blue, gold, and green house fabrics, cut:

- One 1-inch crosswise strip, for a total of 12 strips

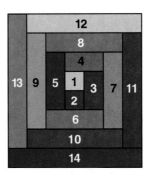

**Cabin Block
Piecing Diagram**

Make It EASY

Since there are no templates for this pattern, you will be cutting out lots of small pieces that you will need to identify later by their dimensions. To avoid having to measure and remeasure pieces in order to find them, label them with their dimensions as you cut. Attach a removable sticky note or scrap of masking tape, or put each size in a labeled envelope to keep organized. ∎

Piecing the Cabin Block

STEP 1. Refer to the **Cabin Block Piecing Diagram** as you piece the Log Cabin House. Lay a blue strip on a gold square with right sides together and raw edges even, as shown in **Diagram 1**. Stitch, press open, and trim the blue strip to ¾ inch from the seam.

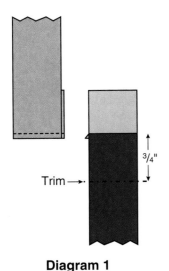

Trim →

¾"

Diagram 1

STEP 2. Lay a red strip on the unit from Step 1 with right sides together and raw edges even, as shown in **Diagram 2**. Stitch, press open, and trim the red strip even with the gold/blue unit.

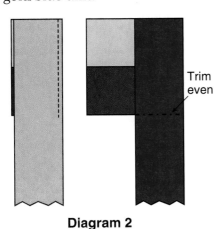

Trim even

Diagram 2

STEP 3. Continue in this manner, working around the block in the order given in the **Cabin Block Piecing Diagram**. Here's a hint: If you use green fabric for Piece 14, it will look like grass in your finished block. You should have a total of 14 pieces in the completed 4 × 4½-inch block.

STEP 4. To make the roof, use a ruler and pencil to draw a line from corner to corner on one 2¼-inch tan background square. Lay this piece on a roof piece with right sides together, as shown in **Diagram 3**. Make sure the line is oriented as shown. Sew along the marked line. Trim the seam allowances to ¼ inch. Fold the background piece back and press.

Cutting line

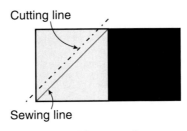

Sewing line

Diagram 3

STEP 5. Place another background square at the other end of the roof piece, as shown in **Diagram 4**. Repeat the marking, sewing, and trimming as described in Step 4. Press.

Cutting line

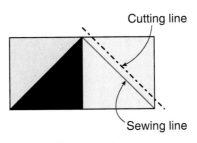

Sewing line

Diagram 4

STEP 6. Join the roof section to the cabin and press, as shown in **Diagram 5** (watch the position of your "grass" strip, if any). The completed block should measure 4 × 6¼ inches. Repeat to make a total of five blocks.

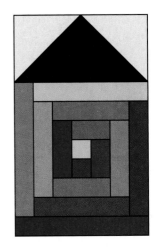

Diagram 5

Make It FAST

For quick and easy marking, place a small cutting mat, pencil, and ruler next to your sewing machine on the left side. Use the pencil and ruler to mark the sewing lines on the pieces. The fine point of a mechanical pencil and a 1 × 12-inch see-through ruler are especially handy for this marking. The textured surface of the cutting mat keeps the fabric from slipping as you mark. ∎

Cutting 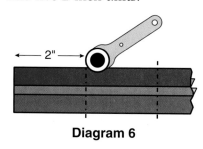 for Tree Block (make 5)

From the tan, cut:

♦ Two 1¼-inch crosswise strips; from these strips, cut ten 1¼ × 2-inch pieces and ten 1¼ × 2¼-inch pieces

♦ One 1¾ × 16-inch strip; from this strip, cut four 1¾ × 4-inch pieces

♦ Two 1½-inch crosswise strips; from these strips, cut the following:

  ♦ Ten 1½-inch squares
  ♦ Ten 1½ × 1¾-inch pieces
  ♦ Ten 1½ × 2-inch pieces

From the brown scrap, cut:

♦ Five 1 × 1¼-inch pieces (Trunk)

If you haven't done so already, from each of the 4 green tree fabrics, cut:

♦ Two ¾-inch crosswise strips, for a total of 8 strips

Piecing the Tree Block

STEP 1. Sew three ¾-inch green strips together lengthwise, as shown in **Diagram 6**. Press both seams in the same direction, taking care not to distort the fabric. The center strip should measure ¼ inch and the outside strips ½ inch. Crosscut into five 2-inch units.

Diagram 6

STEP 2. Add a fourth ¾-inch strip of green to the remainder of the strip set from Step 1, as shown in **Diagram 7A**. Then sew the remaining four green strips together in the same order, as shown in 7B. Press both strip sets. Crosscut into five 3-inch units, five 3½-inch units, and five 4-inch units.

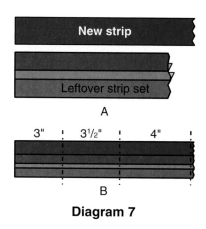

Diagram 7

STEP 3. To make the top row of the tree block, lay a 2¼ × 1¼-inch background piece on one of the 2-inch tree units from Step 1 with right sides together, as shown in **Diagram 8A**. Mark and sew across the background piece diagonally in the direction shown. Trim the seam allowance to ¼ inch. Press. Repeat with another background piece on the other side to create a finished unit, as shown in **8B**.

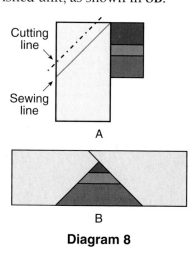

Diagram 8

STEP 4. To make the second row, lay a 2 × 1½-inch background piece on one of the 3-inch tree units from Step 2 with right sides together, as described in Step 3. Mark, sew, trim, and press following those directions. Repeat with another background piece on the other side.

STEP 5. Make the third row in a similar manner, using 1¾ × 1½-inch background pieces and a 3½-inch tree piece from Step 2.

STEP 6. Make the bottom row in a similar manner, using 1½-inch background squares and a 4-inch tree piece from Step 2.

STEP 7. Assemble the rows to make a tree that looks like the one in **Diagram 9**. Press.

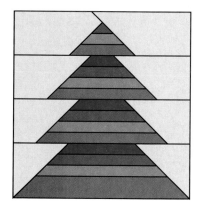

Diagram 9

STEP 8. To make the trunk section, sew a 2 × 1¼-inch background piece to each side of a trunk piece, as shown in **Diagram 10**. Press.

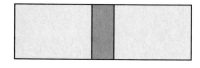

Diagram 10

STEP 9. Join the trunk section to the tree section. Press. Repeat to make a total of five blocks.

STEP 10. Sew 4 × 1¾-inch background pieces to the tops of four of the tree blocks. Press. These four blocks should measure 4 × 6¼ inches.

Cutting for Star Block (make 3)

From the tan, cut one 1¼-inch crosswise strip; from this strip, cut the following:

◆ Twelve 1¼-inch squares
◆ Three 1¼ × 1¾-inch pieces
◆ Three 1¼ × 2-inch pieces
◆ Three 1¼ × 2¼-inch pieces

From the gold, cut:

◆ One 1¼ × 23-inch strip; from this strip, cut nine squares and three 1¼ × 3½-inch pieces

Piecing the Star Block

STEP 1. To make the top row, lay a 1¼-inch gold square on the right end of a 2¼ × 1¼-inch background piece with right sides together, as shown in **Diagram 11A**. Mark and sew across the square diagonally in the direction shown. Trim the seam allowance to ¼ inch. Press open. Sew a 1¾ × 1¼-inch background piece to the right side of this unit, as shown in **11B**. Press.

STEP 2. To make the second row, lay a 1¼-inch background square on each end of a 3½ × 1¼-inch gold piece with right sides together, as shown in **Diagram 12A**. Mark and sew

across the squares in the directions shown. Trim and press to make a unit that looks like the one in **12B**.

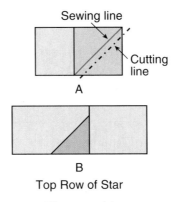

Top Row of Star

Diagram 11

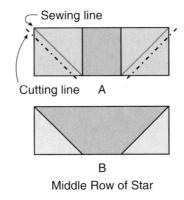

Middle Row of Star

Diagram 12

STEP 3. To make the bottom row, lay a 1¼-inch gold square on a 2 × 1¼-inch background piece with right sides together, as shown in **Diagram 13A**. Mark and sew across the square diagonally in the direction shown. Trim and press open. Lay another 1¼-inch gold square on the other end of this unit, as shown in **13B**. Mark, sew, trim, and press. Attach a 1¼-inch background square to each end of the unit, as shown in **13C**. Press.

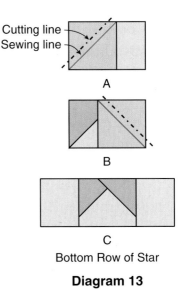

Bottom Row of Star

Diagram 13

STEP 4. Assemble the rows to complete the block. Press. Repeat to make a total of three 3½ × 2¾-inch blocks.

ASSEMBLING the CENTER

Cutting for Center

From the tan, cut one 2¾ × 15-inch strip; from this strip, cut:

◆ Two 2¾ × 2½-inch pieces
◆ One 2¾ × 3½-inch piece
◆ One 1½ × 5-inch piece (Setting Pieces for Star section)

From the rust, cut four 1½-inch crosswise strips; from these strips, cut the following:

◆ Twelve 1½ × 4-inch pieces
◆ Two 1½ × 5-inch pieces
◆ Twelve 1½ × 6¼-inch pieces
◆ One 1½ × 13-inch piece (Sashing)

From the gold, cut:

◆ One 1½-inch crosswise strip; from this strip, cut 18 squares (Corner Squares)

Piecing the Center

STEP 1. To make the top horizontal sashing unit, sew a gold corner square to each end of the 13 × 1½-inch rust piece, as shown in **Diagram 14**.

Make 1

Diagram 14

STEP 2. To make the four other horizontal sashing units, join three 4 × 1½-inch rust pieces and four gold corner squares, as shown in **Diagram 15**. Repeat to make a total of four units.

Make 4

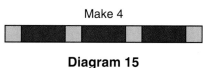

Diagram 15

STEP 3. Referring to **Diagram 16**, join tan setting pieces, 1½ × 5-inch sashing strips, the short tree block, and the star blocks to complete the star section.

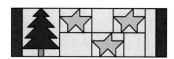

Diagram 16

STEP 4. Referring to **Diagram 17**, join house and tree blocks

to 1½ × 6¼-inch sashing pieces. Make two rows with a cabin at each end and one row with a cabin in the middle.

Make 2

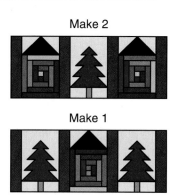

Make 1

Diagram 17

STEP 5. Referring to **Diagram 18**, join the rows with the sashing units from Step 2 to complete the center.

Diagram 18

BORDERS

Cutting for Borders

From the green for the inner border, cut:

◆ Three 1¼-inch crosswise strips; cut one strip in half

From the check for the outer border, cut:

◆ Four 2½-inch crosswise pieces

Attaching the Borders

STEP 1. Refer to the **Quilt Diagram** while following these directions. Measure through the center of your quilt vertically. Cut two inner border strips to this exact measurement. (Use the two longer strips.)

STEP 2. Attach these strips to the sides of your quilt top. Press toward the border.

STEP 3. Measure across the center of the quilt horizontally. Include the side borders in your measurement. Cut the remaining two inner border strips to this exact measurement.

STEP 4. Attach these strips to the top and bottom of your quilt top. Press toward the border.

STEP 5. Repeat Steps 1 through 4 for the outer borders.

QUILTING

STEP 1. Press the finished quilt top. Mark the quilting design, using one of your own or following these suggestions.

■ Quilt in the ditch around the cabins, trees, and stars.

■ Stitch large, medium, and small stars randomly throughout the inner and outer borders. (Some of these stars can even extend into the outside sashing strips.)

■ For fun, add lines radiating from the pieced stars.

■ As a finishing touch, quilt small stars in the center of each cabin.

STEP 2. Layer the quilt top, batting, and backing. Baste the layers together.

STEP 3. Quilt by hand or machine.

STEP 4. Trim the batting and backing even with the quilt top. Remove the basting.

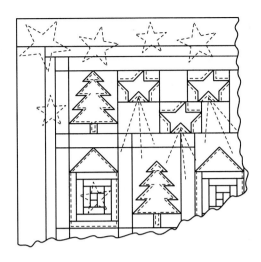

Quilting Diagram

BINDING

STEP 1. Cut three 2½-inch crosswise strips to prepare 120 total inches of double-fold straight-grain binding.

STEP 2. Join the strips end to end with diagonal seams. Fold them in half lengthwise with wrong sides together and press. Attach the binding to the quilt, following the instructions on page 242.

Quilt Diagram

Oh My Dialing!

Judith Hughes Marte, *Around the Block Quilt Designs*

*O*ld-fashioned crank and rotary phones may be gone, but they're not forgotten, thanks to this playful quilt. Supereasy piecing and quick fusible appliqué make this a great weekend project. If you love to embellish your quilts, you'll have lots of fun adding the buttons, ribbons, and fabric strips.

SIZE

Finished quilt is 32 inches square
Finished blocks are 9 × 12 and
   9 × 7 inches

FABRICS and SUPPLIES

Yardage based on 44-inch-wide fabric

- ⅝ yard gold-and-brown plaid for outer border
- ⅛ yard black solid for inner border
- Scraps of two brown prints for dial phone bases (each at least 4 × 6 inches)
- Scraps of four additional gold-and-brown plaids for crank phones and dial phone receivers

- Scraps of a variety of lights for background and checkerboard sashing (⅜ yard total)
- Scraps of a variety of red plaids for checkerboard sashing, hearts, and binding (⅝ yard total)
- Scraps of a variety of fabrics for phone details
- Scraps of four gold prints for corner squares (each at least 6 inches square)
- 1 yard for backing
- Batting, larger than 32 inches square
- 1¼ yards of ⅛-inch-wide flat black ribbon
- Twelve ⅝-inch wooden or plastic buttons for dials
- Eighteen ¾- to ⅞-inch buttons for border
- Fusible web
- Rotary cutter, ruler, and mat

GETTING READY

COLOR and FABRIC TIPS:

The prevailing gold and brown plaids in this quilt help capture the vintage mood of the telephones. But don't be afraid to pick a color scheme totally unrelated to reality. This quilt would be just as darling done up in black, red, and white or teal, gold, and purple. Notice the gold plaid in the border in the quilt shown. A wide border like this is the perfect place to showcase a large-scale plaid. Also pay attention to how plaids of all different scales are mixed together effectively in the quilt center. This mingling of different sizes makes any quilt more interesting.

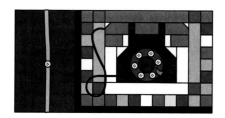

Alternate Color Idea

■ Parts to be rotary-cut and pieced are identified by letters; no templates are provided for these, only cutting dimensions. Appliqué pieces are identifed by numbers; templates are provided for these. You may want to label all of these pieces with their letter or number as you cut to help keep track of them.

■ Wash, damp dry, and press all fabrics before using.

■ All seam allowances are ¼ inch and should be pressed to one side, unless otherwise indicated.

■ In preparation for rotary cutting, trim the selvages off the border fabrics and square off one crosswise edge of each fabric, as described on page 236.

■ This project was designed especially for fusible appliqué. See "Appliqué Basics" on page 238 for details on this method. Trace templates **1–13,** the **Heart,** and the **Receiver** on pages 186–187 onto fusible web.

■ Cutting directions for each part of the quilt are provided in the sections indicated by the yellow rotary cutters. This format allows you to cut what you need as you get ready to assemble each part of the quilt. If you prefer to cut all the pieces at once, skip ahead, looking for the yellow rotary cutters, and cut all the pieces before starting to sew.

ASSEMBLING the BLOCKS

Cutting for Dial Phone Blocks (make 2)

From each of the brown fabrics (base), cut:

♦ One 5½ × 3½-inch piece (A)

♦ One 3½ × 1½-inch piece (B)

♦ Two 1 × 1½-inch pieces (C)

From each of two gold-and-brown scraps (receiver), cut:

♦ Three 2½ × 1½-inch pieces (D)

♦ Two 2 × 1½-inch pieces (F)

Select two light-colored fabrics for the backgrounds. From each fabric, cut:

♦ Two 1-inch squares (E; do not cut into triangles)

♦ Two 1 × 1½-inch pieces (G)

♦ Two 1½-inch squares (H; do not cut into triangles)

♦ Two 1½ × 3½-inch pieces (I)

From the remaining light scraps, cut:

♦ Four 1½ × 5½-inch pieces (J)

♦ Four 7½ × 1½-inch pieces (K)

From the red scraps, cut:

♦ Eight 1½-inch squares (L)

Using the pattern pieces traced onto fusible web and the fabric scraps for the phone details, prepare two *each* of appliqué pieces 1, 2, and 3.

Make 2

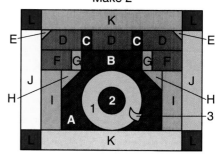

Dial Phone Block Diagram

Making the Dial Phone Blocks

STEP 1. Refer to the **Dial Phone Block Diagram** as you make this block. With right sides together, position E in the upper left corner of D, as shown in **Diagram 1A**. With a pencil and ruler, draw a line from corner to corner. Stitch across the square, following the line. Trim ¼ inch beyond this line. Open E and press flat on the right side. Sew a second E to the upper right corner of another D in the same way, as shown in **1B**. Make sure the stitching line faces in the correct direction, as shown in the diagram.

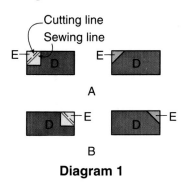

Diagram 1

STEP 2. Sew a C to each side of the remaining D, as shown in **Diagram 2**. Press.

Diagram 2

STEP 3. Join the units from Steps 1 and 2 together, as shown in **Diagram 3**. Press.

Diagram 3

STEP 4. Sew two F, two G, and B together, as shown in **Diagram 4**. Press.

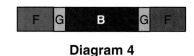

Diagram 4

STEP 5. With right sides together, place an H on each upper corner of A. Using a pencil and ruler, draw lines from corner to corner, as shown in **Diagram 5**. Sew across the squares, following the lines. Trim ¼ inch beyond these lines. Open the H pieces and press flat on the right side.

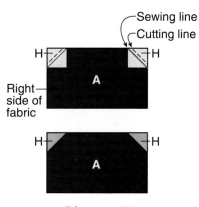

Diagram 5

STEP 6. Sew an I to each side of the A/H unit, as shown in **Diagram 6**. Press.

Diagram 6

STEP 7. Join the three units, as shown in **Diagram 7**. Press.

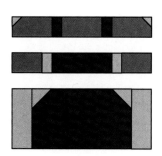

Diagram 7

STEP 8. Sew a J to each side of the center section. Press. Sew an L to each end of each K and press. Add these units to the top and bottom of the center section to complete the block piecing, as shown in **Diagram 8**. Press.

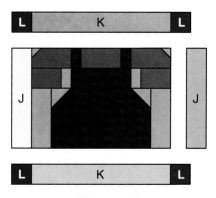

Diagram 8

STEP 9. Fuse appliqué pieces 1, 2, and 3, using the **Dial Phone Block Diagram** on page 180 and the photograph on page 178 for placement.

STEP 10. Using a straight stitch, sew around the inside edges of the appliqué pieces with contrasting thread. This helps secure the pieces and adds decorative details. Fabric "cords" and buttons will be added after the completed top is quilted and bound.

Make It FAST

For quick and easy marking, place a small cutting mat, pencil, and ruler next to your sewing machine on the left side. Use the pencil and ruler to mark the sewing lines on the pieces. The fine point of a mechanical pencil and a 1 × 12-inch see-through ruler are especially handy for this marking. The textured surface of the cutting mat keeps the fabric square from slipping as you mark. ∎

STEP 11. Repeat Steps 1 through 10 to make a total of two blocks.

Cutting for Crank Phone Blocks (make 2)

From each of two gold-and-brown scraps, cut:

♦ One 5½ × 10½-inch piece (M)

♦ One 5½ × 1¼-inch piece (N)

♦ Two 1½-inch squares (O; do not cut into triangles)

Select two lights for the backgrounds; from each fabric, cut:

♦ Two 2½ × 12½-inch pieces (R)

From the remaining scraps, cut:

♦ Two 5½ × 1½-inch pieces (P)

♦ Two 5½ × ¾-inch pieces (Q)

♦ Using the pattern pieces traced onto fusible web and the fabric scraps for the phone details, prepare four of template 4 and two *each* of templates 5 through 13

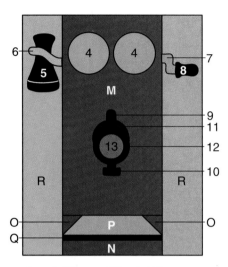

Crank Phone Block Diagram

Making the Crank Phone Blocks

STEP 1. Refer to the **Crank Phone Block Diagram** as you make this block. With right sides together, place an O on each upper corner of P and, with a pencil and ruler, mark lines from corner to corner, as shown in **Diagram 9.** Sew across the squares, following the diagonal lines. Trim ¼ inch beyond these lines. Open the O pieces and press flat on the right side.

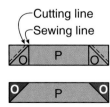

Diagram 9

STEP 2. Sew Q to the bottom of this unit, as shown in **Diagram 10.** Press.

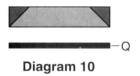

Diagram 10

STEP 3. Join the unit to the bottom of piece M, then add piece N to the bottom, as shown in **Diagram 11.** Press. Sew an R to each side. Press.

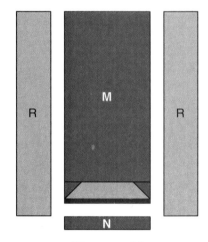

Diagram 11

STEP 4. Fuse appliqué pieces 4 through 13, using the **Crank Phone Block Diagram** and the photograph on page 178 for placement.

STEP 5. Using a straight stitch, stitch around the inside edges of the appliqué pieces.

STEP 6. To make the phone cord, cut the ⅛-inch-wide flat black ribbon into 2-, 3-, and 14-inch pieces. Position the pieces on the block, as shown in **Diagram 12.** By hand or machine, stitch down the center of the ribbons, using black thread. Leave the curving portions of the ribbon free, as shown.

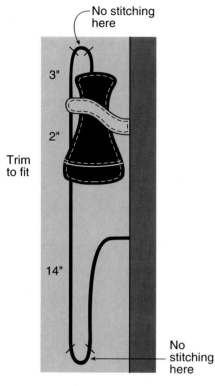

3"

2"

Trim to fit

14"

No stitching here

No stitching here

Diagram 12

STEP 7. Repeat Steps 1 through 6 to make a total of two blocks.

ASSEMBLING the CENTER

Cutting for the Checkerboard Sashing

From the red scraps, cut:

◆ Forty-nine 1½-inch squares

From the light scraps, cut:

◆ Fifty 1½-inch squares

Piecing the Center

STEP 1. Sew a crank phone block to the *top* of one of the dial phone blocks. Sew the other crank phone block to the *bottom* of the other dial phone block.

STEP 2. To make the checkerboard sashing, sew dark and light 1½-inch squares alternately into the following five sets, as shown in **Diagram 13**:

■ 3 strips of 19 squares each, beginning and ending with a light square

■ 2 strips of 21 squares each, beginning and ending with a red square

STEP 3. Sew a phone unit to each side of a 19-square strip, as shown in **Diagram 14**.

Make It FAST

If your scraps are large enough, rotary cut the squares to save time. Stack several fabrics, cut them into 1½-inch strips, then crosscut the strips into squares. ■

Make 3 (19 squares)

Make 2 (21 squares)

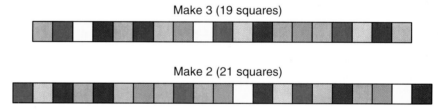

Diagram 13

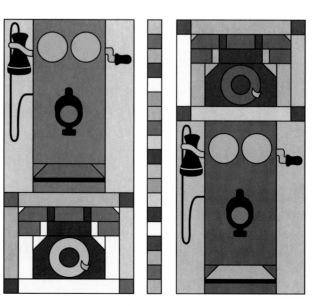

Diagram 14

Make It FUN

- Add ½ × 12-inch torn strips of fabric to the two dial phones, tacking them in place, as shown in the diagram.

- Sew six ⅝-inch buttons to the dials on the dial phones (see photo for placement).

- To make the cord in the border, use ¾-inch-wide ripped strips, joining pieces as necessary to achieve a total length of approximately 120 inches (seams can be hidden under buttons).

- Sew one end of the cord to the appliquéd phone receiver. Tack the rest to the center of the outer border by sewing on large buttons through all layers, approximately every 5 inches and in the center of each corner heart.

- Bring the end of the cord up and over the binding at the top right corner, as shown in the photo, and tack the end down on the back. ■

STEP 4. Sew the other two 19-square strips to the sides.

STEP 5. Sew the 21-square strips to the top and bottom to complete the center, as shown in Diagram 15.

BORDERS

Cutting for Borders

From the black for the inner borders, cut:

- Two 1 × 21½-inch strips (Sides)
- Two 1 × 22½-inch strips (Top and Bottom)

From the gold-and-brown plaid for the outer border, cut:

- Four 5½ × 22½-inch strips

From the gold scraps, cut:

- Four 5½-inch squares (Corner Squares)

Using the pattern piece traced onto fusible web and the red fabric scraps, prepare:

- 4 Hearts

Using the pattern piece traced onto fusible web and the dark scrap, prepare:

- 1 Receiver

Attaching the Borders

STEP 1. Sew 21½-inch black inner border strips to the sides of your quilt top, then add 22½-inch strips to the top and bottom. Press toward the border.

STEP 2. Sew a plaid outer border strip to each side of the quilt.

Diagram 15

Sew a 5½-inch gold corner square to each end of the remaining two outer border strips, then sew these to the top and bottom of the quilt, as shown in the **Quilt Diagram.** Press toward the border.

STEP 3. Fuse one heart to each corner square, with points facing toward the center. Add the telephone receiver to the upper right corner. Stitch around the inside edges of the appliqué shapes and add additional stitching on the receiver, as shown on the **Appliqué Pattern** on page 186 and as in the photograph on page 178.

QUILTING

STEP 1. Press the finished quilt top. Mark the quilting design, using one of your own or following these suggestions.

- Stitch a scant ¼ inch around the phones and hearts.

- Quilt in the ditch around the blocks.

- Quilt in the ditch between the borders.

STEP 2. Layer the quilt top, batting, and backing. Baste the layers together.

STEP 3. Quilt by hand or machine.

STEP 4. Trim the batting and backing even with the quilt top. Remove the basting.

BINDING

STEP 1. From the red scraps, cut enough 2½-inch crosswise strips to prepare 140 inches of double-fold straight-grain binding.

STEP 2. Join the strips end to end with diagonal seams. Fold in half lengthwise with wrong sides together and press. Attach the binding to the quilt, following the instructions on page 242.

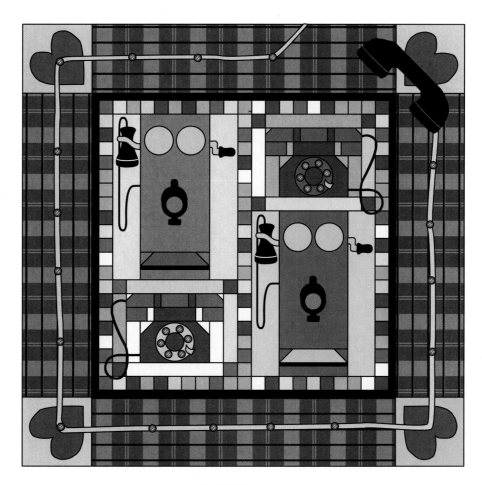

Quilt Diagram

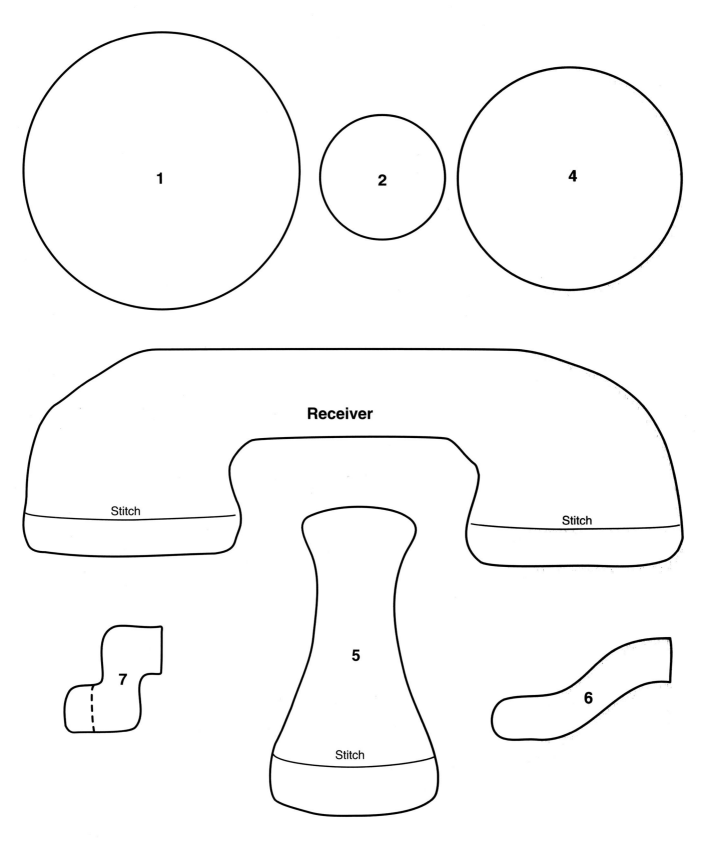

Receiver

Stitch

Stitch

1

2

4

Stitch

5

7

6

Stitch

Appliqué Patterns

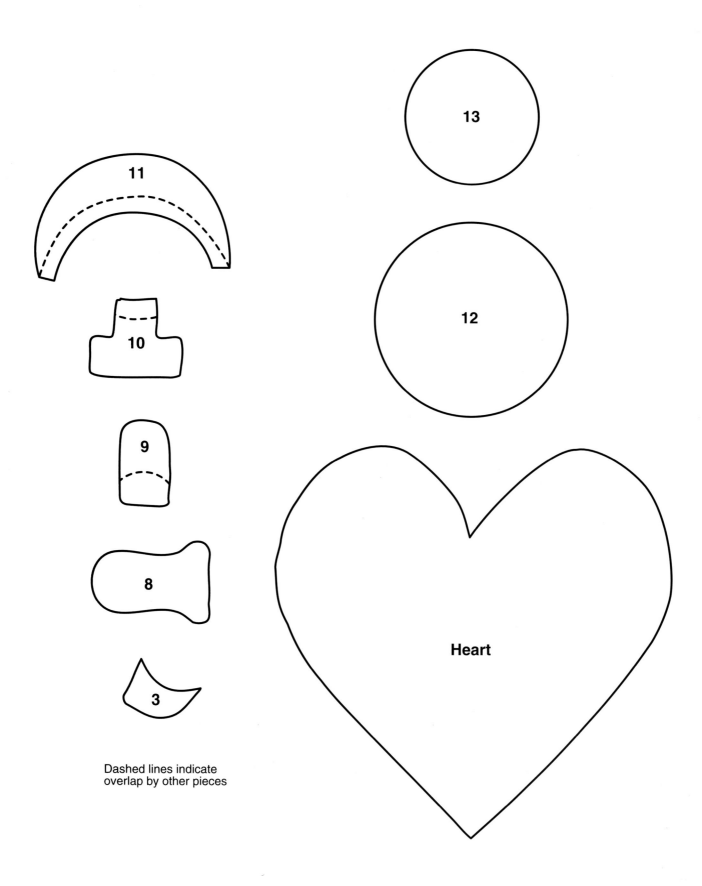

13

11

10

12

9

8

Heart

3

Dashed lines indicate
overlap by other pieces

the
Osage County Quilt Factory

Harvest Medallion

Virginia Robertson, *Osage County Quilt Factory*

The perfect size for a cuddly lap quilt, this design-as-you-go star medallion project offers unlimited room for creativity. The easy half-a-square triangle technique lets you make the basic building blocks for this quilt quickly and easily.

SIZE

Finished quilt is 73½ inches square

FABRICS and SUPPLIES

Yardage based on 44-inch-wide fabric

- Fabric 1: 2⅜ yards black corn print for blocks and border (or 1⅞ yards for a pieced border)
- Fabric 2: ⅝ yard brown star print
- Fabric 3: Scrap of black wave print (at least 10 inches square)
- Fabric 4: 2 yards medium yellow for blocks and border (or ⅞ yard for a pieced border)
- Fabric 5: ⅝ yard orange corn print
- Fabric 6: ⅝ yard orange swirl print
- Fabric 7: ⅜ yard black print
- Fabric 8: Scrap of gold print (at least 10 inches square)
- Fabric 9: ⅜ yard gold swirl print
- Fabric 10: ⅞ yard light yellow paisley
- Fabric 11: ⅓ yard yellow geometric
- Fabric 12: ⅜ yard rust-and-black check
- Fabric 13: ⅞ yard brown-and-black plaid
- Fabric 14: ⅝ yard medium rust paisley
- Fabric 15: ⅜ yard medium rust mini floral print
- Fabric 16: ⅜ yard rust-and-green print
- Fabric 17: ⅜ yard tan geometric
- Fabric 18: Scrap of gold swirl (at least 10 inches square)
- 4½ yards brown for backing and binding
- Rotary cutter, ruler, and mat

189

GETTING READY

COLOR and FABRIC TIPS:

The Corn Quilt has a total of 18 different fabrics that span the range of light, medium, and dark. Only a few of the fabrics are busy prints. The rest are tone-on-tone prints with low contrast. To maintain the star design and patterns formed by the light and dark fabrics in the bands surrounding it, follow these guidelines as you assemble your fabrics.

Darks: Fabrics 1, 3, 7, 8, and 12.
Mediums: Fabrics 2, 5, 6, 9, 13, 14, 15, 16, 17, and 18.
Lights: Fabrics 4, 10, and 11.

In place of the harvest golds and browns shown, imagine how striking this quilt would be in blacks and bright Amish colors. Or picture an assortment of jewel-tone blues, greens, and purples. The basic design of this quilt lends itself well to whatever color scheme you like.

- Wash, damp dry, and press all fabrics before using.
- All seam allowances are ¼ inch and should be pressed to one side, unless otherwise indicated.
- In preparation for rotary cutting, trim the selvages off all fabrics and square up one crosswise edge of each fabric, as described on page 236.
- Cutting directions for the blocks are included in the piecing directions.

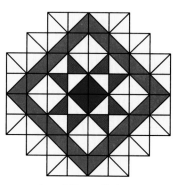

Jewel Tone Palette

SPEEDY HALF-A-SQUARE TRIANGLE UNITS

This quilt is made up of 256 blocks, each 4 inches square, set in 16 straight rows of 16 blocks each. Many of the blocks are half-a-square triangle units, which combine to create the illusion of concentric diagonal bands. Here's an easy way to make these units. (These are the general instructions for this technique; specifics on which fabrics to use for each part of the quilt will be given later in the directions.)

STEP 1. Select two fabrics and cut a piece of each to the dimensions specified in the directions. In this example, we will use 5 × 10-inch pieces.

STEP 2. Draw a 4⅞-inch grid on the wrong side of one fabric, as shown in **Diagram 1A. (All grids used throughout this project will measure 4⅞ inches.)** Draw a diagonal line through each square, as shown in **1B.** Mark ¼ inch on both sides of the diagonal lines with dashed lines, as shown in **1C.**

STEP 3. Lay the marked fabric on top of the second piece, right sides together and raw edges even. Pin in the open areas.

STEP 4. Sew along the dashed lines. *Important:* Do not sew across the solid line into the corner of the adjacent square

unless you like to use a seam ripper! See **Diagram 2.** Remove the pins.

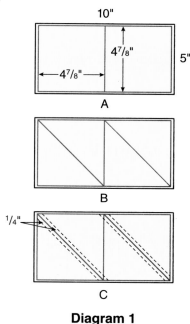

Diagram 1

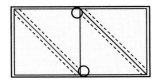

Do not stitch into circled areas

Diagram 2

STEP 5. Cut on the solid lines around the squares and on the diagonals, as shown in **Diagram 3.** Open the units and press the seam allowances toward the darker fabric. In this example, you would get four 4½-inch half-a-square triangle units (finished size: 4 inches).

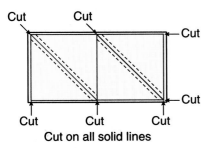

Cut on all solid lines

Diagram 3

Make It EASY

Osage County Quilt Factory Publications sells a 4-inch Half-a-Square Triangle Grid that eliminates the marking step. One package makes 96 units. (See page 248 for ordering information.) ■

CUTTING and PIECING the BLOCKS

As you sew, lay each finished block in position on a large, flat surface or design wall if one is available. This will make both design and assembly easier. (Don't give in to temptation and start to sew the blocks together right away; it's much easier to wait until they're all done before assembling them together.) Refer to the numbered diagonal bands in the **Quilt Diagram** and to the assembly diagrams that accompany the steps that follow. These will make it easy to figure out where all the blocks will go. Also, follow Steps 1 through 5 under "Speedy Half-a-Square Triangle Units" on page 191.

STEP 1. To make the 4 half-a-square triangle units in the center of the quilt, cut 5 × 10-inch pieces of Fabrics 1 and 2. Mark a grid of 2 squares, sew, cut, and press.

STEP 2. To make the 8 outer units in the center star, cut 10-inch squares of Fabrics 3 and 4. Mark a grid of 4 squares (2 by 2), sew, cut, and press. Arrange as shown in **Diagram 4.**

Diagram 4

Quilt Diagram

STEP 3. To complete the star and begin the first band, cut 20-inch squares of Fabrics 5 and 6. Mark a grid of 16 squares (4 by 4). Sew, cut, and press, to make a total of 32 units. Use 4 units now, discard 4 units, and set 24 units aside. Arrange as shown in **Diagram 4** on page 191.

STEP 4. To fill in the 4 light center diamonds and continue the first band, cut 10-inch squares of Fabrics 4 and 8. Mark a grid of 4 squares (2 by 2). Sew, cut, and press to make 8 units. Arrange as shown in **Diagram 5.**

Diagram 6

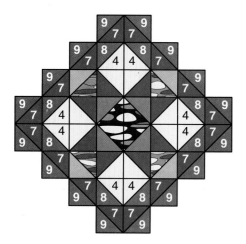

Diagram 5

STEP 5. To finish the first band and start the second band, cut 10 × 20-inch pieces of Fabrics 7 and 9. Mark a grid of 8 squares (2 by 4). Sew, cut, and press to make 16 units. Arrange as shown in **Diagram 5.**

STEP 6. For the second band, cut 10 × 15-inch pieces of Fabrics 10 and 11. Mark a grid of 6 squares (2 by 3). Sew, cut, and press to make 12 units. Cut 5 × 10-inch pieces of Fabrics 1 and 10 and mark a grid of 2 squares.

Diagram 7

Sew, cut, and press to make 4 units. Cut the same size pieces from Fabrics 10 and 12 and repeat to make 4 units. Arrange as shown in **Diagram 6.**

STEP 7. To complete the second band and start the third band, cut 10 × 25-inch pieces of Fabrics 4 and 12. Mark a grid of 10 squares (2 by 5). Sew, cut, and press to make 20 units. Cut 5 × 10-inch pieces of Fabrics 1 and 4. Make a grid of 2 squares, sew, cut, and press to make 4 units. Arrange as shown in **Diagram 6.**

STEP 8. For the third band, cut twenty 4½-inch squares of Fabric 13. Cut 10-inch squares of Fabrics 10 and 13. Sew, cut, and press to make 8 units. Mark a grid of 4 squares (2 by 2). Arrange as shown in **Diagram 7.**

STEP 9. To complete the third band and start the fourth band, cut 20-inch squares of Fabrics 1 and 10. Mark a grid of 16 squares (4 by 4). Sew, cut, and press to make 32 units. Arrange as shown in **Diagram 7.**

STEP 10. For the fourth band, cut 20-inch squares of Fabrics 2 and 14. Mark a grid of 16 squares (4 by 4). Sew, cut, and press to make 32 units; use 28 units and discard 4 units. Arrange as shown in **Diagram 7.**

STEP 11. To complete the fourth band and start the fifth band, use the 24 units of Fabrics 5 and 6 set aside in Step 3. Arrange as shown in **Diagram 7.**

STEP 12. For the fifth band, cut 10 × 25-inch pieces of Fabrics 15 and 16. Mark a grid of 10 squares (2 by 5). Sew, cut, and

press to make 20 units. Arrange as shown in **Diagram 7.**

STEP 13. To complete the fifth band and start the sixth band, cut 10 × 20-inch pieces of Fabrics 1 and 17. Mark a grid of 8 squares (2 by 4). Sew, cut, and press to make 16 units. Arrange as shown in **Diagram 8.**

STEP 14. For the sixth band, cut twelve 4½-inch squares of Fabric 13. Arrange as shown in **Diagram 8.**

STEP 15. To complete the sixth band, cut 10-inch squares of Fabrics 7 and 18. Mark a grid of 4 squares (2 by 2). Sew, cut, and press to make 8 units. Arrange as shown in **Diagram 8.**

STEP 16. For the corners, cut four 4½-inch squares of Fabric 5. Arrange as shown in **Diagram 8.** Now the piecing is done!

Make It FUN

To keep track as you lay out the squares and half-a-square triangle units, take photographs with an instant camera. Using the photos as a reference of your layouts, you can shift the blocks without worry. ■

Diagram 8

ASSEMBLING the CENTER

STEP 1. Arrange the blocks on a large surface or design wall (if you have not already done so) and make sure the design works. Note the orientations of the half-a-square triangle units. In some the seam is parallel to the bands, in others perpendicular. Adjust and correct the bands as desired. Since the technique for making half-a-square triangle units is so simple and quick, don't hesitate to make some replacement blocks to create better contrast or otherwise improve the design.

STEP 2. Sew the blocks together in rows. Experiment to find the easiest method. Instead of sewing blocks together into long—and sometimes unwieldy—single rows, some quiltmakers like to sew units together into pairs, pairs into fours, then join four sets of four. See **Diagram 9**. Press, alternating the direction of the seam allowances from row to row.

STEP 3. Pin the first two rows or sets of 16 blocks together, nesting the opposing seams. Sew and press. Add rows or block groups until the quilt is assembled.

BORDERS

Cutting for Borders

Measure the quilt center. If it does not measure 64½ inches square, adjust the border measurements accordingly.

From the medium yellow (Fabric 4), cut:

♦ Four 1 × 70-inch pieces (Inner Border)

From the black corn print (Fabric 1), cut:

♦ Four 4½ × 80-inch pieces (Outer Border)

Attaching the Borders

STEP 1. The borders on this quilt are mitered. To start, fold each border piece in half crosswise. Mark the center point with a pin or sharp crease.

STEP 2. Sew an inner and an outer border together along the long edges, matching center points, as shown in **Diagram 10**. Press. Repeat to make a total of four border units.

STEP 3. Sew border units to the top and bottom of your quilt top, matching center points and beginning and ending the seams ¼ inch from the ends. Press toward the border.

STEP 4. Sew border units to the sides of your quilt in the same manner. Begin and end your stitching ¼ inch from the ends. Press.

STEP 5. Fold the quilt diagonally, wrong sides together, placing adjoining borders exactly on top of each other. Use a 45 degree triangle or fold a piece of paper in half diagonally to create a perfect 45 degree angle, and place the triangle or the paper angle on the border, aligning it with the end of your stitching line. With a pencil or fabric marker, mark the miter line from the end of your stitching to the outer edge of the border. See **Diagram 11**.

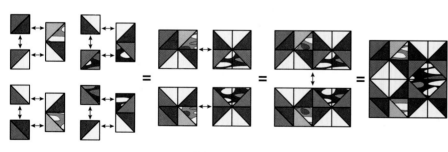

Diagram 9

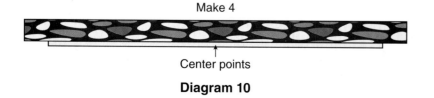

Make 4

Center points

Diagram 10

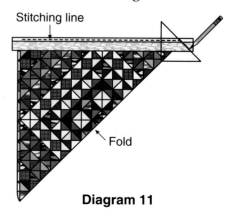

Stitching line

Fold

Diagram 11

STEP 6. Stitch on the marked line, beginning this seam exactly at the point where the border seam ended. Check the miter from the right side of your quilt and trim the excess fabric to ¼ inch. Press the seam open. **See Diagram 12.**

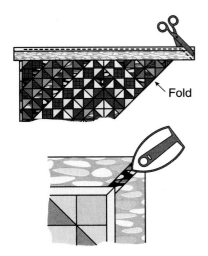

Diagram 12

QUILTING

STEP 1. Cut the backing in half crosswise and sew the halves together along the long edges with a ½-inch seam, as shown in **Diagram 13.** Press the seam *open.* The resulting backing should be about 81 inches square.

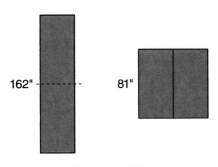

Diagram 13

STEP 2. Press the finished quilt top. Mark the quilting design, using one of your own or following these suggestions.

- Quilt in the ditch along all the patchwork seams.
- Quilt in the ditch along the inner border.
- Channel quilt along the *length* of the borders, spacing four lines approximately ¾ inch apart.

STEP 3. Layer the backing, batting, and quilt top, centering the top on the backing. (The extra backing fabric will be used to bind the quilt.) Baste all the layers together.

STEP 4. Quilt by hand or machine.

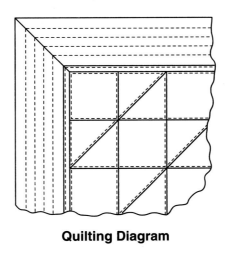

Quilting Diagram

BINDING

STEP 1. Trim the batting even with the quilt top. Trim the backing, leaving 1 inch on all sides. See **Diagram 14A.**

STEP 2. To neatly miter the corners of the binding, fold the

corners in first, as shown in **Diagram 14B.** Fold the 1 inch of extra backing along the sides in half and then bring it to the front, as shown in **14C** and **14D.** Pin. Slip stitch the binding to the front by hand with hidden stitches or topstitch by machine very carefully with matching thread, as shown in **14E.**

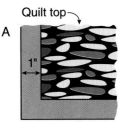

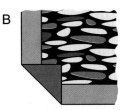

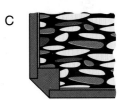

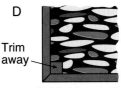

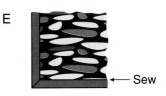

Diagram 14

MUMM'S™
THE WORD

Heart of the Home

Debbie Mumm, *Mumm's the Word*

*H*ere's a housing project that won't break the bank! The perfect antidote to a bulging scrap bag, this wall quilt is easy to put together using bits and pieces left over from other projects. Quick rotary cutting and clever assembly shortcuts guarantee speedy results.

SIZE

Finished wall quilt is 27 × 28 inches
Finished block is 4 × 6 inches

FABRICS and SUPPLIES

Yardage based on 44-inch-wide fabric

- ⅓ yard tan check for lattice
- ⅓ yard brown for binding
- ⅙ yard *each* of six different fabrics for houses and pieced border
- ⅛ yard *each* of six different fabrics for roofs and pieced border (or one 8 × 12-inch scrap of each)*
- ⅛ yard burgundy for corner squares (or one 1½-inch strip)*
- ⅛ yard brown for accent border*

- Scraps of six different lights for backgrounds (each at least 3½ × 11 inches)
- Scraps of six different fabrics for hearts and doors
- ⅞ yard for backing
- Lightweight batting, larger than 27 × 28 inches
- Black embroidery floss
- Ten assorted buttons
- Fusible web (lightweight, sewable type)
- Rotary cutter, ruler, and mat

*Some fabric shops will not cut ⅛-yard pieces. Purchase ¼ yard and save the extra for other projects, or check your scrap bag to see if you have any suitable leftovers on hand. Check the size of the scrap against the size of the pieces that need to be cut to confirm that you have enough fabric.

GETTING READY

COLOR and FABRIC TIPS:

Don't be afraid to use a wide mix of different scraps for all the houses and roofs (just keep in mind that directional fabrics are not recommended). And throw in a healthy assortment of varied fabrics for the doors and hearts. The lattice strips and corner squares provide a unifying setting that will calm down even the most eclectic collection of scraps. Another tactic to keep a scrappy quilt from looking too chaotic is to pick several color families to guide your choices. In this quilt brown, red, black, and gold are the featured colors. For a special Christmas quilt, pick red, green, and tan as the main color groups.

- Wash, damp dry, and press all fabrics before using.
- All seam allowances are ¼ inch and should be pressed to one side, unless otherwise indicated.
- In preparation for rotary cutting, trim the selvages off the lattice, border, and binding fabrics and square up one crosswise edge of each fabric, as described on page 236.
- This project was designed especially for fusible appliqué. Trace the patterns for the **Heart** and **Door** on page 203 onto fusible web, following the directions on page 238.
- Cutting directions for each part of the quilt are provided in the sections indicated by the yellow rotary cutters. This format allows you to cut what you need as you get ready to assemble each part of the quilt. If you prefer to cut all the pieces at once, skip ahead, looking for the yellow rotary cutters, and cut all the pieces before starting to sew.

Holiday Color Scheme

ASSEMBLING the BLOCKS

Cutting 🔧 for Blocks (make 12)

From each of the six house fabrics, cut:
- Two 4½-inch squares

From each of the six roof fabrics, cut:
- Two 2½ × 4½-inch pieces

From each of the six background fabrics, cut:
- Four 2½-inch squares

Using the pattern pieces traced onto fusible web and the fabric scraps, prepare the following (directions for fusible appliqué are on page 238):
- 6 Hearts
- 6 Doors

Piecing the Blocks

You will be making a total of 12 blocks, 2 each of 6 different fabric combinations. Before you start sewing, choose the fabrics for each of the 6 combinations (a house, roof, background, and an appliqué fabric). Keep track of the combinations as you sew.

STEP 1. With a pencil, draw a diagonal line from corner to corner on the wrong side of each of the 2½-inch background squares, as shown in **Diagram 1**. This will be your sewing line.

Make 24

Diagram 1

Make It FAST

Instead of piecing an entire block at one time and then another, repeat each step for all 12 blocks at the same time. This assembly line method speeds up the piecing process. ∎

STEP 2. To make the roof section, place twelve 2½-inch background squares right sides together on twelve 4½ × 2½-inch roof pieces, as shown in **Diagram 2**. Align raw edges, pin, and sew on the drawn line.

Make 12

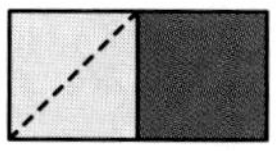

Diagram 2

STEP 3. Trim the excess fabric, leaving a ¼-inch seam allowance, as shown in **Diagram 3**. Press the seam away from the roof fabric.

¼"

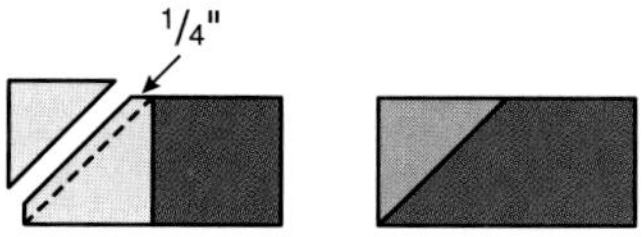

Diagram 3

STEP 4. Sew 12 additional 2½-inch background squares to the units from Step 3, making sure the diagonal lines are in the position shown in **Diagram 4**. Also be sure to use matching background squares for each roof. Trim and press.

Make 12

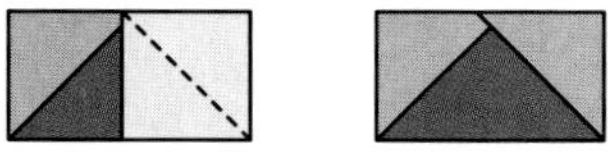

Diagram 4

STEP 5. Sew a 4½-inch house square to the bottom of each roof section to complete the blocks, as shown in **Diagram 5**. Press the seam toward the house fabric. The blocks will now measure 4½ × 6½ inches.

Make 12

Diagram 5

ASSEMBLING the CENTER

Cutting for the Center

From the tan check, cut:

◆ One 4½ × 32-inch piece (Horizontal Lattice)

◆ Three 1½-inch crosswise strips; from these strips, cut fifteen 6½-inch pieces (Vertical Lattice)

From the burgundy, cut:

◆ One 1½-inch crosswise strip; from this strip, cut one 32-inch piece and one 8-inch piece (Corner Squares)

Piecing the Center

STEP 1. Lay out the blocks in a pleasing arrangement of three rows of four blocks each. Keep track of your layout while attaching the lattice.

STEP 2. Sew a 1½ × 6½-inch tan check lattice strip to the right side of each house block. On three of those blocks, add another strip to the left side (these will be the blocks on the left end of each row). See **Diagram 6**. Press toward the lattice. Sew the blocks together into rows. Press toward the lattice.

Make 9

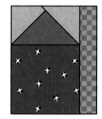

Make 3

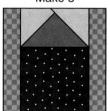

Diagram 6

STEP 3. To make the horizontal lattice, sew the 1½ × 32-inch burgundy strip to the 4½ × 32-inch tan strip, as shown in

Diagram 7. Press toward the tan. Cut the resulting 5½ × 32-inch unit in half crosswise.

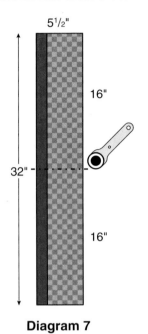

Diagram 7

STEP 4. Resew the halves together to make a 10½ × 16-inch unit, as shown in **Diagram 8.** Press toward the tan. Cut this unit in half again crosswise.

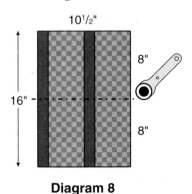

Diagram 8

STEP 5. Resew the halves together to make a 20½ × 8-inch strip set, and sew the 1½ × 8-inch burgundy piece to the right side, as shown in **Diagram 9.** Press toward the tan.

STEP 6. With your rotary cutter and ruler, crosscut this strip set into four 1½ × 21½-inch strips, as shown in **Diagram 10.**

STEP 7. Pin in position and sew one lattice strip to the bottom of each row of blocks, matching intersecting seams. Add the fourth strip to the top of the top row, as shown in **Diagram 11.** Press toward the lattice. Sew the three rows together. Press.

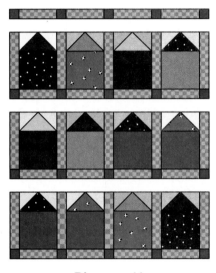

Diagram 11

Appliquéing the Blocks

STEP 1. Using the photograph on page 196 as a placement guide, fuse the hearts and doors onto the houses. You may want to alternate the positions of hearts and doors within each row, as in the quilt shown.

STEP 2. Using two strands of black embroidery floss, hand stitch around the hearts and doors. Use a primitive stitch for the hearts, making the stitches approximately ¼ inch apart and ⅛ to ¼ inch long, as shown in **Diagram 12.** For the doors, use a ⅛-inch-long running stitch outside the edge of the appliqué.

Diagram 12

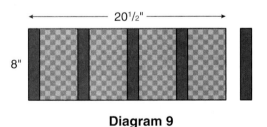

Diagram 9

Cut 4 strips

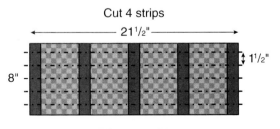

Diagram 10

Make It FUN

Sew a button in the center of each heart and one in each corner of the quilt. ■

BORDERS

Cutting for Borders

From the brown, cut:

♦ Four 1-inch crosswise strips (Accent Border)

From each of the 12 house and roof fabrics, cut:

♦ Two 12-inch strips; strips should vary in width from 1½ to 2½ inches. Sew together along the 12-inch sides to make a 12 × 30-inch strip set, as shown in **Diagram 13** on page 202. Crosscut into four 2½ × 30-inch strips (Pieced Border).

Quilt Diagram

Cut 4 strips

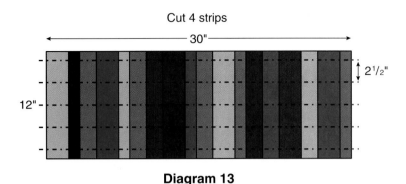

30"

12"

2½"

Diagram 13

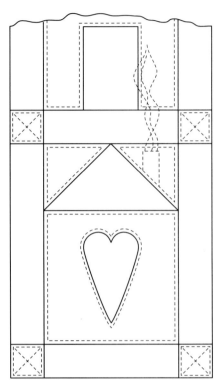

Quilting Diagram

Attaching the Borders

STEP 1. Measure across the center of your quilt horizontally. Cut two brown border strips to this exact measurement.

STEP 2. Attach these strips to the top and bottom of your quilt top. Press toward the border.

STEP 3. Measure through the center of the quilt vertically. Include the top and bottom borders in your measurement. Cut the remaining two brown accent border strips to this exact measurement.

STEP 4. Attach these strips to the sides of your quilt top. Press toward the border.

STEP 5. Repeat Steps 1 through 4 for the pieced borders. Press toward the brown accent border.

QUILTING

STEP 1. Press the finished quilt top. Mark the quilting design, using one of your own or following these suggestions.

- Stitch in the ditch around the houses, roofs, lattice, and accent border.
- Outline quilt ¹⁄₁₆ inch outside the doors.
- Outline quilt ¼ inch outside the hearts.
- Quilt ½-inch-wide chimneys at random on five houses.
- Quilt smoke swirls coming out of one chimney in the top row.
- Quilt in the ditch along the pieced border.
- Quilt an X in each burgundy square in the lattice.

STEP 2. Layer the quilt top, batting, and backing. Baste the layers together.

STEP 3. Quilt by hand or machine.

STEP 4. Trim the batting and backing even with the quilt top. Remove the basting.

BINDING

STEP 1. Cut four 2¾-inch crosswise strips. Press each strip in half lengthwise with wrong sides together.

STEP 2. With raw edges even, lay the binding strips on the top and bottom edges of the quilt top. Sew ¼ inch from the edge, through all layers. Press binding away from the quilt top (with seam pressed toward binding). Trim the binding strips even with the quilt top.

Make It EASY

Stay stitch ⅛ inch from the raw edge of the quilt top to keep the seams of the scrap border from coming apart before the binding is added. ∎

STEP 3. Sew the remaining two binding strips to the sides of your quilt top, including the top and bottom bindings in the seam. Press binding away from the quilt top (with seam pressed toward binding). Trim the side bindings even with the folded edges of the top and bottom bindings, as shown in **Diagram 14**.

STEP 4. Fold the binding around to the back, top and bottom bindings first. Press and pin in position. Hand stitch in place. Repeat with the side bindings.

Diagram 14

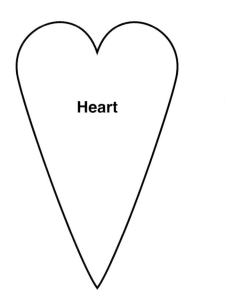

Heart

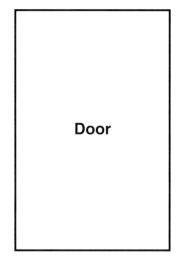

Door

Young at Heart

Bear with Us

❀

Playmates

❀

Floppy Ears

❀

Cat and Mouse

fabric
EXPRESSIONS

Bear with Us

Toni Phillips and Juanita Simonich, *Fabric Expressions*

*T*eddy and Tina Bear are pretty irresistible, especially when they're dressed up in their Sunday finest. Quick-piecing techniques make short work of assembling this quilt. The perfect baby shower gift, this quilt is an equally appropriate present for any adult smitten with teddies.

SIZE

Finished quilt is 40 × 48 inches
Finished block is 14 × 16 inches

FABRICS and SUPPLIES

Yardage based on 44-inch-wide fabric
- ⅝ yard blue plaid for outer border
- ½ yard *each* of two ivory prints for background
- ½ yard dark brown check for feet, ears, and inner border
- ⅜ yard light brown check for bear bodies
- ⅜ yard navy solid for binding
- ¼ yard tan solid for muzzles and checkerboard sashing
- ¼ yard blue-and-gold star print for Bear's Paw blocks and checkerboard sashing
- ¼ yard light red print for dress skirts and sleeves
- ⅛ yard dark red print for dress tops (or one 12 × 4-inch scrap)*
- ⅛ yard blue solid for pants (or one 12 × 4-inch scrap)*
- ⅛ yard blue print for shirts (or one 12 × 4-inch scrap)*
- Scrap of dark brown solid for eyes and noses
- 1½ yards for backing (more if fabric is less than 42 inches wide after washing)
- Dark brown embroidery floss for faces
- 4-inch doily (see page 248 for source)
- Lightweight fusible interfacing
- Fusible web
- Rotary cutter, ruler, and mat

*Some fabric shops will not cut ⅛-yard pieces. Purchase ¼ yard and save the extra for other projects, or check your scrap bag to see if you have any suitable leftovers on hand. Check the size of the scrap against the sizes of the pieces to be cut to confirm you have enough fabric.

G E T T I N G   R E A D Y

COLOR and FABRIC TIPS:
For a softer look, try dressing the teddies in pastel shades of pink and blue. If you'd prefer a more uniform background, use just one shade of ivory for all four teddy bear blocks. The blue plaid borders give this teddy quartet a decidedly country flair; for a totally different look, try a paisley or floral print—or even a polka dot.

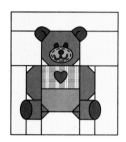

Alternate Color Ideas

- Wash, damp dry, and press all fabrics before using.
- All seam allowances are ¼ inch and should be pressed to one side, unless otherwise indicated.
- In preparation for rotary cutting, trim the selvages off the blue plaid, dark brown check, tan, and blue-and-gold star fabrics and square up one crosswise edge of each fabric, as described on page 236.
- Trace the patterns for the **Muzzle, Eyes, Nose,** and **Heart** on page 215 onto the paper side of the fusible web. The **Muzzle** pattern is also the pattern for the bear's feet. Make 3 copies of the **Muzzle** pattern for each bear, or a total of 12. Because these patterns are all symmetrical, there's no need to reverse them before tracing onto the fusible web.
- Cutting directions for each part of the quilt are provided in the sections indicated by the yellow rotary cutters. This format allows you to cut what you need as you get ready to assemble each part of the quilt. If you prefer to cut all the pieces at once, skip ahead, looking for the yellow rotary cutters, and cut all the pieces before starting to sew.

ASSEMBLING the BLOCKS

Cutting for Teddy Bear Blocks (make 2)

NOTE: The width of each piece is listed first and the length second. This is important to remember when working with directional prints.

From one of the ivory prints, cut:
- Two 14½ × 3-inch pieces (Piece 1)
- Two 4½ × 5-inch pieces (Piece 2)
- Four 2-inch squares (Pieces 3A and 3B)
- Twelve 1½-inch squares (Pieces 3C, 3D, 8A, 8B, 11A, and 11B)
- Two 5½ × 5-inch pieces (Piece 4)
- Two 5½ × 3½-inch pieces (Piece 7)
- Four 2½-inch squares (Pieces 10 and 13)
- Two 2½ × 9½-inch pieces (Piece 14)
- Two 3½ × 9½-inch pieces (Piece 15)

From the light brown check, cut:
- Two 5½ × 5-inch pieces (Piece 3)
- Four 2½ × 5-inch pieces (Pieces 8 and 11)
- Four 2½ × 3-inch pieces (Pieces 9 and 12)
- Eight 1½-inch squares (Pieces 6A, 6B, 7A, and 7B)

From the blue print, cut:
- Two 5½ × 3½-inch pieces (Piece 5)

From the blue solid, cut:
- Two 5½ × 3½-inch pieces (Piece 6)

From the dark brown check, cut:
- 4 Feet

From the tan, cut:
- 2 Muzzles

From the light red, cut:
- 2 Hearts

From the dark brown solid, cut:
- 4 Eyes
- 2 Noses

Teddy Bear Block Diagram

Piecing for Teddy Bear Blocks

STEP 1. Trace four **Ear** patterns onto interfacing, leaving at least ½ inch between ears, as shown in **Diagram 1**.

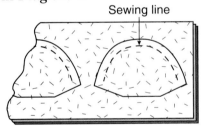

Sewing line

Diagram 1

Make It EASY

As you cut, write the piece number on a label and pin it to each piece or group of pieces. This will make assembling the bear blocks a snap. ■

STEP 2. Stack two layers of brown fabric right sides togeth-er. Fuse interfacing to wrong side of top fabric. Sew on drawn lines between arrows, leaving the bottom open. Trim to ¼ inch around each ear, as shown in **Diagram 2A**, and turn.

Make 2

A

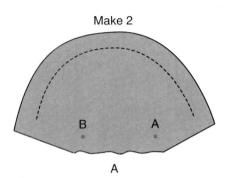

B ◄——— A

B

C

Diagram 2

STEP 3. Fold point A over to meet point B, forming a pleat in the ear, as shown in **Diagram 2B**. Pin to secure the pleat, as shown in **2C**. Repeat to make a second ear.

STEP 4. Mark diagonal seam lines on Pieces 3, 3A, and 3B, as shown in **Diagram 3**. Mark the *right* side of Piece 3 and the *wrong* sides of Pieces 3A and 3B.

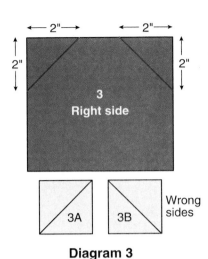

Diagram 3

STEP 5. Lay a folded ear on Piece 3 with the folded edge extending ¼ inch past the drawn line, as shown in **Diagram 4**.

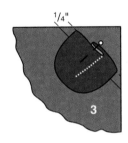

Diagram 4

STEP 6. Lay Piece 3B right side *down* over the ear, raw edges even with the edges of Piece 3, as shown in **Diagram 5**. Pin. Sew along the drawn line. Trim, leaving a ¼-inch seam allowance. Repeat Steps 4 and 5 with the second ear and Piece 3A in the other corner.

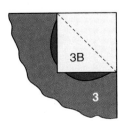

Diagram 5

STEP 7. Mark diagonal seam lines on the wrong sides of Pieces 3C, 3D, 6A, 6B, 7A, 7B, 8A, 8B, 11A, and 11B. Join them to Pieces 3, 6, 7, 8, and 11 in the following manner (also refer to **Diagram 6**): Lay the square on the piece with right sides together and raw edges even. Sew along the drawn line. Press and check that raw edges of newly formed triangle and background block match. Trim the bottom two layers leaving ¼-inch seam. Press.

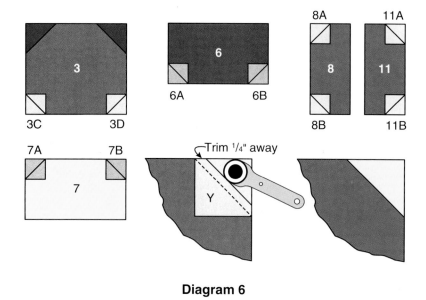

Diagram 6

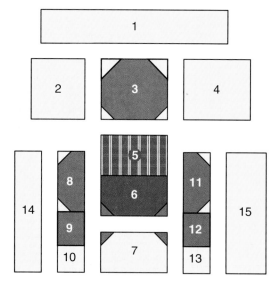

Block shown is for lower right of quilt. To make block for upper left, reverse positions of Pieces 2 and 4, and 14 and 15.

Teddy Bear Block Assembly Diagram

STEP 8. Referring to the **Teddy Bear Block Assembly Diagram**, join the pieces in numerical order. Make the lower right-hand Teddy Bear block as shown in the diagram. Repeat to make the upper left-hand block, switching the positions of Pieces 2 and 4, and Pieces 14 and 15.

STEP 9. Referring to the **Teddy Bear Block Diagram** and the photograph on page 206, and following the directions for fusible appliqué on page 238, appliqué the eyes, muzzle, nose, heart, and feet to the bear.

Cutting for Tina Bear Blocks (make 2)

From the second ivory print, cut:

◆ Two 14½ × 3-inch pieces (Piece 1)

◆ Two 4½ × 5-inch pieces (Piece 2)

◆ Four 2-inch squares (Pieces 3A and 3B)

◆ Eight 1½-inch squares (Pieces 3C, 3D, 16A, and 18A)

◆ Two 5½ × 5-inch pieces (Piece 4)

◆ Two 2½ × 7½-inch pieces (Piece 20)

◆ Two 3½ × 7½-inch pieces (Piece 21)

◆ Two 14½ × 2½-inch pieces (Piece 22)

From the light brown check, cut:

◆ Two 5½ × 5-inch pieces (Piece 3)

◆ Four 2½-inch squares (Pieces 19A and 19B)

From the light red, cut:

◆ Four 2½ × 3½-inch pieces (Pieces 16 and 18)

◆ Two 9½ × 4½-inch pieces (Piece 19)

From the dark red, cut:

♦ Two 5½ × 3½-inch pieces (Piece 17)

From the dark brown check, cut:

♦ 4 Feet

From the tan, cut:

♦ 2 Muzzles

From the dark brown solid, cut:

♦ 2 Noses

Tina Bear Block Diagram

Piecing for Tina Bear Blocks

STEP 1. Repeat Steps 1 through 6 under "Piecing for Teddy Bear Blocks" on page 209.

STEP 2. Mark diagonal seam lines on the wrong sides of Pieces 3C, 3D, 16A, 18A, 19A, and 19B, as shown in **Diagram 7.** Join them to Pieces 3, 16, 18, and 19, as described in Step 7 on page 210.

STEP 3. To make the collar, cut the doily in half on the diagonal. The doily in the photograph on page 206 was tea-

dyed to give it a soft, antiqued look (see "Make It Fun" on page 63).

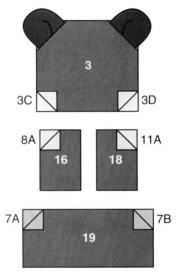

Diagram 7

STEP 4. Referring to the **Tina Bear Block Assembly Diagram,** join the pieces in numerical order. (Note that the numbers

skip from 4 to 16 to avoid any confusion between the pieces for the Tina Bear and the Teddy Bear blocks.) Insert the collar into the seam when joining Pieces 3 and 17. Make the lower left-hand Tina Bear block as shown in the diagram. Repeat to make the upper right-hand block, switching the positions of Pieces 2 and 4, and Pieces 20 and 21.

Make It FUN

Using two strands of embroidery floss, embroider a mouth on each teddy with a backstitch (see page 131). Sew ⅛ inch from the inside edge of the muzzle with a running stitch. ■

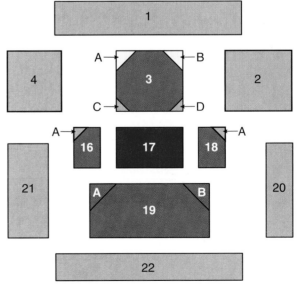

Block shown is for lower left of quilt. To make block for upper right, reverse positions of Pieces 2 and 4, and 20 and 21.

Tina Bear Block Assembly Diagram

STEP 5. Referring to the **Tina Bear Block Diagram** and the photograph on page 206, fuse the eyes, muzzle, nose, and feet to the bear.

ASSEMBLING the CENTER

Cutting for the Center

From the blue-and-gold, cut:

◆ One 2½-inch crosswise strip

From the tan, cut:

◆ One 2½-inch crosswise strip

Piecing the Center

STEP 1. To make the checkerboard sashing, join the tan solid and the blue-and-gold star print strips along the long edges. Press. Crosscut this unit into fourteen 2½-inch segments, as shown in **Diagram 8A.** Sew the fourteen segments together, alternating the blue and tan squares, as shown in 8B. Press.

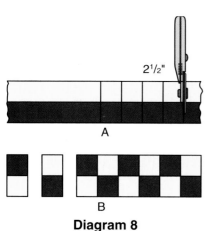

2½"

A

B

Diagram 8

STEP 2. Referring to the **Quilt Diagram,** sew upper left-hand Teddy Bear to upper right-hand Tina Bear. (A tip here is to orient the blocks so the thinner background pieces are always toward the inside of the quilt.) Press. Sew the checkerboard sashing to the bottom of this unit. Press.

STEP 3. Sew lower left-hand Tina Bear to lower right-hand Teddy Bear. Press. Join this unit to the bottom of the checkerboard to complete the center. Press.

Make It FAST

The quickest way to piece the checkerboard is to first chain piece seven pairs of blue and tan segments together. Stack the segments as they are to be sewn, remembering to flop the colors in each pair. Starting with the first pair, begin sewing. When you come to the end of the seam, slide the next pair of segments right up against the first. Continue sewing onto this second pair without stopping or cutting the thread. Continue this way until all the pairs are sewn. Press the seams, clip the threads, then join the seven units together to complete the checkerboard. ■

BORDERS

Cutting for Bear's Paw Block (make 4)

From the blue-and-gold, cut:

◆ Four 3½-inch squares

◆ Eight 2⅜-inch squares

From the tan, cut:

◆ Four 2-inch squares

◆ Eight 2⅜-inch squares

Piecing Bear's Paw Border Block

STEP 1. Lay a tan 2⅜-inch square on a blue-and-gold 2⅜-inch square with right sides together. Draw a diagonal line on the wrong side of the tan square, as shown in **Diagram 9.** This will be your *cutting* line.

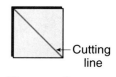

Cutting line

Diagram 9

STEP 2. If your presser foot is an accurate guide, stitch ¼ inch away from this line on either side, as shown in **Diagram 10.** If it's not an accurate ¼ inch, draw accurate sewing lines ¼ inch on either side of your cutting line, then sew. After sewing, cut on the center drawn line to make two pieced squares. Press toward the darker fabric. Repeat to make a total of four pieced squares.

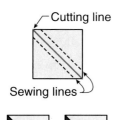

Cutting line

Sewing lines

Diagram 10

STEP 3. Sew the pieced squares into units, orienting the squares as shown in **Diagram 11**. Press.

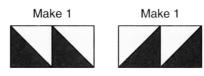

Make 1   Make 1

Diagram 11

STEP 4. Join one unit to a 3½-inch blue-and-gold square, as shown in **Diagram 12**. Press.

STEP 5. Sew a 2-inch tan square to one end of the other unit, as shown in **Diagram 13A**. Press. Join this unit to the unit from Step 4, as shown in **13B**. Press.

STEP 6. Repeat Steps 1 through 5 to make a total of four blocks.

Diagram 12

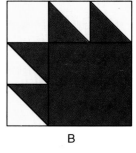

A   B

Diagram 13

Cutting for Inner and Outer Borders

From the dark brown check for the inner border, cut:

◆ Two 2 × 36½-inch strips (Sides)

◆ Two 2 × 28½-inch strips (Top and Bottom)

From the blue plaid for the outer border, cut:

◆ Four 2-inch squares (Corner Squares)

From the blue plaid for the outer border, cut:

◆ Two 5 × 39½-inch strips (Sides)

◆ Two 5 × 31½-inch strips (Top and Bottom)

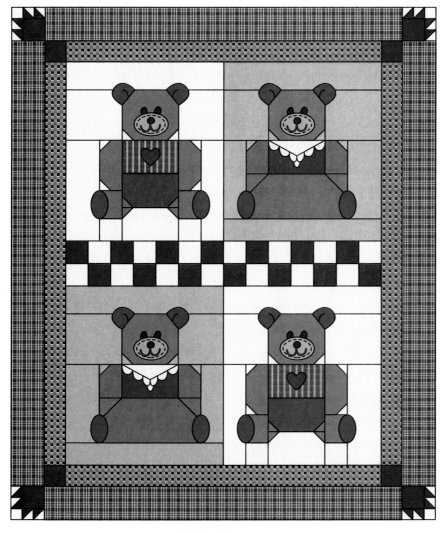

Quilt Diagram

Piecing and Attaching the Borders

STEP 1. Refer to the **Quilt Diagram** on page 213 as you attach the borders. For the inner border, attach 36½-inch strips to the sides of the quilt top. Press toward the border.

STEP 2. Sew a blue-and-gold corner square to each end of the 28½-inch strips. Press toward the border strips.

STEP 3. Attach these strips to the top and bottom of your quilt top. Press toward the border.

STEP 4. For the outer border, repeat Steps 1 through 3, using blue plaid outer border strips and substituting completed Bear's Paw blocks for the corner squares.

QUILTING

STEP 1. If your washed backing fabric is less than 42 inches wide, cut and add a strip of fabric to one long edge so that the backing extends at least 2 inches beyond the quilt top on all sides.

STEP 2. Press the finished quilt top. Mark the quilting design, using one of your own or following these suggestions.

■ Quilt in the ditch around all blocks.

■ Quilt in the ditch between the inner and outer borders.

■ Stitch diagonal lines through the checkerboard sashing squares.

■ Outline quilt the Teddy and Tina Bear shapes.

■ Stitch ¼ inch inside all the shapes except the ears.

■ Fill the background area behind each teddy with a simple design. This quilt features a simple continuous line motif perfect for machine quilting.

■ Channel quilt approximately 1¼ inches apart in the border, running the lines along the length of the borders.

STEP 3. Layer the quilt top, batting, and backing. Baste the layers together.

STEP 4. Quilt by hand or machine.

STEP 5. Trim the batting and backing even with the quilt top. Remove the basting.

BINDING

STEP 1. Cut five 2¼-inch crosswise strips to prepare 190 total inches of double-fold straight-grain binding.

STEP 2. Join the strips end to end with diagonal seams. Fold in half lengthwise with wrong sides together and press. Attach the binding to the quilt, following the instructions on page 242.

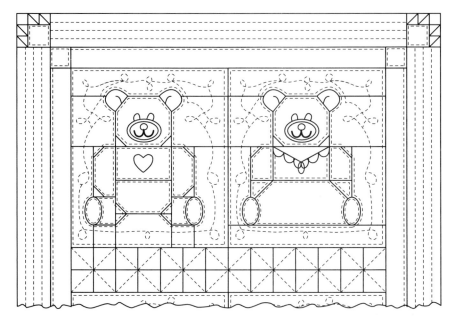

Quilting Diagram

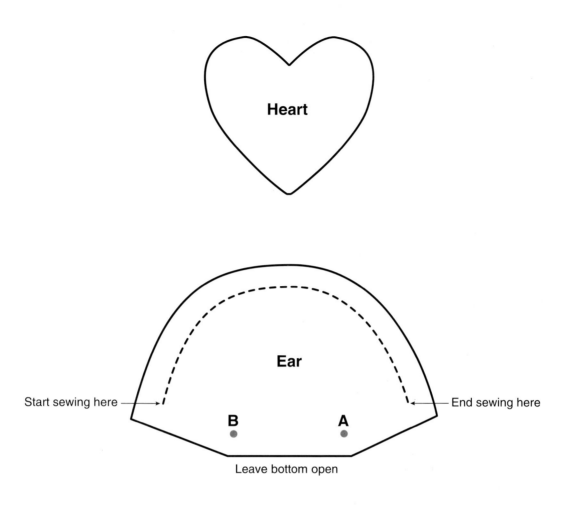

Heart

Ear

Start sewing here →

End sewing here ←

B

A

Leave bottom open

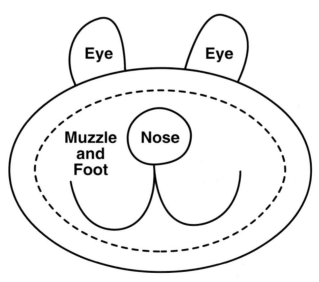

Eye   **Eye**

Muzzle and Foot   **Nose**

Little Quilts

Playmates

Alice Berg, Mary Ellen Von Holt, and Sylvia Johnson, *Little Quilts*

This nostalgic quilt captures the look of the 1930s and '40s, but benefits from the most up-to-date quiltmaking techniques. If you choose to fuse the Scotties in place, you could start and finish this quilt easily in a weekend. A wonderful all-occasion gift, this little quilt looks equally at home in a new baby's room or gracefully tumbling out of a basket in a country kitchen.

SIZE

Finished quilt is 20½ × 25½ inches
Finished block is 5 inches square

FABRICS and SUPPLIES

Yardage based on 44-inch-wide fabric
- ⅜ yard unbleached muslin for background
- ¼ yard tan plaid for border
- ¼ yard black solid for binding
- Scraps of 12 different prints for dogs (each at least 5 inches square)
- ¾ yard for backing
- Thin quilt batting, larger than 20½ × 25½ inches
- Black embroidery floss (optional)
- 12 tiny black buttons for eyes
- Template plastic or fusible web, depending on appliqué method
- Rotary cutter, ruler, and mat
- Tea for dyeing (optional)

GETTING READY

COLOR and FABRIC TIPS:
These projects can be made from all new fabrics, or from a combination of old and new fabrics. Many fabrics available today easily adapt to an antique look. Choose bright florals, checks, polka dots, plaids, and geometrics, along with black and sage green solids.

Polka dots are fun

- Wash, damp dry, and press all fabrics before using.
- All seam allowances are ¼ inch and should be pressed to one side, unless otherwise indicated.
- In preparation for rotary cutting, trim the selvages off the muslin, tan plaid, and black fabrics, and square off one crosswise edge of each print fabric, as described on page 236.
- See "Appliqué Basics" on page 238 and choose a method. Then, trace the **Scottie Dog** pattern on the opposite page onto template plastic or fusible web, depending on the method you've chosen. If you are using fusible web, remember to *reverse* the pattern before tracing onto the web.
- Cutting directions for each part of the quilt are provided in the sections indicated by the yellow rotary cutters. This format allows you to cut what you need as you get ready to assemble each part of the quilt. If you prefer to cut all the pieces at once, skip ahead, looking for the yellow rotary cutters, and cut all the pieces before starting to sew.

ASSEMBLING the BLOCKS

Cutting for Blocks (make 12)

From the muslin, cut:

◆ Two 5½-inch crosswise strips; from these strips, cut 12 squares (Background)

From each of the 12 prints, cut:

◆ One Scottie Dog, following the directions for the appliqué method you have chosen

Appliquéing the Blocks

Appliqué or fuse a dog to each background square, then embroider around the dog with a buttonhole stitch, if desired (see page 61). Repeat to make a total of 12 blocks.

Make It FAST

If your machine has a buttonhole stitch, try it on these Scottie blocks. To help stabilize the blocks (especially if you have appliquéd by hand), put a piece of tear-away or tracing paper underneath the blocks before you stitch. ■

ASSEMBLING the CENTER

Arrange the appliquéd blocks as desired and sew together into four rows of three blocks each, referring to the **Quilt Diagram**.

Press, alternating the direction of the seam allowances from row to row. Join the rows to complete the center of the quilt. Press.

BORDERS

Cutting for Borders

From the tan, cut:

◆ Two 3-inch crosswise strips; from these strips, cut four 21-inch pieces

ATTACHING the BORDERS

STEP 1. Measure through the center of your quilt vertically. Trim the side border strips to this exact measurement.

STEP 2. Attach these strips to the sides of the quilt, as shown in the **Quilt Diagram.** Press the seam allowances toward the border.

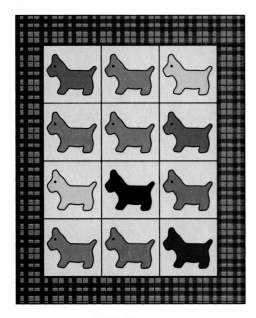

Quilt Diagram

STEP 3. Measure across the center of the quilt horizontally. Include the side borders in your measurement. Cut the remaining two border strips to this exact measurement.

STEP 4. Attach these strips to the top and bottom of your quilt top. Press the seam allowances toward the border.

QUILTING

STEP 1. Press the finished quilt top. Mark the quilting design, using one of your own or following these suggestions.

■ Quilt around each Scottie dog.

■ Quilt ¼ inch inside each square.

■ Stitch a diagonal crosshatch in a 1-inch grid in the borders.

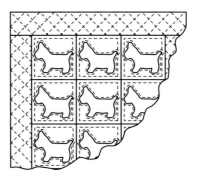

Quilting Diagram

STEP 2. Layer the quilt top, batting, and backing. Baste all the layers together.

STEP 3. Quilt by hand or machine.

STEP 4. Trim the batting and backing even with the quilt top. Remove the basting.

BINDING

STEP 1. Cut three 1¼-inch crosswise strips to prepare 110 inches of single-fold straight-grain binding.

STEP 2. Join the strips end to end with diagonal seams. Fold in half lengthwise with wrong sides together and press. Attach the binding to the quilt, following the instructions on page 242.

Make It FUN

Go through your button collection and pick out 12 to sew on for eyes. In this quilt, the same size and color buttons were used for all the dogs, but you can vary the button color from dog to dog. As a final finishing touch, you could give this quilt a gentle tea bath to enhance the vintage look. For directions on tea dyeing, see page 63. ■

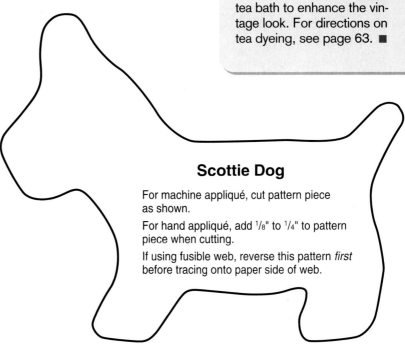

Scottie Dog

For machine appliqué, cut pattern piece as shown.

For hand appliqué, add ⅛" to ¼" to pattern piece when cutting.

If using fusible web, reverse this pattern *first* before tracing onto paper side of web.

Bears Paw Designs

Floppy Ears

Jill Kemp, *Bears Paw Designs*

*H*ere's a cluster of country bunnies with a plaid attitude. Three-dimensional ears set these rabbits head-and-shoulders above the rest—and the best part is, these extra-special features are easy to make. Appealing enough to hang on your wall all year long, you might also want to make one of these quilts in light and bright Easter colors to give as a gift or use as a seasonal decoration in the spring.

SIZE

Finished quilt is 29 inches square
Finished block is 5 inches square

FABRICS and SUPPLIES

Yardage based on 44-inch-wide fabric

- ¾ yard tan solid for bunnies and heart border
- ⅝ yard dark red solid for sashing, inner border, and binding
- ½ yard tan print for block backgrounds
- ¼ yard black check for middle border
- Scraps of 9 different prints for dresses
- Scraps of 36 different fabrics for hearts (can use some dress fabrics)
- 1 yard for backing
- Batting, larger than 29 inches square
- Black, fine-point, permanent felt-tip marker
- Powdered blush
- Template plastic or fusible web, depending on appliqué method
- Rotary cutter, ruler, and mat

GETTING READY

COLOR and FABRIC TIPS:

The tan used for the bunnies and the heart-filled border and the deep golds and reds work together to set a definite country mood. For a lighter, brighter palette, choose a pale tan with less brown in it for the bunnies, dress them in pastels (how about some of the light-hearted 1930s reproduction prints?), and choose a print or plaid for the border. Whatever color scheme you choose, remember to keep good contrast between the hearts and border, and between the rabbit ears and sashing.

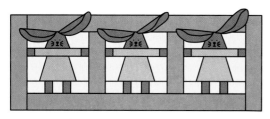

Alternate Color Idea

- Wash, damp dry, and press all fabrics before using.

- All seam allowances are ¼ inch and should be pressed to one side, unless otherwise indicated.

- In preparation for rotary cutting, trim the selvages off the tan print and the border and binding fabrics, and square off one crosswise edge of each fabric, as described on page 236.

- See "Appliqué Basics" on page 238 and choose a method for appliquéing the hearts to the outer border. Then, trace the **Heart** pattern on page 226 onto template plastic or fusible web, depending on the method you've chosen.

- Trace the templates for the **Ear** and pieces **A, B, E,** and **F** on pages 226–227 onto template plastic and cut them out. To speed up the cutting of these lettered pieces, see the rotary/template method described in "Make It Fast" on page 223.

- This quilt includes some templates that must be used both right side up and reversed. This is always specified in the instructions, and is denoted on the pattern pieces with (r) following the pattern letter name.

- Cutting directions for each part of the quilt are provided in the sections indicated by the yellow rotary cutters. This format allows you to cut what you need as you get ready to assemble each part of the quilt. If you prefer to cut all the pieces at once, skip ahead, looking for the yellow rotary cutters, and cut all the pieces before starting to sew.

ASSEMBLING the BLOCKS

Cutting  for Blocks (make 9)

From the tan solid, cut:

- 9 B
- 36 Ears
- Two 1⅛-inch crosswise strips; from these strips, cut eighteen squares (C) and eighteen 1½-inch pieces (H)

From the tan print, cut:

- 9 A and 9 A Reverse
- 9 E and 9 E Reverse
- Two 1½-inch crosswise strips; from these strips, cut eighteen 2-inch pieces (G) and nine 1¼-inch pieces (I)

From each of the nine dress prints, cut:

- 1 F
- One 4¼ × 1⅛-inch piece (D)

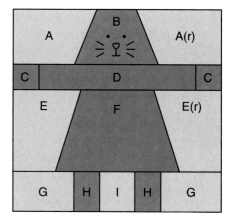

Block Diagram

Make It FAST

To save time and cut more accurately, use your rotary cutter with templates A, B, E, and F. Trace around the plastic templates onto the right sides of the fabric. To get the reverse pieces for A and E, place two layers of fabric wrong sides together before you trace on the top. When you cut the pieces out of these two layers, the ones underneath will automatically be the reverse. Align the edge of a rotary ruler exactly along the lines you've drawn and cut with the rotary cutter. For more accurate pieces, use the thin lead of a mechanical pencil to draw the cutting lines. ■

Piecing the Blocks

STEP 1. Sew A and A Reverse to the sides of B to make the Head Unit, as shown in **Diagram 1**. Press.

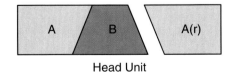

Head Unit

Diagram 1

STEP 2. Sew a C to each end of D to make the Arm Unit, as shown in **Diagram 2**. Press.

Join the Arm Unit to the bottom of the Head Unit. Press.

Arm Unit

Diagram 2

STEP 3. Sew E and E Reverse to the sides of F to make the Dress Unit, as shown in **Diagram 3**. Press. Attach the Dress Unit to the bottom of the Head/Arm Unit. Press.

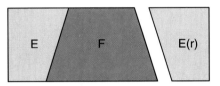

Dress Unit

Diagram 3

STEP 4. Referring to the **Block Diagram**, sew G, H, and I pieces together to make the Leg Unit. Press. Attach this unit to the bottom of the Dress Unit. Press.

STEP 5. Draw a face on the bunny with the pen, using the face on pattern piece B as your guide. Repeat to make a total of nine blocks.

STEP 6. With right sides together, sew two ears together, leaving the bottom (straight) edge open, as shown in **Diagram 4**. Clip the curves, then turn right side out. (Tweezers can come in handy for turning the ears.) Use the powdered blush to tint the center of the ear pink. Repeat to make a total of 18 ears.

Diagram 4

STEP 7. Fold each ear in half lengthwise and pin to the bunny's head with the open side facing toward the outside edge of the head, as shown in **Diagram 5**. Baste in place less than ¼ inch from the raw edge. Sew two ears to each bunny.

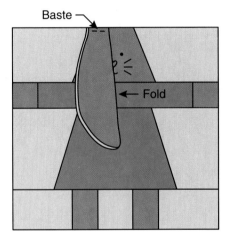

Diagram 5

ASSEMBLING the CENTER

Cutting for the Center

From the red, cut:

◆ Two 2-inch crosswise strips; from these strips, cut six 5½-inch pieces (Vertical Sashing Strips) and two 18½-inch pieces (Horizontal Sashing Strips)

Piecing the Center

STEP 1. Sew bunny blocks and 5½-inch sashing strips into three horizontal rows of three blocks each, as shown in **Diagram 6**. Press toward the sashing strips.

STEP 2. Join rows to 18½-inch sashing strips to complete the center, as shown in **Diagram 7**. (You may want to pin the bunny ears out of the way so they aren't accidently sewn into the seams.) Press toward the sashing strips.

Make It EASY

Before you join the heart blocks into rows, lay them out around the quilt top to find the best color placement. ■

Make 3

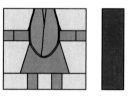

Diagram 6

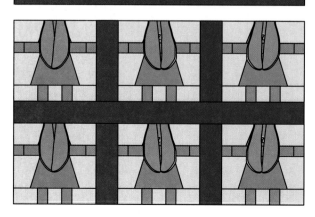

Diagram 7

BORDERS

Cutting for Borders

From the red, cut:

◆ Four 2-inch crosswise strips; from these strips, cut two 18½-inch Top and Bottom Inner Borders and two 21½-inch Side Borders. (Cut one of each length from each strip.)

From the black check, cut:

◆ Two 1½ × 21½-inch strips (Top and Bottom Middle Borders)

◆ Two 1½ × 23½-inch strips (Side Middle Borders)

From the tan solid, cut:

◆ Three 3⅜-inch crosswise strips; from these strips, cut 36 squares

From the assorted prints, cut:

◆ 36 Hearts (fabrics can be repeated 2 or 3 times), following the directions for the appliqué method you have chosen

Attaching the Borders

STEP 1. For all of the directions on adding the three borders, refer to the **Quilt Diagram**. Attach 18½-inch red strips to the top and bottom of the quilt top. Press the seams toward the border.

STEP 2. Attach 21½-inch red strips to the sides of the quilt top. Press toward the border.

STEP 3. Repeat Steps 1 and 2 for the black check middle border.

STEP 4. Fuse or appliqué hearts to the centers of the 3⅜-inch tan squares.

STEP 5. Join eight heart blocks *side to side* to make the top pieced border. Press. Repeat to make the bottom border. Attach these rows to the top and bottom of the quilt top, being careful to keep the hearts upright. Press.

STEP 6. Join ten heart blocks *top to bottom* to make a side pieced border. Press. Repeat to make the other side border.

Attach these borders to the sides of the quilt top, again keeping the hearts upright. Press.

QUILTING

STEP 1. Press the finished quilt top. Mark the quilting design, using one of your own or following these suggestions.

- Outline the bunnies by stitching in the ditch.
- Quilt in the ditch around the blocks.
- Accent the shape of the dresses by stitching across the neckline, the ends of the sleeves, and the hemline.
- Stitch in the ditch between the inner and middle border, and between the middle and outer border.

8 blocks

10 blocks

Inner Border

Middle Border

Outer Border

Quilt Diagram

■ Quilt ¼ inch outside the hearts in the outer border.

STEP 2. Layer the quilt top, batting, and backing. Baste the layers together.

STEP 3. Quilt by hand or machine.

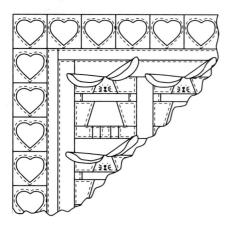

Quilting Diagram

STEP 4. Trim the batting and backing even with the quilt top. Remove the basting.

STEP 5. Tack the bunny ears in place, positioning one up and out to the side, as shown in the photograph on page 220.

BINDING

STEP 1. Cut three 2-inch crosswise strips to prepare 126 inches of double-fold straight-grain binding.

STEP 2. Join the strips end to end with diagonal seams. Fold in half lengthwise with wrong sides together and press. Attach the binding to the quilt,

following the instructions on page 242.

Make It FUN

Personalize this quilt for "somebunny" special by fusing plain muslin hearts onto the dresses. Have people sign these hearts for a friendship quilt. Or use light-colored fabrics for the dresses and have kids autograph them for a teacher's end-of-the-year gift from the class. ■

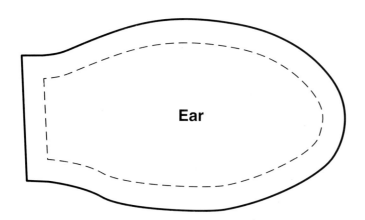

Ear

Heart

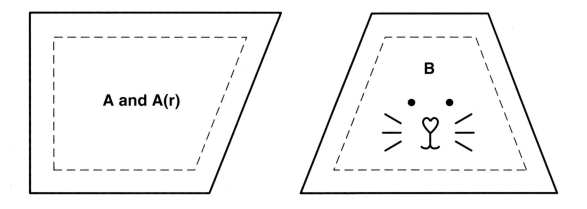

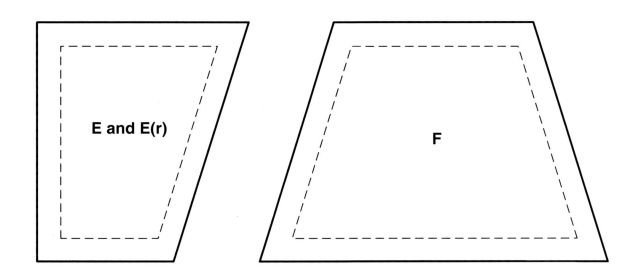

Cat and Mouse

Kathy Boudreau, *Katrinka Designs*

*F*or anyone who enjoys feline companion-
ship in the sewing room, this quilt is a must!
Quilt-makers have long understood the natural
affinity between cats and quilts. Celebrate this
bond by stitching this delightful wall quilt. As
a sign of true devotion, hang it above your cat's
bed or feeding bowl, or display it in your
sewing room.

SIZE

Finished quilt is 17½ × 19 inches

FABRICS and SUPPLIES

Yardage based on 44-inch-wide fabric

- ¼ yard blue stripe for upper background
- ¼ yard rust stripe for lower background
- ¼ yard dark-blue-and-tan stripe for outer border. **Note:** Buy ½ yard if the stripes run crosswise.
- ¼ yard tan print for cat body (or a scrap at least 5 × 8 inches)
- ⅛ yard light-blue-and-tan stripe for outer border. (See **Note** above.)
- ⅛ yard blue-and-white stripe for inner border. (See **Note** above.)

- ⅛ yard blue-and-white check for inner border
- Scraps for stripes, tail, inner ears, nose, and mouse body
- ¼ yard black solid for binding
- ⅝ yard for backing (⅜ yard for a pieced backing)
- Batting, larger than 17½ × 19 inches
- Two ¼-inch buttons for mouse feet
- 2-inch length of black cord for mouse tail
- One 1-inch or smaller wooden heart or heart button
- Black, fine-point, permanent felt-tip pen
- Clear nylon fishing line for whiskers (optional)
- Template plastic or fusible web, depending on appliqué method
- Rotary cutter, ruler, and mat

GETTING READY

COLOR and FABRIC TIPS:
This scrappy little feline is an easy project to make from the leftover bits and pieces you have stashed in your sewing room. If your scrap collection is bulging, the only fabric you may need to buy is the backing. As you combine your fabrics, make sure the cat body contrasts well with the upper and lower backgrounds. Also notice in this quilt how five different stripes are used. Instead of looking too busy or distracting, these stripes work together to create an interesting and energetic border and backdrop for the cat and his buddy. The key to this successful look is that all the stripes are in the same color family.

Substitute red or green for blue fabrics

■ Wash, damp dry, and press all fabrics before using.

■ All seam allowances are ¼ inch and should be pressed to one side, unless otherwise indicated.

■ You may need to back light-colored fabrics with interfacing to prevent shadowing.

■ See "Appliqué Basics" on page 238 and choose a method. Then, using the patterns on page 233, trace the cat's body, stripes, tail, inner ears, and nose, and the mouse's body, onto template plastic or fusible web, depending on the method you've chosen. If you are using fusible web, remember to *reverse* the patterns first before tracing onto the web.

■ Cutting directions for each part of the quilt are provided in the sections indicated by the yellow rotary cutters. This format allows you to cut what you need as you get ready to assemble each part of the quilt. If you prefer to cut all the pieces at once, skip ahead, looking for the yellow rotary cutters, and cut all the pieces before starting to sew.

ASSEMBLING the CENTRAL MOTIF

Cutting for the Center

From the tan print, following the directions for the appliqué method you have chosen, cut:

◆ The cat's body

From the scraps, following the directions for the appliqué method you have chosen, cut:

◆ The cat's stripes
◆ The cat's tail

◆ The cat's inner ears
◆ The cat's nose
◆ The mouse's body

From the blue stripe, cut:

◆ One 11½ × 7½-inch piece (Upper Background)

From the rust stripe, cut:

◆ One 11½ × 4-inch piece (Lower Background)

Piecing and Appliquéing the Center

STEP 1. Sew the upper background to the lower background along the 11½-inch sides. Press.

STEP 2. Referring to the **Patterns and Placement Guides** on page 233, fuse or appliqué the inner ears, nose, and stripes to the cat's body.

STEP 3. Referring to the **Quilt Diagram**, center the cat on the background with the lower edge approximately 1½ inches below the background seam. Tuck the tail under the body. Position the mouse's body 1½ inches from the lower edge of the background and 2 inches from the left edge. It will overlap the lower left corner of the cat.

Make It FAST

If you are doing machine appliqué, use clear nylon monofilament thread for the top thread. This will blend with any color fabric, making it unnecessary to stop and switch thread colors with every new appliqué piece. Use a close zigzag stitch and loosen the top tension. ■

STEP 4. Fuse or appliqué the cat's tail in place first, then the cat's body, and then the mouse. Position the cord for the mouse's tail before appliquéing the mouse down.

STEP 5. Referring to the **Patterns and Placement Guides**, draw faces on the cat and mouse with the permanent pen. (See "Make It Fun" on page 232 for tips on creating whiskers.) Sew buttons to the bottom of the mouse for his feet. Glue the cat's heart in place with a hot glue gun, or

sew it on by drilling two small holes in it and using it as a button. (If you find the perfect heart button, skip the drilling and just sew it in place.)

BORDERS

Cutting the Borders

Cut all striped borders with the stripes parallel to the *short* ends of the border strip.

From the blue-and-white check for the inner border, cut:

◆ Two 1¾ × 11-inch pieces (Sides)

From the blue-and-white stripe for the inner border, cut:

◆ Two 1¾ × 14-inch pieces (Top and Bottom)

From the light-blue-and-tan stripe for the outer border, cut:

◆ Two 2¼ × 13½-inch pieces (Sides)

From the dark-blue-and-tan stripe for the outer border, cut:

◆ Two 17½ × 3¼-inch pieces (Top and Bottom)

Attaching the Borders

STEP 1. Attach the 11-inch check borders to the sides of the quilt top. Press toward the border.

STEP 2. Attach the 14-inch striped borders to the top and bottom of the quilt top. Press toward the border. Repeat for outer borders, using the 13½-

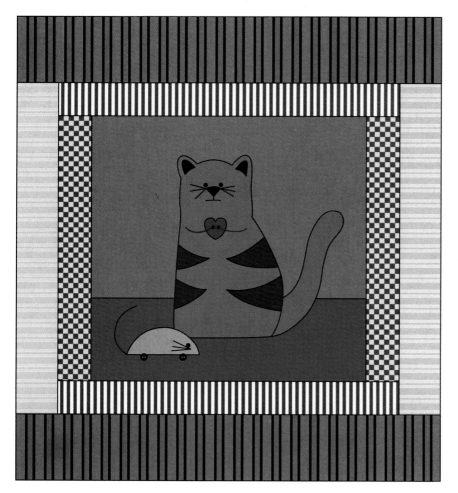

Quilt Diagram

inch light striped side borders and the 17½-inch dark striped top and bottom borders.

QUILTING

STEP 1. Press the finished quilt top. Mark the quilting design, using one of your own or following these suggestions.

■ Quilt ¼ inch outside the cat.

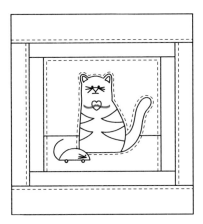

Quilting Diagram

■ Quilt ¼ inch inside the background section.

■ Stitch in the outer borders ¼ inch away from the seams.

STEP 2. Layer the quilt top, batting, and backing. Baste all the layers together.

STEP 3. Quilt by hand or machine.

STEP 4. Trim the batting and backing even with the quilt top. Remove the basting.

BINDING

STEP 1. Cut two 2-inch crosswise strips to prepare 90 inches of double-fold straight-grain binding. (Cut and add another short strip if necessary.)

STEP 2. Join the strips end to end with diagonal seams. Fold in half lengthwise with wrong sides together and press.

Attach the binding to the quilt, following the instructions on page 242.

Make It FUN

You can draw the cat's whiskers with the pen, or you can make them out of clear nylon fishing line using the following method: Thread a large needle with a single strand of fishing line and knot it at one end. Working from the back of the quilt, insert the needle close to the top of the nose and come out on the front. Leave extra length and repeat for a total of three whiskers on each side. Trim to the desired length. ■

Button Placement

For machine appliqué, cut pattern pieces as shown. For hand appliqué, add ⅛" to ¼" to pattern pieces when cutting. For fusible web, reverse the patterns *first* before tracing onto paper side of web.

Patterns and Placement Guides

All the Basics

❖

QUILTMAKER'S BASIC SUPPLY LIST

Here's a list of items you should have on hand before beginning a project.

■ **Iron and ironing board:** Set these up near your sewing machine. Careful pressing leads to accurate piecing.

■ **Needles:** The two types of needles commonly used by quilters are *betweens,* short needles used for quilting, and *sharps,* long, very thin needles used for appliqué and hand piecing. The thickness of hand-sewing needles decreases as the size designation increases. (A size 12 needle is thinner than a size 10.)

■ **Rotary cutter, acrylic rotary ruler, and cutting mat:** Fabric can be cut quickly and accurately with rotary-cutting equipment. There are a variety of cutters available, all with slightly different handle styles and safety latches. Rigid, see-through acrylic rulers are used with rotary cutters. A 6 × 24-inch ruler is a good size; for the most versatility, be sure it has 45 degree and 60 degree angle markings. A 14-inch square ruler will also be helpful for making sure blocks are square.

Always use a special mat with a rotary cutter. The mat protects the work surface and helps to grip the fabric. Purchase the largest mat practical for your sewing area. A good all-purpose size is 18 × 24 inches.

■ **Safety pins:** These are generally used to baste quilts for machine quilting. Use rustproof, nickel-plated brass safety pins, preferably size 0.

■ **Scissors:** You'll need several pairs of scissors: shears for cutting fabric; general scissors for cutting paper, fusible web, and template plastic; and small, sharp embroidery scissors for trimming threads.

■ **Sewing machine:** Any machine with a straight stitch is suitable for piecing quilt blocks. For machine quilting, an even-feed foot (for straight lines) and a darning foot (for free-motion curving, meandering lines) are essential. Follow the manufacturer's recommendations for cleaning and servicing your sewing machine.

■ **Straight pins:** Choose long, thin pins with glass or plastic heads that are easy to see against fabric so that you are sure to remove them all.

■ **Template material:** Sheets of clear and opaque template plastic can be purchased at most quilt and craft shops. Gridded

plastic is also available and may help you draw shapes more easily. Various weights of cardboard can also be used for templates, including common household items like cereal boxes, posterboard, and manila file folders.

■ **Thimbles:** For hand quilting, a thimble is almost essential. Buy one that fits the finger you use to push the needle. The thimble should be snug enough to stay on when you shake your hand. There should be a bit of space between the end of your finger and the tip of the thimble.

■ **Thread:** For hand or machine piecing, 100 percent cotton thread is a traditional favorite. Cotton-covered polyester is also acceptable. For hand quilting, use 100 percent cotton quilting thread. For machine quilting, you may want to try clear nylon thread as the top thread, with cotton thread in the bobbin.

❖

SELECTING and PREPARING FABRICS

The traditional fabric choice for quilts is 100 percent cotton. It handles well, is easy to care for, presses easily, and frays less than synthetic blends.

The yardages in this book are generous estimates based on 44/45-inch-wide fabrics. It's a good idea to always purchase a bit more fabric than necessary to compensate for shrinkage and occasional cutting errors.

Prewash your fabrics using warm water and a mild soap or detergent. With dark colors, test for colorfastness first. Snip a 2-inch square from the fabrics you want to test and safety pin them to a piece of a white terry washcloth. Put them through the washer and then check for any signs of color bleeding onto the white. If colors bleed, repeat the cycle with a new piece of washcloth, adding a cup of vinegar to the rinse water. If, after two spins through the washer, the color still bleeds, don't use that fabric in a quilt that will need laundering—save it for a wallhanging that won't get a lot of use.

After washing, preshrink your fabric by damp drying it in a dryer on the medium setting. To keep wrinkles under control, remove the fabric from the dryer while it's still slightly damp and press it immediately with a hot iron.

❖

ROTARY CUTTING

The cutting instructions in this book are written to take advantage of quick rotary-cutting techniques whenever possible. Rotary cutting is not only faster than the traditional template method, but it also ensures much better accuracy.

Follow these two safety rules every time you use a rotary cutter: Always cut by moving the blade *away* from yourself, and always slide the blade guard into place the *second* you stop cutting.

Step-by-Step Rotary Cutting

STEP 1. You can cut several layers of fabric at a time with a rotary cutter. Fold the fabric with the selvage edges together (many quilters like to trim away these woven edges of the fabric before they fold the fabric). You can fold it again if you want, doubling the number of layers to be cut. This second fold also shortens the length of the cut that needs to be made, which many quilters, especially beginners, find easier to handle.

STEP 2. Before cutting any strips, square up the end of the fabric, as shown in **Diagram 1**. Place a ruled square even with the fold and slide a 6 × 24-inch ruler against the side of the square. Hold the ruler in place, remove the square, and cut along the edge of the ruler. (If you are left-handed, work from the other end of the fabric.)

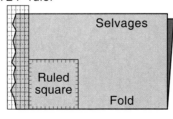

6" x 24" ruler

Diagram 1

STEP 3. As needed for your project, cut strips on the crosswise grain, then cut them into smaller pieces as the project directions specify. **Diagram 2** shows a strip cut into squares. Find the strip

width specified in the cutting directions, then locate that number on the ruler. Align that number's guide line on the ruler with the squared-up edge of the fabric. The other edge of the ruler serves as the cutting guide; slide the rotary cutter along the edge of the ruler, making the cut *away* from yourself. Inch the fingers of the hand holding the ruler up the length of the ruler as you cut; this will overcome the tendency the ruler has to slip out of position.

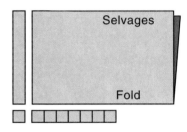

Diagram 2

STEP 4. Open up and check your cut strips periodically to make sure they're straight and not angled, as shown in **Diagram 3**. If they start looking V-shaped, refold the fabric and square up the edges again, then resume cutting strips.

Diagram 3

Special Rotary Cuts

Turning squares into triangles: A square can be cut into two triangles by making one diagonal cut (**Diagram 4A**). Two diagonal cuts yield four squares (**4B**).

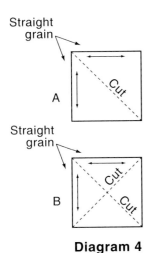

Diagram 4

Rotary cutting single squares:
Some projects call for just a single square or two to be cut from a certain fabric. Slicing a strip, then cutting off just one or two squares leaves you with a lot of leftover strip. Instead, use your square rotary ruler and find the lines that match the cutting dimension of the fabric square you need. With a single or double layer of fabric, position one of the ruler's guidelines close to the edge of the fabric, as shown in **Diagram 5A**. In this example, a square of 3 inches is needed. The first cut is made using the 3½-inch guidelines (to leave a little extra for "insurance"). Rotary cut along the right and top edges of the ruler. Rotate the cutting mat so that the two edges of the fabric you just cut are closest to you.

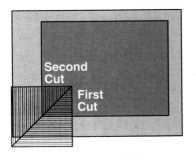

Diagram 5A

Reposition the ruler, aligning the guidelines with the two sides of the square that were just cut. Finish cutting the square by slicing along the right and top edges, as shown in **5B**.

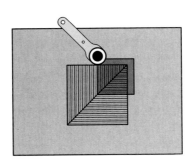

Diagram 5B

Rotary cutting with templates:
First, prepare your templates as described in "Templates" on this page, using either template plastic or cardboard. Then layer as many fabrics as you need, right sides facing up. On the top layer (it's helpful if this is a light-colored fabric), trace around the template, leaving ¼ to ½ inch between traced shapes. Lay the edge of your rotary ruler exactly along the lines you've drawn and cut through all layers with a rotary cutter, as shown in **Diagram 6**. To ensure more accurate pieces, use the thin lead of a mechanical pencil to draw the cutting lines.

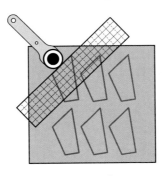

Diagram 6

If you need to cut any reverse pieces, here's a shortcut. As you layer the fabrics to be cut, put the one for the reverse pattern in the pile with the *wrong side* facing up. When you trace the template and cut, that piece will automatically become the reverse. For more on reverse pieces, see page 238.

❖

TEMPLATES

Although the bulk of the pieced projects in this book feature rotary cutting, patterns have been provided for shapes that do not lend themselves to this cutting technique. Appliqué projects also include patterns. For some of these, you will need to convert the pattern on the book page into a template you can then use to cut your fabric. (For some of the projects specially designed for fusible appliqué, you can skip making templates and trace the appliqué shapes directly from the book onto fusible web. See page 239 for more details.)

Making templates: Place template plastic over the book page, trace the pattern onto the plastic using a pencil or an extrafine-point permanent marker, and carefully cut out the template. To make a cardboard template, copy the pattern onto tracing paper, glue the paper to the cardboard, and cut out the cardboard template. Record on every template the project name, any identification letters and grain lines, as well as the size and name of the block and the number of pieces needed. Always check your templates against the printed pattern for accuracy.

Seam allowances: The patchwork patterns in this book are printed with double lines. The inner dashed line is the finished size of the piece, while the outer solid line includes the seam allowance. For machine piecing, trace the outer solid line on the printed pattern to make templates that include the seam allowance. Draw around the templates on the wrong side of the fabric and cut out the pieces on this line, as shown in **Diagram 7.**

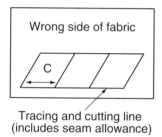

Diagram 7

Reverse pattern pieces: For some projects, you will need a pattern piece plus its reverse, or mirror image. In the cutting lists and directions, these will be called Reverse pattern pieces (A Reverse, for example); on the pattern piece itself, these are denoted with an (r) following the pattern letter. To create a reverse pattern piece, simply take the template you have created and turn it over to the reverse side, as shown in **Diagram 8.** Place this reversed template on the fabric, then trace and cut as usual.

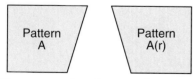

Turn over pattern to create its reverse

Diagram 8

Appliqué patterns: Patterns for appliqué pieces in this book have only a single line and are shown finished size. Trace around this line to make templates for traditional hand appliqué. As you cut, allow a scant ⅛-inch seam allowance outside the drawn line, as shown in **Diagram 9.** If you are using fusible or machine appliqué, you do *not* need to include a seam allowance as you cut. Refer to the instructions for specific appliqué projects for information on whether reversing your pattern pieces is necessary for the appliqué method you choose. Pay particular attention to reversing if you are using fusible appliqué.

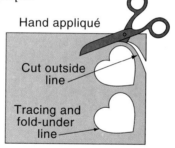

Diagram 9

❖

MACHINE PIECING

The standard seam allowance for piecing is ¼ inch. Machine sew a sample seam to test the accuracy of the seam allowance; adjust as needed. If you have a hard time maintaining an accurate ¼ inch, consider purchasing a Little Foot attachment for your machine (see page 248 for source). Available for nearly every model of sewing machine, this foot provides an accurate sewing guide for quilters.

Step-by-Step Machine Piecing

STEP 1. Cut the fabric pieces using templates with seam allowances included, or using a rotary cutter and ruler. Set the stitch length at 10 to 12 stitches per inch.

STEP 2. Place the fabric pieces right sides together, then sew from raw edge to raw edge. Press the seams to one side before crossing them with other seams, pressing toward the darker fabric whenever possible.

❖

APPLIQUÉ BASICS

All of the appliqué projects in this book are suitable for no-sew or *fusible* appliqué, the fastest method around. You can also use machine appliqué, which provides significant time savings. For people who love handwork, hand appliqué is also an option for some of the projects—admittedly not a fast method, but for its fans, a soothing technique nonetheless.

Step-by-Step Fusible Appliqué

STEP 1. Lay the fusible web, paper side up, on the pattern in the book and trace. You need a fusible web pattern for every repetition of an appliqué shape. You do not need to add seam allowances for fusible appliqué.

The shape you trace onto the paper needs to be the *reverse* or mirror image of the final shape that appears on your quilt. The project directions will tell you when you need to reverse. Symmetrical shapes like hearts or circles don't need to be reversed. To reverse the pattern, trace it from the book onto a piece of plain paper, using a very dark black fine-point marker. Flip the paper over; if you can't see the pattern lines clearly through the paper, retrace them. Place a piece of fusible web, paper side up, over this reversed pattern and trace it.

STEP 2. Cut out the pattern, not following the drawn lines exactly, but leaving a generous margin (at least 1/4 inch) outside the lines, as shown in **Diagram 10**.

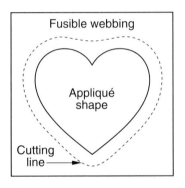

Diagram 10

STEP 3. Using a dry iron on a medium setting, fuse the web to the *wrong* side of the fabric. Be sure to follow the manufacturer's directions about heat setting and how long to hold the iron in place. Leaving the iron on for too long can remove the adhesive from the fabric.

STEP 4. Once the fabric and fusible web have cooled, cut the pattern out exactly along the drawn lines, as indicated in **Diagram 11**. To fuse to your pro-

ject, simply peel away the paper backing, position carefully, and press, following the manufacturer's directions.

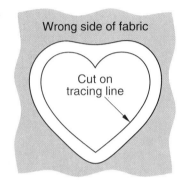

Diagram 11

Tips for Fusible Appliqué

■ Fusible web comes in two different weights. Use the lightweight type if you plan to embellish your appliqué with any sort of embroidery, like a decorative buttonhole stitch. Use the heavyweight for extrastrong hold.

■ Pay attention to the order in which the pieces need to be fused in place. Look for overlapping pieces and start with the ones that are in the background, then work your way to the foreground. In some projects the pieces are numbered in order of fusing to make it easy for you to follow.

■ To manipulate small appliqué pieces, use tweezers or a straight pin.

■ Protect the surface of your ironing board from the sticky adhesive of the fusible web with a scrap piece of muslin or an old towel. If the adhesive builds up

on your iron, check your sewing or quilting shop for special products designed to clean away all traces of stickiness.

■ Once the appliqué shapes are in place on your quilt, you can leave the edges alone or finish them with a machine satin stitch or other decorative stitch of your choice.

Step-by-Step Machine Appliqué

Not quite as speedy as fusible appliqué, but often quicker than hand appliqué, this satin stitch technique gives you nice, clean, finished edges on simple appliqué shapes. (Smaller, more detailed shapes are trickier to machine appliqué.)

STEP 1. Using templates *without* seam allowances, cut the appliqué shapes from your fabric. For best results, stabilize the appliqué shape by using either fusible interfacing or lightweight fusible web. Press the interfacing to the wrong side of the appliqué fabric before cutting the shape, as shown in **Diagram 12**. For fusible web, see "Step-by-Step Fusible Appliqué" on page 238.

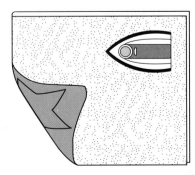

Diagram 12

STEP 2. Position the appliqué on the background fabric with basting stitches (for fusible interfacing) or with a warm iron (for fusible web).

STEP 3. Attach an appliqué foot or zigzag foot to your machine. Loosen the top tension a bit to keep the bobbin thread from showing through on the top. Set your machine for a close zigzag satin stitch (with stitch width approximately ⅛ inch).

STEP 4. Begin stitching so the thread just barely covers the edges of the appliqué shape. When you reach a corner, lower the needle into the background fabric, lift the presser foot, and turn the fabric so you can stitch in the next direction, as shown in **Diagram 13**. Lower the presser foot and continue stitching.

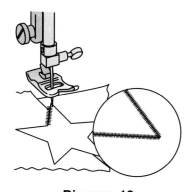

Diagram 13

STEP 5. To end a line of satin stitches, leave a 3-inch tail free, pull the thread to the back of the fabric, and tie a knot.

Step-by-Step Hand Appliqué

Admittedly a bit more time consuming than the quick fusible appliqué method, there is still something to be said for the leisurely pace of needle-turn appliqué. Appliqué patterns with lots of tiny pieces are not good candidates for this hand technique, but larger, simpler shapes like hearts are easy for anyone to master.

STEP 1. Review "Templates" on page 237 to learn how to prepare templates for hand appliqué. Lightly draw around each template on the right side of the fabric using a pencil or a nonpermanent marker. These are the fold-under lines. Cut out the pieces ⅛ to ¼ inch outside the marked lines.

STEP 2. Pin the appliqué pieces into position on the background fabric, always working in order from the background to the foreground. To ensure best results, don't turn under or appliqué edges that will be covered by other appliqué pieces. Use a thread color that matches the fabric in the appliqué piece itself.

STEP 3. Be sure to bring the needle up from under the appliqué patch exactly on the drawn line. Fold under the seam allowance on the line to neatly encase the knot.

STEP 4. Insert the tip of the needle into the background fabric right next to where the thread comes out of the appliqué piece. Bring the needle out of the background fabric approximately ¹⁄₁₆ inch away from and up through the very edge of the fold, completing the first stitch. See **Diagram 14**.

Diagram 14

STEP 5. Repeat this process for each stitch, using the tip and shank of your appliqué needle to turn under ½-inch-long sections of seam allowance at a time. As you turn under a section, press it flat with your thumb and then stitch it in place. Clip any concave curves or clefts before turning under to ensure smooth curves and crisp inner points.

❖

MARKING QUILTING DESIGNS

To mark a quilting design, use a commercially made stencil, make your own stencil using a sheet of plastic, or trace the design from a book or magazine page. Use a nonpermanent marker, such as a silver or white pencil, chalk pencil, or chalk marker, that will be visible on the fabric. You can even mark with a 0.5mm lead pencil, but be sure to mark lightly.

For light-colored fabrics you can see through, place the pattern under the quilt top and trace the quilting design directly onto the right side of the fabric. Mark in a thin, continuous line that will be covered by the quilting thread.

With dark fabrics, mark from the top by drawing around a hard-edged design template. To make a simple template, trace the design onto template plastic and cut it out around the outer edge. Trace the outside edge of the template onto the fabric, then add the inner lines by eye. If you're not comfortable "eyeballing" it, you could trace the inner lines onto the template, then cut skinny slits with a craft knife through the plastic. Use those slits as guides to trace the inner lines onto the quilt top.

❖

LAYERING and BASTING

Carefully preparing the quilt top, batting, and backing will ensure that the finished quilt will lie flat and smooth. Place the backing wrong side up on a large table or clean floor. Center the batting on the backing and smooth out any wrinkles. Center the quilt top right side up on the batting, smoothing it out.

If you plan to hand quilt, baste the quilt with thread. Use a long darning needle and white thread. Baste outward from the center of the quilt in a grid of horizontal and vertical rows approximately 4 inches apart.

If you plan to machine quilt, baste with safety pins. Thread basting does not hold the layers securely enough during machine quilting, and the thread is difficult to remove when quilting is completed. Use size 0 rustproof, nickel-plated brass safety pins, pinning from the center of the quilt out approximately every 3 inches.

❖

HAND QUILTING

For best results, use a hoop or a frame to hold the quilt layers taut and smooth during quilting. Work with one hand on top of the quilt and the other hand underneath, guiding the needle. Don't worry about the size of your stitches; they will get smaller over time.

Getting started: Thread a needle with quilting thread and knot the end. Insert the needle through the quilt top and batting about 1 inch away from where you will begin stitching. Bring the needle to the surface in position to make the first stitch. Gently tug on the thread to pop the knot through the quilt top and bury it in the batting, as shown in **Diagram 15**.

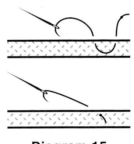

Diagram 15

Taking the stitches: Insert the needle through the three layers of the quilt. When you feel the tip of the needle with your underneath finger, gently guide it back up through the quilt. When the needle comes through the top of the quilt, press your thimble on the end with the eye to guide it down again through the quilt layers. Continue to quilt in this manner, taking two or three small running stitches at a time. Refer to **Diagram 16**.

Diagram 16

Ending a line of stitching: Bring the needle to the top of the quilt just past the last stitch. Referring to **Diagram 17**, make a knot at the surface by bringing the needle under the thread where it comes out of the fabric and up through the loop of thread it creates. Repeat this knot and insert the needle into the hole where the thread comes out of the fabric. Run the needle inside the batting for an inch and bring it back to the surface. Tug gently on the thread to pop the knot through the quilt top and into the batting layer. Clip the thread.

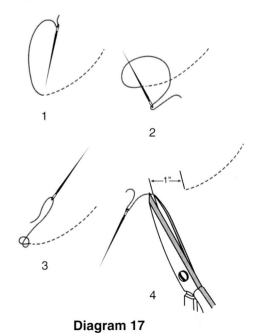

Diagram 17

MACHINE QUILTING

For best results when doing machine-guided quilting (for example, quilting in the ditch, creating grids, or channel quilting), use a walking foot (also called an even-feed foot) on your sewing machine. For free-motion quilting (for example, stipple or meander quilting, or overall freeform or continuous quilting lines), use a darning or machine-embroidery foot. Use thread to match the fabric colors, or use clear nylon thread in the top of the machine and white or colored thread in the bobbin.

Getting started: To secure the thread at the beginning of a line of stitches, adjust the stitch length on your machine to make several very short stitches, then gradually increase to the regular stitch length. As you near the end of the line, gradually reduce the stitch length so that the last few stitches are very short.

Machine-guided quilting: Keep the feed dogs up and move all three layers as smoothly as you can under the needle. To turn a corner in a quilting design, stop with the needle inserted in the fabric, raise the foot, pivot the quilt, lower the foot, and continue stitching.

Free-motion quilting: Disengage the feed dogs so you can manipulate the quilt freely as you stitch. Guide the quilt under the needle with both hands, coordinating the speed of the needle with the movement of the quilt to create stitches of consistent length.

BINDING

Each project in this book tells you whether to use single-fold or double-fold binding, and it also gives the width to cut the strips and the number of strips you'll need. With those specifics in mind, follow these general techniques for making and attaching the binding to your quilt.

Making binding: Cut strips from the binding fabric in the desired width, cutting across the width of the fabric, unless specified otherwise. Sew the strips together end to end with diagonal seams. Place the strips right sides together so that each strip is set in ¼ inch from the end of the other strip, as shown in **Diagram 18**. Sew a diagonal seam and trim the excess fabric, leaving a ¼-inch seam allowance. Press the seam open.

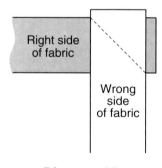

Diagram 18

Double-fold binding: Fold the resulting long binding strip in half lengthwise, wrong sides together, and press. To apply, place the pressed strip on the quilt top with raw edges even.

Single-fold binding: Fold the edges of the strips in toward the middle until they meet (a handy little tool, available in fabric shops, does the folding for you). Press. To apply single-fold binding, open out one fold and place the binding on the quilt with right sides together and raw edges even.

Step-by-Step Attaching Binding

STEP 1. Trim the excess batting and backing even with the quilt top. If you choose to, you can leave ¼ inch extending past the quilt top to make a firm, filled binding. Beginning in the middle of a side, not in a corner, place the strip right sides together with the quilt top, align the raw edges, and pin.

STEP 2. Fold over approximately 1 inch at the beginning of the strip and begin stitching ½ inch from the fold, as shown in **Diagram 19**. Sew the binding around the entire perimeter of the quilt, using a ¼-inch seam for double-fold binding, or stitching along the crease for single-fold binding. Stitch through all layers of the quilt.

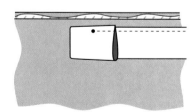

Diagram 19

STEP 3. As you approach a corner, stop stitching ¼ inch from the raw edge of the corner. Backstitch and remove the quilt from the machine. Fold the binding strip up at a 45 degree angle, as shown in **Diagram 20A**. Fold the strip back down so there is a fold at the upper edge, as shown in **20B**. Begin sewing at the top edge of the quilt, continuing to the next corner. Miter all four corners in this manner.

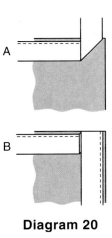

Diagram 20

STEP 4. To finish the binding seam, overlap the folded-back beginning section with the ending section, as shown in **Diagram 21**. Stitch across the fold, allowing the end to extend approximately ½ inch beyond the beginning.

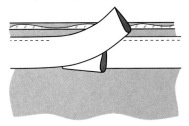

Diagram 21

STEP 5. Turn the binding to the back of the quilt and blind stitch the folded edge in place, covering the machine stitches with the folded edge, as shown in **Diagram 22**. Fold in the

adjacent sides on the back and take several stitches in the miter. In the same way, add several stitches to the miters on the front.

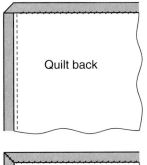

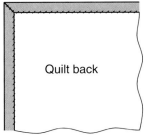

Diagram 22

Quilter's Resource

DIRECTORY of DESIGNERS

Here's your chance to learn more about the talented designers whose wonderful projects are featured in this book. Use the addresses and phone numbers provided to find out more about the other patterns and projects they have designed.

Alice Berg
Mary Ellen Von Holt
Sylvia Johnson

Little Quilts
4939 Lower Roswell Road #204C
Department R
Marietta, GA 30068

Projects featured in the book:
Star & Nine Patch Quilt (page 58) and Playmates (page 216)

Little Quilts is a pattern and kit business located in Marietta, Georgia. Designers Alice Berg, Mary Ellen Von Holt, and Sylvia Johnson are also authors of *Little Quilts, All through the House,* and design a line of fabric for Fabri-Quilt. Traditional designs on a small scale are their specialty, with influence from antique doll quilts. Little Quilts are textile paintings and work well in most decorating schemes. For a catalog, send $2 to the address above. ❖

Kathy Boudreau

Katrinka Designs
4 Robin Drive
Brunswick, ME 04011
(207) 725-8027

Projects featured in the book:
Saint Nicholas (page 98), Homestead Hearts (page 134), and Cat and Mouse (page 228)

I reside in Maine along with my husband, twin sons, psychotic dog, and killer cat. Originally from Amish country in Ohio, I have long been surrounded by beautiful antique quilts, handed down through my family. Needlework has always been an interest, but it wasn't until I took a quilting class in the 1980s that the quilting bug really bit (and left a permanent mark!). My design inspirations have come from many directions, including childhood Christmas memories, growing up on a farm, and, more recently, living on the Maine coast. ❖

Glenda Carr

Blue Whale Designs
120 South Terrace
Liberty, MO 64068

Project featured in the book:
Starry Night (page 44)

I first started my business in 1979 by selling finished quilt items to local retailers. All of my work was based on my original designs and, after a while, I started receiving requests for the designs in pattern form. As a result, I published my first collection of quilt designs in 1982, and soon after that I began my line of counted cross-stitch leaflets.

As my business grew I continued to expand both lines: Blue Whale Designs became mostly country cross-stitch and I began publishing the quilt designs under the trademark Liberty Homestead. I originally started my business so that I could work at home and be with my daughter, Jessy (who was 2 at the time and has just now graduated from high school). My son, Jordan, is just starting junior high. I feel very fortunate to have been successful enough in my business that I could be here for my children these last 16 years while doing the work that I love. It is my hope that my success continues for one more trip through junior high, high school, college, and graduate school. ❖

Sandy Gervais

Pieces from My Heart
Dept. rdp
P.O. Box 112
Algona, IA 50511
(515) 295-5672 (phone/fax)

Projects featured in the book:
Christmas Angel (page 112) and Heart and Hand (page 128)

I'm a self-taught artist. I combine my art with my sewing ability to create patterns, which I've been designing since 1992. My patterns feature quilted wallhangings using simple piecing and fusible appliqué, as well as some soft-sculpture items. I'm known for using unusual embellishments on patterns, such as tin, twigs, wire, and antique buttons. I also design fabrics and greeting cards, and I have written and illustrated a humorous book entitled *Living the Life of a Fabric-aholic.*

I live in Algona, Iowa, with my husband Bruce and my two children, Antony and Abby. ❖

Lynette Jensen

Thimbleberries, Inc.
205 Jefferson Street
Hutchinson, MN 55350
(612) 587-3944

Project featured in the book:
Homespun Stars Tree Skirt (page 92)

Thimbleberries grew out of a love for the needle arts, color, and design. Quiltmaking is a perfect mix for all these interests of mine. Over the past 20 years of teaching and the most recent 6 years of owning Thimbleberries, I'm constantly reminded that today's quilters want designs that are doable in a fairly short period of time. When designing a project, the number-one Thimbleberries goal is to hear our customers say "I can do that!". A touch of good color, wonderful fabrics, and a bit of stitching will always add warmth to a room. ❖

Jill Kemp

Bears Paw Designs
7500 Greenwich Road
Seville, OH 44273

Projects featured in the book:
Gingerbread Cookies (page 118), Birdhouse Alley (page 160), and Floppy Ears (page 220)

Bears Paw Designs was established in 1987 as a result of my love of quilting and a friend's suggestion that I should turn some of my original wallhangings into patterns. Up to that time I had been designing counted cross-stitch patterns for about 3 years. A little more than 8 years later, my business is still growing. So is my 20-year obsession with quilting, although it seems that I don't get to quilt as much as I used to because of running my business. I feel fortunate to be able to make a living doing something I love. Hopefully, with God's blessing, I will be able to keep designing and share my designs with other quilters for years to come. ❖

Paula Kemperman
Susan Rand

Wild Goose Chase
P.O. Box 1166
Grand Rapids, MI 49501

Project featured in the book:
Sew So Easy (page 22)

We have known each other almost all our lives, having grown up attending the same church. We enjoy the same hobbies: gardening, camping, bicycling, and cooking. We're presently working on perfecting five-minute meals so that we can enjoy all the varied things we like to do without hav-

ing to spend too much time in the kitchen (just ask our husbands).

The bicentennial year, 1976, was the beginning of our interest in quilting. It wasn't long before we started selling wallhangings and quilts at art fairs in order to support our love for buying fabrics. Shortly after that, we began teaching in our homes and in local community education classes.

In 1982 we began designing patterns. Over the years we have designed a total of 77 patterns, including some counted cross-stitch. One of our first designs, Lonely Teddy, is still selling—and is now being translated into German!

Sharing new and innovative designs has always been our goal. We have thoroughly enjoyed what we do. Quilting has really taken us many places, and making so many new friends has been our greatest treasure. ❖

Gerry Kimmel

Red Wagon
P.O. Box 520
Liberty, MO 64068
(816) 792-1540 (phone)
(816) 781-3197 (fax)

Projects featured in the book:
Bird Parade (page 2) and 1776 (page 38)

I began Red Wagon in the fall of 1987. My mom loaned me the money to publish my first pattern, 1776, and my first book, *Snowbound.*

It has been a roller coaster ride ever since: 29 patterns, 15 books, plus a large collection of homespun fabrics for Indo-US Sales.

My quilt style can be categorized as folk art, while I tend to create quilts that are seemingly antique in age. Stressing a primitive style, I feel I have generated a great deal of interest in appliqué, especially with the apprehensive stitcher.

I have had the opportunity to do some teaching, but the greatest asset of Red Wagon has been the people I've been fortunate to meet and the friends I have made. ❖

Judith Hughes Marte

Around the Block Quilt Designs
P.O. Box 25
Genesee, ID 83832

Projects featured in the book:
Stars and Scraps Forever (page 64) and Oh My Dialing! (page 178)

What do you get when you mix a love of art, math, fabric, and color, with a degree in Wildlife Management? You get me, quilt designer Judith Hughes Marte. OK, the degree doesn't have anything to do with quilting, but it was while in college in the late 1970s that I began handpiecing original quilt designs. This hobby grew while I worked as an outdoor writer in Louisiana.

After moving to the Northwest and starting a family, I decided to turn my passion for quilting into a profession. I started Around the Block Quilt Designs in 1989 to market my original patterns for wallhangings, quilts, and wearables. My patterns are now available in quilt and fabric shops all over the United States and in many foreign countries.

I live with my husband and two children in Genesee, Idaho, where I am very active in the Genesee Quilter's Guild. I teach a variety of classes for local guilds and quilt

shops. I especially enjoy working with beginners—introducing them to the joys of fabric, color, design, and "finishing a project" in the wonderful world of quilting! ❖

Debbie Mumm

Mumm's the Word, Inc.
2900 North Nevada
Spokane, WA 99207
(509) 482-0210

Project featured in the book:
Heart of the Home (page 196)

I'm a quilt and fabric designer, author, and illustrator. My quilt pattern company, Mumm's the Word, Inc., is run from my design/production center in Spokane. Quilt enthusiasts worldwide have come to know and respect the creativity and accuracy of the patterns I provide. My country-style designs feature quick cutting and sewing techniques that appeal to today's busy quilters of all skill levels, from novice to expert.

I've written three hardcover books, the most recent one being *Quick Country Christmas Quilts.* My latest designing venture adds designs for home and gift products to my existing lines of fabrics and patterns.

I live with my husband Steve and son Murphy in a home overlooking Mount Spokane. Since my career keeps me running during the day, I devote my evenings and weekends to my family.

By using the address and phone number above, you can request ordering information and a catalog. Patterns, books, notecards, and country fabric packets of six fat quarter pieces are among the products available. ❖

Toni Phillips
Juanita Simonich

Fabric Expressions
5950 South Platte Canyon Road #D4
Littleton, CO 80123
(303) 798-2556

Projects featured in the book:
These Guys Don't Melt (page 74), Farmer's Market (page 154), and Bear with Us (page 206)

Our partnership combines a diversity of background, experience and education with a common love for creating, teaching, and encouraging our customers in the art of quiltmaking.

Toni, born in New York City and raised in Houston, first learned needlework through embroidery and cross-stitch. But once she was introduced to quilting, it became her passion. Fine hand appliqué was her specialty, and soon she introduced her glue stick/freezer paper method through her pattern company, Quilt Classics.

Juanita, born and raised in rural northeastern Montana, learned to sew as a child and continued her education at Montana State University, where she did graduate work in Clothing and Textiles. Juanita's love of color and design led her into painting and drawing, each of which influenced her quiltmaking.

We met in 1990, and soon the creative juices were flowing. The pattern company expanded and was renamed Fabric Expressions. We expanded our activities to include writing books: *T.L.C., Tender Loving Covers, and Quilt*A*Saurus.* In 1994 we opened a retail quilt shop in Littleton, Colorado. The cozy shop (motto: "Give the customer more than they expect") is filled with warmth and enthusiasm.

The projects included in this book are typical of our designs, which feature template-free machine piecing and appliqué. Quilters tell us they enjoy making our designs because they are fast, nonrepetitive, and give instant gratification. ❖

Marilyn Reardon

Churn Dash Designs
P.O. Box 60056
Department RP
Seattle, WA 98160-0056
(206) 546-8904 (fax)

Projects featured in the book:
Friendship Plaids (page 10) and Stars & Stripes (page 52)

I have been involved with sewing and stitchery all my life. Having sewn and knitted throughout my school years, I then became interested in stitches—needlepoint, cutwork, pulled thread, cross-stitch, and so on. I began teaching these classes in 1971. My quilting began in the mid 1960s with embroidered blocks that were sewn into baby quilts and tied. The 1970s brought a quilting class, and I began teaching quilting myself in 1981.

I began working in the sewing industry in a retail needlework shop, managing a full-line fabric store, working in an independent retail quilt shop, and working for a wholesale fabric distributor.

Teaching quilting led to self-publishing some of my designs under the name Churn Dash Designs. I wanted patterns that would teach specific skill-building techniques. By designing my own

patterns for classes, I could very specifically provide practice in needed skills. The classes also provided wonderful opportunities for feedback from the students that further guided my designing.

I now own a wholesale distributorship of sewing-related products called The Reardon Company and a retail mail-order company. I also work as the product specialist for Morning Glory Products.

I live in Seattle with my husband, Jim, and am frequently visited by our four daughters and three grandchildren. I enjoy all forms of needlework and read a lot. I am active in my local and regional quilting and needle arts guilds. ❖

Virginia Robertson

Osage County Quilt Factory
400 Walnut
Box 490
Overbrook, KS 66524
(913) 665-7500

Project featured in the book:
Harvest Medallion (page 188)

I've been in the fabric and quilt business for 26 years. I've managed a chain-store fabric department, owned a quilt shop for 12 years, taught college-level quilting in three universities, and for the last 15 years operated Osage County Quilt Factory, a quilt pattern publishing business. Three years ago I began designing my own line of fabrics with Fabri-Quilt, Inc.

I come from a culture of home sewing that includes five generations of quilters. My full-time venture into quiltmaking as a satisfying form of self-expression was inspired by a successful show of art quilts after my master of fine

arts thesis. After a university teaching career, I returned to my home state of Kansas and started Osage County Quilt Factory in the bedroom and garage. When the demand for my designs outgrew the space, my husband, Lynn, and I purchased a 105-year-old country church, which now houses the design center and shipping facilities for the publishing business. ❖

Connie Tesene
Mary Tendall

Country Threads
2345 Palm Avenue
Garner, IA 50438

Projects featured in the book:
Plaid Patches (page 16), Father Christmas (page 104), and Hearts and Spools (page 146)

Country Threads is located in north-central Iowa on a small farm in a renovated chicken coop surrounded by not only trees, shrubs, and flowers, but also goats, chickens, ducks, geese, cats, and Red, Mary's dog. This peaceful setting is the inspiration and the focus of the Country Threads look created by Connie and Mary.

Located just 3 miles west of Garner on U.S. Highway 18, the quilt shop provides shoppers with the latest in patterns, books, notions, and 3,000 bolts of fabric, with heavy emphasis on plaids, stripes, and checks. Also offered are many services that include machine quilting, a fabric club, a newsletter, classes, quilt retreats, and the ever-expanding mail-order business that helps friends across the country get the latest patterns, fabrics, and kits from Country Threads.

Mary lives on the farm where

Country Threads is located and enjoys collecting folk art and antiques, reading, caring for her lawn and garden, watching all of her animals grow, and eating chocolate.

Connie lives in Garner with husband, Roy, and three boys. Gardening, reading, collecting primitive folk art, rug hooking, tending family pets, and eating pie are some of Connie's favorites. Sewing, designing, and creating are the best parts of every work day. It's great when you can't wait to get to your job. Just ask us! ❖

Retta Warehime

Sew Cherished
2630 South Kellogg
Kennewick, WA 99337
(509) 783-2795

Projects featured in the book:
Flying Flags (page 28) and Summer Camp (page 170)

Only with 100 percent support from my husband Dan (who cooks six nights a week) and my four wonderful children, Shawna, Jayme, Marci, and Gregg, have I been able to devote 10 hours a day to sewing, designing, and managing my pattern business.

My love of needle and thread began when my mom introduced me to sewing; because of her patience, my skills grew. I began with clothing, moved to crafts, then to piecing. While I was a good sewer, classes at a local quilt shop fine-tuned my piecing ability.

One step led to another. I began assisting at the classes, then teaching some of my own, and next I was receiving custom-piecing orders. These projects led to drafting my own patterns, which

became the basis for my own pattern business, Sew Cherished.

Running my own business takes a lot of time and energy, but it's worth it since designing and piecing are the things I love to do. Everywhere I go, everything I see triggers ideas in my mind. My desire to create is being fulfilled one piece at a time with each new project I complete. ❖

Johanna Wilson

Plum Creek Patchwork
Route 2, Box 95
Walnut Grove, MN 56180
(507) 859-3030

Project featured in the book:
Hearts (page 140)

I was a teacher and high school librarian in Connecticut before moving with my husband, Ormon, to a farm on the Minnesota prairie. The Wilson farm is in Walnut Grove, very near the site of Laura Ingalls Wilder's dugout home on Plum Creek in the 1870s.

In the early 1980s, I began designing and creating quilt patterns. Many of my patterns, published as Plum Creek Patchwork, are based on traditional blocks reminiscent of another era, made from fabrics our grandmothers never imagined. Other designs, like Hearts, are fast, fun, and whimsical designs that will quickly put a quilt on your wall and a smile on your face.

In the past several years I have exhibited my quilts in shows, museums, and exhibitions across the United States and Europe. In 1990 I was the recipient of the first Master/Apprentice Folk Arts Teaching Grant in quilting from the Minnesota Arts Board. My

quilt designs have won various awards and I have enjoyed teaching and lecturing to promote the art of quilting. ❖

MAIL-ORDER SOURCES

Wimpole Street Products is the source for the 4-inch doily used in Bear with Us on page 206. This doily is available through:

Barrett House
(801) 299-0700

❖

Little Foot (sewing machine attachment for ¼-inch seam allowances)

Little Foot Ltd.
605 Bledsoe NW
Albuquerque, NM 87107
(505) 345-7647

❖

Half-a-Square Triangle Grid Papers: 4-inch grid papers to use for the Harvest Medallion quilt on page 188. Grid papers eliminate the marking step. A package of 4-inch papers makes 96 units.

Osage County Quilt Factory
400 Walnut
Box 490
Overbrook, KS 66524
(913) 665-7500

❖

Handmade ceramic buttons (as seen on cover of book and in photographs throughout)

Something Pretty
Route 1, Box 93C
Big Sandy, TN 38221
(901) 593-3807